WORK IN THE
◆
NEW
ECONOMY
◆

The New Labor Market
Dramatic changes in our economy
and work lives

Effective Job Search Skills
Now an essential survival tool

Providing Job Search Assistance
Innovative approaches get results

WORK IN THE NEW ECONOMY

◆ Careers and Job Seeking into the 21st Century ◆

REVISED EDITION

Robert Wegmann
Robert Chapman
Miriam Johnson

and

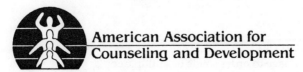

American Association for
Counseling and Development

Production Manager: Carole Black
Cover-Interior Design: Ron Troxell

First edition published in 1985 under the title *Looking for Work in the New Economy*

Co-published by:

JIST Works, Inc.
720 North Park Avenue, Indianapolis, Indiana 46202-3431
Toll free order number: 800/648/5478 or 317/637/6643

American Association for Counseling and Development
5999 Stevenson Avenue, Alexandria, VA 22304

Library of Congress Cataloging-in-Publication Data

Wegmann, Robert G.
    Work in the New Economy: careers and job seeking into the 21st
    century / Robert Wegmann, Robert Chapman, Miriam Johnson. —
    Rev. ed.

    p.   cm.
    Bibliography: p.
    Includes index.
    ISBN 0-942784-19-7
        1. Job hunting — United States. 2. United States —Occupations.
    3. Employment forecasting — United States. 4. Economic forecasting —
    United States. 5. United States — Economic conditions — 1981-
    I. Chapman, Robert B. II. Johnson, Miriam, 1918- . III. Wegmann, Robert
    G. Looking for work in the new economy. IV. Title.
    HF5382.75.U6W44   1988
    650.1'4--dc19   88-24147
                         CIP

ISBN 0-942784-19-7
See last page to order single or multiple copies

WHY YOU SHOULD READ THIS BOOK

This book is a *must* for anyone interested in helping others plan their careers or find jobs. It contains information every working person needs to get ahead. A careful analysis of labor market information allows the authors to project the changes in our economy and work lives through the year 2000. It is the most thoroughly researched book on this topic (over 330 references!).

We are now, for example, far more likely to change jobs and careers. Competition for available jobs will increase and the gap between high and low earners will widen. Many will experience unemployment. Technology and the shift to a service economy will change the types of jobs people have.

A Revolutionary Conclusion

Amidst this rapid change, there is a low technology and cost-effective solution that can help people get ahead. It is, simply, to learn more effective methods for getting a good job.

A New Survival Skill

Substantial economic benefits can go to those who use more effective career planning and job seeking techniques. People can get better jobs and do so in less time. And they will know how to move up to new jobs and opportunities.

The authors present the best methods and provide specific suggestions on how to use them. They demystify the job search process for all time. More importantly, they provide a guide for individual empowerment and a common sense model for a national employment policy.

An Important Source Book

Work In The New Economy is destined to be an essential source for journalists, futurists, labor market analysts, job search trainers and instructors, career counselors, authors of job search books, program planners, administrators, and other change agents. But it is also for you and me as job seekers and people of the twentieth (and soon to be the twenty-first) century.

For A Quick Overview

Start with Chapter Eleven if your time is short. This chapter gives an excellent summary of the book's major observations and conclusions.

Each of the three sections begin with a three- to four-page overview that gives additional insights into the topics covered. In addition, the Table of Contents and List of Tables will provide a useful way to find specfic topics of interest to you.

CONTENTS

The Labor Force Is Growing Rapidly • Unemployment Increases
And Jobs Change • The Work Force Is Changing, Too • Increased
Foreign Trade • Is The U.S. Exporting Jobs? • A Negative Trade
Balance Increases Job Loss • For The First Time, The U.S. Is A
Debtor Nation • More Permanent Job Loss, Lower Wages Become
The Norm • Fewer Jobs For Those With Low Skills • Computers
Effect More People's Jobs • Are The Robots Coming? • A
Summary Of The Changes

The Action Shifts To Smaller Organizations • Business Instability
Results In More Job Changing • As Self Employment Increases
And Organizations Shrink, Compensation Goes Down • Mergers
And Takeovers Increase Corporate Turbulence • Productivity
Pressures Result In Even More Layoffs • The Shift To A "Service"
Economy Will Dramatically Reduce Manufacturing Jobs • A
Diverse And Growing Service Sector • The Impact Of New
Technologies • Competition For Government Jobs Increase •
Displaced Workers Face Lower Living Standards • Longer
Periods Of Unemployment, Particularly For Older Workers • New
Workers Find It Harder To "Break-in" — Earn Less Even When
Employed • Minority And Older Workers • Weakening Union
Influences • The Growing Demand For Educated Workers • For
Many, Family Income Is Going Down • Labor Market Changes
Affect Society • Notes

TABLES

FOREWORD

The American economy is being transformed by a number of forces that affect the lives of everyone in the United States — indeed, of everyone on earth. These include the globalization of economic activity; technology, especially the pervasive information technologies; and very important demographic changes that will literally transform the American population, economy, and work force. Those who would perform successfully in this new labor force must, therefore, understand its imperatives. This is as true of people who are concerned about job search as it is for managers, labor leaders, and public officials — elected or appointed. In fact, job search is one of the most important activities in an individual's life, but, amazingly, it is one of the activities we do not do very well or systematically in the United States. We do an especially poor job for that half of our youth population (20 million people) 16 to 24 years of age who are not college bound and for the millions of adults who change jobs every year but who are not "well connected" with labor market insitutions.

This book is valuable for individuals, employers, schools, unions, labor market institutions, and public officials concerned with job search. It is written by people whose knowledge and skills complement each other nicely. Robert Wegmann is an academic who has synthesized the research on job search and has been a close observer of labor markets. Robert Chapman is a partner in a successful management consulting firm with intimate knowledge of corporate personnel needs and procedures. Miriam Johnson has had rich experiences observing and operating labor market institutions, especially those concerned with matching workers and jobs. The experience of these authors is reflected in their synthesis of knowledge, ideas, and practical insights into the job search process. They bring order and clarity to this important subject.

Chair, Economic and Public Affairs   Ray Marshall
University of Texas
U.S. Secretary of Labor 1977-1981

PART ONE
The New Labor Market — Dramatic Changes Through The Year 2000

Finding a good job has always been a challenge. Today, that challenge is more difficult than ever. The set of jobs available in the American labor market has changed significantly. This has made finding a job more confusing, and often more prolonged, than it used to be.

Trying to study the job search process without reference to these labor market changes would be like trying to study swimming without any knowledge of where that swimming is being done. It makes a great deal of difference whether a swimmer is diving into a placid pool, a wave-filled ocean or a fast-moving rapids.

The three chapters in Part One discuss how the American labor market has changed. The focus of Chapter One is on the major elements which have generated wide swings in the unemployment rate in an economy which is, paradoxically, generating many new jobs.

Since 1975, the balance of supply and demand in the American labor market has undergone a significant shift. More women seeking paid employment outside the home, increased immigration, and the entrance of the "baby boom" generation into the labor market have all contributed to a significant increase in the number of American workers. A massive new involvement in foreign trade, combined with a negative trade balance, have kept the growth rate of new job openings below what is needed to accommodate all these new entrants to the labor force. This has led to significantly higher levels of unemployment than were typical during the first 30 years of the postwar era (1945-1975).

These post-1975 changes involve much more than increased unemployment. Chapter Two reviews the changing nature of the jobs which *are* available. Here we find several major, interrelated structural shifts. There is a movement of employment opportunity from large corporations to medium and small employers. A declining proportion of the population works in manufacturing and government, while an increasing proportion has jobs in the trade and service sectors.

As a result of these changes, many workers have jobs which are less well paid and less stable than was formerly the case. Jobs must be changed more often, and any such move can involve accepting lower wages. The problem of finding a good job is especially acute for older workers, and for those with low levels of formal education.

The changes discussed in the first two chapters have important economic and social implications. Chapter Three looks in more depth at three particularly important effects of this new labor market.

The first area of concern is the changing pattern of family income that has resulted from these changes. While two-income families have contributed to growing affluence for part of the American population, downward mobility and unemployment have simultaneously increased the proportion of low-income families.

This shift in family income is greatly influenced, of course, by the increasing number of women who are seeking and finding paid employment outside the home. Some of these women work at high salaries, but more often they earn wages well below those typically earned by men.

Pay and level of education are more closely related for women than for men. It should not surprise us, therefore, that the proportion of women seeking paid employment varies with educational level. The probability that a woman has a job increases markedly as her level of education rises. As a result, the U.S. now has a labor force which is significantly more educated than its adult population.

Partly because of the growing probability that a woman college graduate will seek employment, the competition for professional and managerial jobs has increased sharply. This has led, for the first time in American history, to significant underemployment among those who have college degrees

Large numbers of college graduates, unable to find professional, technical or managerial employment, now compete with those who are less educated for less prestigious jobs. This competition, in turn, makes it even more difficult for persons with lower levels of formal education to find well-paid employment.

The total picture presented by the data reviewed in these three chapters makes it abundantly clear that the competition for desirable jobs is much more intense than it used to be. There are multiple applicants for almost every opening. Only rarely do positions remain empty because no qualified person applies. The few exceptions are usually jobs where the pay is quite low for the skills which the job requires.

Anyone who sets out to look for work under these highly competitive conditions needs to be clear about both his or her occupational goals, and the best methods to reach those goals. Success today requires a good idea of where openings are most likely to be found, and what behaviors are usually successful in obtaining interviews once an opening is located. Therefore, we look first at how the labor market has changed and then, in Part Two, at the research findings on the job search.

CHAPTER ONE
Dramatic Changes In Our Economy And Workforce

Somewhere around 1975, the American labor market changed. The number of people who wanted jobs was increasing at a rapid rate. They were having more difficulty than usual in finding them.

New trends began to emerge. Energy prices increased sharply. College graduates had unusual problems finding professional jobs. American involvement in foreign trade began to move to levels not seen in modern times. Unemployment shot up.

Old trends intensified. More and more women sought employment outside the home. Manufacturing jobs became more scarce, and service sector jobs more common. American workers, always mobile, faced frequent changes of employer, occupation and residence.

These trends, new and old, combined and interrelated to produce a labor market that was significantly more competitive, more unstable and more challenging than anything known during the prior 30 years. The American economy changed, and the labor market changed with it.

In the years since 1975, American workers have struggled to adapt to this new situation. Many, in fact, have adjusted surprisingly well. Others have had much more difficulty. All would benefit from a better understanding of what happened, and why. This chapter begins our examination of the major factors creating this new, post-1975 labor market.

TABLE ONE

Labor Force Growth 1950 through 2000
(in millions)

Year	Civilian Labor Force Size	Employed	Unemployed	Unemployment Rate (%)
1950	62.2	58.9	3.4	5.3
1955	65.0	62.2	2.9	4.4
1960	69.6	65.8	3.9	5.5
1965	74.5	71.1	3.4	4.5
1970	82.8	78.7	4.1	4.9
1975	93.8	85.8	7.9	8.5
1980	106.9	99.3	7.6	7.1
1985	115.5	107.2	8.3	7.2
1990	124.5	116.5	7.9	6.4
1995	131.6	122.0	9.6	7.3
2000	138.8	130.4	8.3	6.0

Source: Bureau of Labor Statistics. Figures after 1985 are estimates. Details may not add to totals due to rounding. Unemployment increases in 1995 because the econometric model used forecasts a recession period at that time.

Labor Force Is Growing Rapidly

There has been, since World War II, a continuing increase in the number of persons working or actively seeking employment, as Table One shows. This growth was particularly strong during the 1965-1985 period. These were the years when most of the "baby boom" group, made up of individuals born between 1946 and 1964, left school and sought employment. Just between 1970 and 1982 the labor force grew by over 27 million people. This increased its size by almost one-third during a period of only 12 years.

Until the recession year of 1975, the American economy was able to absorb most of these new workers without undue difficulty. The unemployment rate, depending on the state of the economy, moved between four and six percent during most of the quarter century prior to 1975. Since 1975, however, average annual unemployment has only twice gone below six percent (5.8 percent in 1979, and 5.5 percent in 1988).

It is hard to tell whether the recent decline in unemployment will continue. Department of Labor projections have average yearly unemployment rates holding at or above six percent through the year 2000 (Saunders, 1987).

Unemployment Increases And Jobs Change

It is important to note, first, that continuing high unemployment has occurred in an economy where there is significant growth. The number of available jobs has been increasing, not decreasing. Between 1970 and 1980 employment went up by over 20 million, an extraordinarily large increase, with another increase of over 10 million between 1980 and 1986. These increases, however, have not been large enough to absorb the even greater numbers of people seeking work.

Furthermore, this growth has been quite uneven. Some areas of the economy grew while others declined. As a result, the total set of available job possibilities has, over the last decade, become significantly different from the mix of jobs typical of the 1945-1975 period. Some employment possibilities are now much more common, others much more scarce.

An initial sense of how the mix of available jobs has been changing can be gotten by examining the pattern of employment increases during the latter part of the 1970s. Approximately 16 million new jobs were created during the 1972-1980 period. Detailed examination of these positions shows that growth occurred in three-fourths of the 235 occupational categories used by the Department of Labor. However, almost half of this growth occurred in just 20 of these occupations. These new jobs were almost entirely white-collar positions. Overall, white-collar employment increased by 30 percent, while blue-collar positions grew by less than 8 percent.

This pattern of differential growth has continued since 1980. For the 1986-2000 period, the Bureau of Labor Statistics projects a drop of manufacturing employment each year, while the number of jobs in other parts of the economy will be increasing steadily (Personick, 1987).

These differential growth rates will be examined in more detail in Chapter Two. What is important at this point is simply to note that there has been considerable, if uneven, growth in the number of available jobs, though not enough to meet the needs of everyone looking for work.

The Work Force Is Changing, Too

Three major factors have contributed to the rapid increase in the labor force. The first is natural increase. This effect, as has already been noted, was particularly strong during the years when those born during the era of high birth rates came of age. The second major impact is the constantly increasing proportion of American women who have been seeking paid employment outside the home, a phenomenon which will be discussed in detail in Chapter Three. Finally, an unusually large number of immigrants, legal and illegal, have come to the United States in recent years, and they too have sought employment.

Any one of these factors would have made an impact on the economy. Because all three occurred simultaneously, the size of the labor force grew very rapidly, especially during the 1965-1985 period. In the future, however, the first of these factors will no longer be producing a large number of entry level workers. As a result, labor force growth will slow notably.

The 16- to 24-year-old labor force reached a peak in October 1979. The last of the baby boom group completed high school around 1982. By the end of 1982, the number of 16- to 24-year-olds with jobs or seeking them had already declined by 850,000. In the years ahead, the number of young persons seeking employment will continue to drop sharply (Young, 1983).

This does not necessarily mean the total number of new entrants to the labor force will drop by an equivalent amount, however. Some of this decline will be made up by immigration, legal and illegal. During the 1970s, legal immigration to the U.S. exceeded 4.4 million, the highest level in half a century. Another 5.5 to 5.7 million legal immigrants are expected to come during the 1980s. It is important to note that each legal immigrant creates the potential for new immigration. American immigration law gives preference to the immediate families of naturalized citizens, thus creating a sort of "echo effect."

If present patterns continue, total immigration will add approximately four million workers to the labor force between now and the year 2000 (Hudson Institute, 1987). In contrast to past patterns, the present stream of immigrants is heavily Hispanic and Asian (Muller, 1984).

The number of illegal immigrants is not known, and estimates vary widely. Freeman (1980) suggests that about ten percent of the work force may be illegal aliens, and Fogel (1977) cites an estimate by the Immigration and Naturalization Service of 8-12 million illegal aliens working in the U.S. The Census Bureau believes that about two million undocumented aliens were included in the 1980 census (Passel, 1986).

Realistically, these estimates are educated guesses. While past and present levels of illegal immigration are undoubtedly substantial, there is no accurate count. Many illegal immigrants, particularly Mexicans, go back and forth regularly between this country and their country of origin, so that net immigration is significantly lower than the number who enter. The new immigration law, with its fines for employers who hire undocumented aliens, also complicates the situation. It is not yet clear what effect this law will have in slowing illegal immigration.

Adult women are the third major group contributing to rapid growth in the number of persons seeking employment. During the 1970-1981 period, the labor force grew by 10.7 million men and 15.2 million women, a roughly two to three ratio. This ratio is expected to hold approximately constant through the 1980's and beyond. During the 1986-2000 period, women are expected to make up 64 percent of the net additions to the labor force (Fullerton, 1987).

It was, then, an increased proportion of women seeking paid employment at the same time that the baby boom cohort came of age and an influx of immigration occurred which produced such sizable increases in labor force size from about 1965 to the early 1980s. Although the entrance of the baby boom group into the workforce is now over, immigration (legal and illegal) is continuing, and the labor force participation rate of women also continues to increase (Klein, 1982).

In the 1960s and early 1970s, the economy was generally able to generate sufficient employment for this increasing number of new workers. Beginning in the mid-1970s, however, the ability of the American labor market to absorb new entrants faltered. The rate of unemployment climbed substantially. What happened?

Increased Foreign Trade

A series of recessions, largely induced by very rapid increases in the price of energy, played a major role. The 1973-1975 downturn was the worst since the Great Depression, with another recession in 1980, followed by a short recovery and then the downturn of 1981-1982. These recessionary conditions were coincident with a very rapid increase in American involvement in foreign trade. The two phenomena are related, of course, since the dollar value of imported oil climbed dramatically during this period.

As Table Two shows, the proportion of goods produced in America and then shipped to other countries (the last column in the table) shot up dramatically after 1970. In 1950 we shipped $10.2 billion dollars worth of merchandise to other countries, 6.3 percent of the goods produced in this country. By 1980 this figure had grown to $225.1 billion, a full 19.2 percent of the goods segment of our gross national product. This is an extraordinary increase, given the huge size of the American economy. After 1980, because of unfavorable exchange rates and other reasons, we continued to import heavily, but were unable to export as much as we had previously.

TABLE TWO

Merchandise Imports and Exports as a Proportion of the Goods Segment of the Gross National Product
(in billions of dollars)

Year	Goods Segment of GNP	Merchandise Imports	%	Merchandise Exports	%
1950	162.4	9.1	5.6	10.2	6.3
1955	216.3	11.5	5.3	14.4	6.6
1960	257.2	15.2	5.9	20.5	8.0
1965	342.9	22.2	6.5	27.8	8.1
1970	467.8	40.9	8.7	44.5	9.5
1975	714.7	99.0	13.9	109.6	15.3
1980	1174.9	247.5	21.1	225.1	19.2
1985	1637.9	341.0	20.8	220.8	13.5

Source: U. S. Bureau of Economic Analysis. Details may not always add to totals due to rounding.

The world today is struggling to cope with a global movement toward industrialization which is hitting with multiplicative force. Not only are there a rapidly growing number of people in the world, but an increasing proportion of that growing number wants to industrialize. Many inhabitants of the so-called "third world" would be happy to leave their villages, which often cannot provide the food and work needed by a growing population, to take a factory job at a dollar an hour. Wages that are a big step down for an American worker can be a big step up for citizens in developing countries. Given free trade and equal technology, this puts the American factory, and factory worker, at a competitive disadvantage.

This would not be of great importance if distance made large scale competition impractical. Modern transportation, however, is rapid and relatively inexpensive. This means that the costs of production in foreign countries, even with transportation expenses included, can be well below American production costs.

Containerized cargo ships, for example, are highly efficient. Cargo handled at the port of San Francisco, to take a concrete instance, increased 292 percent between 1961 and 1983. The number of man-hours required to move this increased tonnage, however, went down 39 percent.

As similar increases in transportation efficiency were lowering costs, another stimulus to increased trade was taking effect. Round after round of mutual tariff reductions lowered the economic barriers which formerly limited involvement in international trade. If the price of a product is not raised by tariffs which must be paid when that product is brought into another country, then the item's selling price is determined primarily by the costs of production and transportation. The natural result of decreased tariffs ("free trade") was increased purchases of American goods by other countries, and of their goods by wholesalers and distributors in the United States.

More and more, we are trading with the newly developing countries as extensively as we do with countries having more developed economies. By 1980, total U.S. trade with developing countries amounted to more than our trade with Europe and Japan combined (Executive Office of the President, 1982). Our trading pattern is to export food (one out of every three acres planted on our highly mechanized farms is for export), high technology goods, services and some raw materials; we import petroleum, low technology goods, consumer goods and automotive products.

Is The U.S. Exporting Jobs?

Because the goods we export are different from those being imported, more American manufacturing jobs are lost due to foreign trade than are gained, even when there is a positive balance of trade. Aho and Orr (1981) report a study of two groups of industries, with 20 industries in each group. These were the industries where employment was most favorably and most adversely affected by foreign trade during the 1964-1975 period. The 20 industries which suffered the greatest job losses included apparel, motor vehicles and parts, furnaces and other steel products, motorcycles and bicycles.

The 20 American industries which gained the most employment by producing for export during this same period included aircraft, computers, oil field machinery, construction machinery, and electric measuring instruments. On the whole, there is more employment for skilled labor in these exporting industries than there is in the industries losing jobs because of import competition. Thus our trading pattern creates a disproportionate loss of unskilled manufacturing jobs.

Equally important, there are fewer workers needed to produce a dollar's worth of goods in the exporting industries. These industries are more automated and more capital-intensive. The industries hurt by imports, on the other hand, are more labor-intensive. To be specific, the 20 industries which lost the most employment because of import competition during the 1964-1975 period suffered a decline of 422,000 jobs; the 20 that gained the most employment producing for export experienced a gain of 316,000 jobs. This is about a four to three ratio, and a net loss.

The balance of merchandise trade was generally positive during 1964-1975. It was negative for only three of those years, with a net positive balance of more than $19 billion for the entire period. Even though the United States was coming out ahead in dollars by exporting more than was being imported, however, we were still losing manufacturing jobs. Our imports were more labor-intensive than our exports.

Specific data on the employment effects of foreign trade have also been reported by Schoepfle (1982). Between 1972 and 1979, 72 of 318 manufacturing groups were "import-sensitive," with their markets having experienced either a sustained high level of import penetration, or a substantial increase in the proportion of sales by imports. Despite the overall growth in employment during much of the 1972-1979 period, about half of the domestic industries which produce products in these import-sensitive groups reported a decline in employment. Such declines were particularly strong in the textile, apparel and leather goods groups.

Although much publicity has been given to the highly paid steel and auto workers who have been displaced by foreign competition, the overall employment impact of foreign trade has actually been more often felt by less highly paid workers. The apparel worker who is paid $5 an hour and must compete with a similar worker in Taiwan receiving $1.32 an hour is as likely as an auto worker to find his or her job disappearing. In fact, the overall data suggest that it is women and minority manufacturing workers who have been disproportionately affected by our increased involvement in foreign trade.

These same effects occur whether the competing company is completely foreign, or is an American firm which has moved some or all of its manufacturing facilities to other countries to take advantage of lower labor costs. Such "exporting of jobs" or "outsourcing" has become common in recent years.

The impact of foreign trade on employment outside of manufacturing is more positive. Imported goods still have to be shipped, stored, sold and serviced, and this work is largely done by American workers. When the cost of imported goods is lower than equivalent domestic products, American consumers have money left over to buy other goods and services, most of which have been made in the United States or are provided by an American source. The net effect of increased foreign trade on overall American employment is thus difficult to estimate.

In a recent attempt to do so, Belous and Wyckoff (1987) did a computer modeling of the employment effect of an additional $10 billion of both imports and exports. Their model showed 179,000 jobs of all types being lost due to the additional imports, with 193,000 jobs gained due to the additional exports. The jobs gained, however, were significantly different from the jobs lost. More blue-collar jobs were lost; more professional, managerial, marketing and clerical jobs were gained.

A Negative Trade Balance Increases Job Loss

Even balanced foreign trade would change the set of the jobs available in this country. In fact, however, our trade situation has become highly unbalanced.

There are many reasons why we are buying so much more than we are selling: the increasing quality of many foreign products, lower foreign labor costs, government subsidization of some foreign industries, and so on. Large American budget deficits also play an important role. When the government spends more than it takes in in taxes, bonds must be sold to raise the difference. This increases the competition for lendable funds, and raises American interest rates. These high interest rates attract foreign investors, who trade in their own currencies to obtain the dollars needed to buy our bonds, thereby affecting the value of the dollar and the flow of trade (Johnson, 1983).

We have been, in effect, trading high-interest treasury bonds and other securities for foreign imports. This has allowed us to buy far more goods than we sell. Because of the many problems this causes, the U.S. government has been trying to reduce both interest rates and the value of the dollar. So long as our budget deficit remains high, however, there are limits to what can be done without generating highly inflationary side effects.

Gall (1983) reports that the U.S. merchandise trade deficit in 1971 was the first such deficit since 1888. Since 1971, however, the problem has become chronic, with an unbroken string of deficits since 1976. The merchandise trade deficit for 1983 went over $60 billion, and the deficit for 1984 was almost double that. Merchandise trade deficits of over $100 billion a year have now become routine.

Such trade deficits mean that jobs are lost in two ways. American industries which must compete with imported goods lose employment as imports rise. So do exporting industries, as

American goods fail to sell to other countries in sufficient quantities to balance our imports. The net effect is to depress growth in employment, and in the gross national product.

Guzzardi (1983) estimates that our trade imbalance cost between one and two million American jobs during 1983. For 1984, Alexander (1984) cites a loss of 2.5 million jobs. Such estimates are not easy to calculate, and are controversial. If even close, however, they would help to explain the unprecedented anomaly, in 1984, of unemployment exceeding seven percent in the middle of the second year of a vigorous economic recovery.

The economic impact of this trade deficit is substantial. Irwin Kellner of Manufacturers Hanover Trust reports that, between 1980 and 1984, the United States experienced a decline of $80 billion in real net exports. As a result, the economy grew only 12.5 percent from the third quarter of 1980 to the same period four years later. Without this decline, the growth would have been 18 percent (Kellner, 1984).

Except for farm and petroleum products, foreign manufacturers now provide 26 per cent of what is sold in the U.S.; ten years ago they supplied 13 percent. While foreign firms have gained market share in this country, American firms have been losing market share abroad. This is true even in high technology areas previously dominated by American companies. In 1984, for the first time ever, America imported more electronics products than were exported (Wilson, 1985).

Our trade with Latin America has been particularly hard hit. Historically, the U.S. has sold large quantities of manufactured goods to this nearby part of the world. This trade is now severely depressed, however, because many of these countries must use their limited funds to pay off their own large foreign borrowings. Little money is left to pay for new purchases.

For The First Time, The U.S. Is A Debtor Nation

As we continue to buy foreign goods without selling an equivalent value of American goods, our foreign debt increases. We used to be a net creditor. In 1982, American investments abroad were worth over $169 billion more than foreign investments in the United States. By early 1985, however, for the first time in 70 years, our position as a net creditor had been lost (Drobnick, 1985). By the end of 1985, the United States was a net debtor for the first time since 1914. In 1986, foreign investors held $1.33 trillion in assets in this country, compared to $1.07 trillion in foreign assets owned by Americans, a difference of $260 billion. By 1988, this gap had more than doubled (Nasar, 1988).

This means that we will be paying more in dividends and interest to other countries than we will be receiving from them, thus decreasing our national wealth. In 1984 the U.S. Treasury Department paid $19 billion to foreign holders of Treasury debt, an amount larger than our entire foreign-aid budget. By 1987, these interest payments had grown to over $23 billion. Other large sums must be paid to foreign holders of corporate stocks and bonds, and foreign owners of American property and corporations. In the third quarter of 1987, for the first time in more than half a century, foreigners earned more on their U.S. investments than U.S. investors earned in other countries.

There is no sign that our trade imbalance will disappear. The Bureau of Labor Statistics projects a trade deficit of nearly $100 billion 1982 dollars in the year 2000 (Saunders, 1987).

Employment losses caused by an imbalance in merchandise trade are partially made up by the income which American firms earn abroad selling services rather than merchandise to foreign customers. American corporations provide accounting, banking, insurance, education, health, communication, advertising and other services to firms in foreign countries, and this generates some additional American jobs. Unfortunately, the quality of data on the dollar value and employment impact of these services is poor (Driscoll, 1980; Yochelson and Cloney, 1982; Executive Office of the President, 1982). It is clear, though, that the level of income from trade in services is not enough to make up for the present imbalance in merchandise trade.

Trade in services undoubtedly increases the number of American jobs, even though the exact size of this increase is unknown. The positions created, however, tend to be skilled, white collar positions, not unskilled or blue collar jobs.

In the future, trade in services is likely to become increasingly important. As the U.S. moves to a knowledge-based economy, many corporations will export both products and services. A publishing firm, for example, will sell either a book or the license to reprint it. A variety of industries such as pharmaceuticals, telecommunications, computers and scientific instruments already operate this way (Drucker, 1986). Computer software royalties, the provision of temporary help, film and TV royalties, management consulting and many other areas are all part of our growing trade in services (Kirkland, 1987).

More Permanent Job Loss — Lower Wages Become The Norm

At the same time that international trade has greatly increased competitive pressures on many American manufacturing firms, domestic deregulation of the transportation, communications and finance industries has simultaneously increased competition in these areas. The government formerly played a major role in deciding who could run a bus service between what cities, the interest rates banks could offer on savings accounts, and how much could be charged for an airline ticket. This is no longer true. Firms in these industries are now much freer to compete without government regulation.

The employment effects of the competition generated by deregulation are essentially identical to those of foreign competition. Both increase the pressure to lower costs in order to keep market share. One obvious way to do this is to shrink the number of employees to the absolute minimum, and if possible to lower wages.

Bankruptcies can result if adjustments to deregulation cannot be made successfully. The price of survival is doing more with less. United Airlines, to give one concrete example of a major firm functioning in a newly deregulated environment, operated during 1982 at 96 percent of its 1978 capacity, but with 21 percent fewer workers. Virtually every major airline has experienced serious difficulties adjusting to deregulation, and many have been acquired by other corporations.

Many small firms have had an equally difficult time adjusting. Deregulation has been coincident with increased oil prices, high interest rates and recessionary conditions. This has presented the managements of these firms with severe tests. More than 300 trucking companies have failed since deregulation went into effect in the transportation industry, for example, and many Teamster locals at other small firms have accepted sizable wage cuts to keep their jobs.

At the same time, many new firms have been formed. Since passage of the Motor Carrier Act of 1980, the number of trucking companies with I.C.C. certification has gone from 18,000 to 32,000. The bright spot in domestic deregulation is that these new firms, formed to compete under deregulated conditions, are American and create new employment opportunities in this country. These opportunities, however, have been created under difficult, even tumultuous conditions, as firms rise and shrink rapidly in size and the market readjusts to a new set of constraints.

When numerous corporations reduce their workforces or go out of business, the effect on employment can be substantial. One indication of this can be found in some data released by the Bureau of Labor Statistics. In the three recessions before the 1981-1982 downturn, 37 percent of the increased unemployment was caused by workers permanently losing their jobs (as opposed to quitting, being temporarily laid off, or being unable to find a job when entering or reentering the labor market). In the 1981-1982 recession, however, the proportion of permanent job loss rose well above this 37 percent level, to a startling 53 percent. As a result, a much larger proportion of those who were unemployed had to look for new employers instead of waiting out the recession and returning to their old employers when business picked up (Bednarzik, 1983).

Corporate managers now see major layoffs as a necessary component of corporate strategy. We suspect that, in the next recession, rapid and large-scale job loss will be common.

More competitive conditions, like the increase in imports, are in many ways good for the economy. They provide consumers with a wider choice of goods and services at lower prices, thus playing a major role in holding down inflation. They stimulate innovation and efficiency, as firms struggle to survive. They also produce a much more unstable employment situation, however, at least in the short run, while simultaneously holding down pay increases and even causing pay cuts.

Such impacts go well beyond lower level workers. Corporate pyramids are being flattened. Many corporate staff jobs are being eliminated. Middle management positions with major corporations are now more difficult to obtain, more competitive, and less secure. In the long run, this too can lead to greater productivity. The immediate effects, however, are turmoil, job losses, and painful readjustments.

Fewer Jobs For Those With Low Skills

Although the future is always uncertain, current patterns seem to be in the direction of strengthening rather than weakening many of the trends we have been discussing. Both imports and exports are expected to rise in the decade ahead (Saunders, 1987). The crash of the world's stock markets in October 1987 illustrated vividly how deeply we are enmeshed in the world economy.

However this may all work out over time, the immediate effect of these trends is to reduce the total number of available jobs below the number which would otherwise exist, and to change the nature of those jobs which remain.

At the same time, it is important to stress that many good jobs are being created. Well paid jobs which used to be open to persons with relatively little formal education, however, seem to be disappearing with particular speed. Such jobs are typically found either in government, in regulated industries or in areas of the economy involving large scale manufacturing by major corporations. It is precisely these sectors of the economy which have been experiencing either slow growth or actual declines in employment.

The inflation-adjusted pay of the remaining unskilled and semi-skilled jobs in these industries is now often considerably below what such jobs paid in the past, particularly for the newly hired. Some labor contracts in industries heavily affected by foreign competition or deregulation specify lower wages for everyone hired after a given date. Flax (1984) reports that such "two-tier contracts" are in effect at a number of major corporations. We will examine these trends toward lower pay in more depth in Chapters Two and Three.

Computers Affect More People's Jobs

Every major technological advance changes both the nature and the mix of available jobs. This was true of the railroad, the telephone, the airplane, the first computers and television, to name some obvious examples, and it is true today of the microchip. As each technology spreads, some jobs disappear and new jobs are created. What is done each day at a given job often changes even when the job title remains the same.

Today, because of the microchip, we are seeing such a phenomenon. Indeed, we seem to be experiencing the "computerization of everything." During 1984 alone, over two million new computers were supplied to American workers, so that one worker in eight was using one (Goldstein and Fraser, 1985). What is done in many jobs is changing as computers are introduced. The computer has also caused some positions to disappear entirely and new ones to be created (Mark, 1987).

On the one hand, some jobs are being "deskilled." Blood samples, for example, were once analyzed by skilled workers. Today computerized machines do far more analysis at considerably lower cost, and much less training is required to operate the machines than when the work had to be done by hand.

An employee transferred to a work station centered around a computer terminal in an insurance company, on the other hand, may now be able to handle all aspects of an account personally. This can greatly improve customer service while simultaneously making the job more interesting, less repetitive, and more responsible (Giuliano, 1982).

One review of the evidence on deskilling versus job upgrading concluded that the effects of the two trends are about equal, so that they cancel each other out (Spenner, 1985). It should be noted, though, that although computer technology had the opposite effect in our two examples, with one job downgraded and another upgraded, in both cases fewer people were needed to do a given amount of work.

New jobs, of course, are also being created by microchip- based technology. Someone has to design and sell the new machines, while others must service, manufacture and transport them. New positions are created to perform these functions.

Are The Robots Coming?

The effects of the microchip are potentially very great in almost all areas of white collar employment: word processing for the secretary, computer search of past cases for the lawyer, immediate access to current data and increased ability to do "what-if" calculations for the manager. It is the manufacturing robot which has attracted the attention of the news media, however, because of its apparent potential to empty the factory of workers. Bylinsky reports, for example, that the Japanese now have a factory (the Yanazaku Machinery Works) which, with 12 workers and a night watchman, produces the same volume of goods that would otherwise take not only 215 workers but four times as many machines. Closer to home, General Electric now builds locomotive frames in one day that used to take 16 days and 70 workers, with the frame now untouched by human hands (Bylinsky, 1983). Walgreen's has installed robots in its warehouses which can handle 900 less-than-case-load shipments per hour. Human packers formerly did 110 per hour (Foulkes and Hirsch, 1984). Since 1982, the number of robots used by Chrysler has increased from 300 to over 1200. The number of manhours which Chrysler needs to build a vehicle has gone from 175 to 102.

Along with these changes in technology, the demands of manufacturing employment are also changing. A few years ago, 11 percent of Chrysler's salaried manufacturing personnel had college degrees; by the end of 1988 it will be 45 percent (Taylor, 1987).

In Japan, where the introduction of robots has proceeded much more quickly than in the United States, manufacturing employment grew by only 70,000 between 1970 and 1981, while trade and service employment grew by 5.2 million. In industries where U.S. employers are willing and able to make the investment (GM will put $1 billion into the installation of 20,000 robots by 1990, for example), the effect of robotics on employment will undoubtedly be substantial. Of course, if these investments were not made, it might not be possible to produce goods at competitive prices, and jobs could be lost anyway. For this reason it is impossible to separate the employment effects of technology and automation from those of foreign competition. It is competition that drives corporations to make the investments in new technology.

Although the robot's potential certainly suggests the possibility of a rapid and radical alteration of employment patterns, particularly in manufacturing, this first impression does not hold up well on closer examination. In fact, a large-scale move to robotics may be surprisingly slow in coming. Robots are, at this point, still somewhat primitive. A significant investment in research and development will be needed to make them fully productive, and this will take time. In addition, robots work best in factories which are specially built for them. What the robot does has to be integrated with what is done by other machines, usually in what is called a "manufacturing cell" (Clark, 1983). It can be difficult to introduce robots into factories which were originally built for other means of production.

A review of the effect of robotics on manufacturing employment by H. Allan and Timothy Hunt estimates that, by 1990, somewhere between 50,000 and 100,000 robots will eliminate 100,000 to 200,000 jobs, about one fourth of them in the auto industry. At the same time, robot manufacturing, sales and service requirements should create between 32,000 and 64,000 new positions. This suggests a net loss of employment due to robotics. It is not a huge loss, however, given the total number of persons employed in manufacturing. These authors do note, though, that while the jobs being eliminated are semi-skilled or unskilled, the jobs being created are much more likely to require significant technical training (Hunt and Hunt, 1983).

The General Accounting Office, in an overview of the potential impact of automation and robotics on employment, looked at over 100 documents on this topic. They, too, found the effect on employment difficult to forecast, given the many factors which influence levels of employment and unemployment.

This GAO report cites information on 33 occupations which are expected to lose employment because of automation in the years ahead, and 26 others which are expected to grow as a result of increased automation. Just reviewing the declining occupations (boiler tender; file clerk; postal clerk; telephone operator, to name a few) and those expected to grow (ceramic engineer; economist; librarian; technical writer), it is clear that the growing occupations are far more white collar or bookish than those expected to decline, and will typically require more formal education (General Accounting Office, 1982).

A Summary Of The Changes

Although there are uncertainties about many important details, the overall pattern of change during the last dozen years is clear enough. On the one hand, the labor force grew at a rapid rate as the baby boom generation reached maturity, more and more women sought employment outside the home, and an increased number of immigrants entered the country. At the same time a rapid increase in foreign trade occurred, followed by a large trade deficit. What was purchased from other countries did not have to be made here, and manufacturing jobs disappeared. Higher energy costs and increased automation and computerization also lowered employment growth. The total number of net jobs being created fell behind the number of people seeking employment. High unemployment became chronic, the available jobs more bookish and white collar, and the competition for desirable openings more intense than in the past. This, in turn, led to important shifts in where jobs were to be found and what they pay. It is to a closer examination of these shifts that we now turn.

Notes✦✦✦

Readers who are unfamiliar with social science citations should note that "Smith (1984)" is a shorthand way of saying that information in this sentence or paragraph has been partially drawn from a book or article published in 1984 by someone named Smith. If you want to find the complete citation, look up Smith in the Reference section in the back of the book, and find his or her 1984 publication. Actual quotations will include the page from which the quote is taken, in the form "(Smith, 1984: 45)."

Because of the introduction of population adjustments in certain years, the data in the tables in this book are not always strictly comparable with prior years. The admission of Alaska and Hawaii to the union, for example, changed the population base of the country in 1960. Before 1947 labor force data were collected for those 14 and over who were employed; today such data are usually collected for those 16 and over, although some tables give figures for those 20 and over. There have also been changes in estimation procedures, and variations in whether or not the armed forces are included. None of these changes, however, hinders our ability to observe the direction of major trends over a long period of time.

Readers should be careful to note that the phrase "labor force" means both those who have jobs and those who are seeking them. Apparent discrepancies between statistics on the labor force and figures on the number of employed persons come from the fact that the figures on employment do not include the unemployed, while data on the labor force do.

Three useful articles in Business Week provided helpful data on the effects of foreign trade and deregulation: "Imports are Still Ripping into the Textile Industry" (September 5, 1983), "Special Report: Deregulating America" (November 28, 1983), and "Special Report: A New Era for Management" (April 25, 1983). The special issue on "The Superdollar" (October 8, 1984) was also used, as was information taken from a variety of reports in the Wall Street Journal. Additional information on pay cutbacks can be found in The Monthly Labor Review for November of 1983, pages 72-75.

A theoretical discussion of how cohort size and other factors affect the probability of promotion can be found in Stewman and Konda (1983).

CHAPTER TWO
Where People Work Is Changing Rapidly

The kind of work we do, and where we do that work, have both changed significantly during the past decade. Compared to only 10 or 12 years ago, a person today is much more likely to find employment in a small or medium-sized business instead of a major corporation. The work that he or she does is more likely to involve the provision of some service (as in a hospital, school, bank or consulting group) rather than the production of a physical product. Government employment, which for decades absorbed a growing part of the country's labor force, no longer does. Layoffs and downsizings have displaced many older workers from jobs they held for years, and which they expected to hold until retirement, and significantly changed the options available to younger workers.

The first thing anyone looking for work needs to know is what jobs are available. The answer to that question is dramatically different today than it was a dozen years ago. The purpose of this chapter is to describe what has changed, where jobs can be found (and where they cannot), and how the demands of those jobs have increased.

The Action Shifts To Smaller Organizations

One of the more important characteristics of the labor market in recent years has been the high proportion of new jobs opening up at recently created, rapidly growing small firms. David Birch analyzed data drawn from the Dun and Bradstreet files (which contain credit reports on an estimated 80 percent of the country's business establishments). He found that 66 percent of the new jobs which became available during the 1969-1976 period were created in establishments of 20 or fewer employees, while only 13 percent of net employment growth was in establishments with 501 or more employees. He also found that 80 percent of the new jobs are created by businesses only four or fewer years old. Large firms, he concluded, are simply no longer the major sources of new employment opportunities in this country (Birch, 1981).

Birch's findings were so striking that they were carefully reexamined by other researchers, who pointed out that many of these small establishments were not independent, but were owned by other (though not necessarily large) corporations. However, even the use of a stricter definition of "small businesses" (firms with fewer than 100 employees in all locations combined) still leads to the finding that these firms generate a disproportionate share of newly created jobs (Armington and Odle, 1982). In addition, there has been an even more rapid increase in the proportion of employment found in small establishments owned by larger corporations (Office of Technology Assessment, 1988).

Birch has continued and expanded his research. By 1986, his files contained data on the employers of approximately 95 percent of all nongovernment workers. His most recent findings are even more striking than the results of his earlier work. He reports that, during the 1981-1985 period, 88 percent of net job creation took place in firms with fewer than 20 employees. Most of this growth occurred in a subset of these smaller firms, about one in five, which had very high growth rates. These same firms had many ups and downs. They both hired and let go a large number of employees (Birch, 1987).

These facts have some important implications for anyone who is looking for work. In a small business economy, workers must find new employment more frequently than they used to. Equally important, they will have to approach many small businesses rather than simply going to a few major corporations as they might have done in the past.

Business Instability Results In More Job Changing

Economic growth and job creation have become major concerns of many American communities. Researchers studying job loss and job creation have discovered a surprising amount of both growth and decline among American businesses. On the average, every percentage point of employment growth is the net result of a point and a half of growth due to new businesses being founded, another point and a half of growth from the expansion of existing businesses, a one point loss because of business contractions, and another point loss from firms going out of business entirely.

Since most communities lose about eight percent of their jobs each year, the key to growth is how many new jobs are created. The rate of job creation varies significantly from city to city (Birch, 1987).

It is important to note that net employment growth can only begin after the lost jobs have been replaced. In Phoenix, Arizona for example, employment increased from 613,000 to 631,000 during 1980. For the Phoenix economy to grow by these 18,000 net new jobs, it was necessary to create approximately 66,700 new jobs: 48,700 to replace jobs which had been lost in declining or dying firms, and then the 18,000 additional jobs for net growth (Greene, 1982).

Because of all this simultaneous growth and decline, the American labor market is characterized by a high degree of movement from job to job and employer to employer, as some firms grow and others fail. So pervasive has this pattern become that, today, there is little difference in the likelihood of losing one's job in a large or small firm (Birch, 1987).

One study based on Unemployment Insurance tax returns for the state of California found that only 30 percent of the new hires in the state were on the same employer's payroll six months later. This percentage is undoubtedly affected by those who work for only a short time at a variety of construction jobs, or who choose to work only during peak holiday periods, or take occasional second jobs, or are summer help, or do only casual labor on a daily or weekly basis, and so on. It does, however, give an overall measure of employment instability.

The same study also found that 66 percent of the new hires in California were replacing departing workers; only two percent represented net growth. The remaining 32 percent expanded the size of some firms; this expansion, however, was balanced off by an equal decline in employment at other firms. These figures, like those already given, emphasize again the degree of volatility in the labor market (Siebert, 1977). The median number of years an American worker has been with his or her employer is only 4.2, and has been declining (Bureau of Labor Statistics, 1987).

As Self Employment Increases And Organizations Shrink, Compensation Goes Down

One potential effect of the role now being played by small businesses in generating employment opportunities is lowered worker income. In general, pay levels increase as employers become larger, with significantly higher pay in the largest firms. Establishments with 10,000 or more employees typically pay 10 to 15 percent above small employers for professional and administrative positions, and 20 percent more for clerical and technical jobs. Even firms with 2500 or more employees pay significantly higher wages than companies of smaller size (Personick and Barsky, 1982; Morton, 1986). Since the larger corporations now have fewer employees, while the workforce in smaller businesses has been growing, average pay tends to go down.

There has also been an increase in the smallest of small businesses, the self-employed. During the 1976-1983 period, nonagricultural wage and salary employment increased by 29 percent. During this same period, however, nonagricultural self-employment increased by 45 percent. Although many view this growing trend toward self-employment as indicative of a new burst of entrepreneurship, it is important to note that the self-employed, who are disproportionately older, white and male, had average annual earnings in 1982 of $12,600, in contrast to the $17,600 earned by wage and salary workers (Becker, 1984). These figures probably overstate the income gap between self-employment and working for someone else. The self-employed learn to charge many expenses to their business. It is important, nonetheless, to note that self-employment does not in itself correlate with high income.

In addition to higher pay, major firms also usually provide a much larger internal labor market, as employees move from one job to another, and from one city to another, while staying with the same corporation. This allows them some choice of occupation and working conditions while continuing to build seniority and pension benefits with the same firm. One study done in Chicago found these internal labor markets to be important in keeping employees with the same corporation (Bridges and Villemer, 1982).

Mergers And Takeovers Increase Corporate Turbulence

This may be changing. More than foreign competition has threatened the security of life in large corporations in recent years. Another phenomenon which appeared in the mid-1970s is the hostile corporate takeover. Because of the high interest rates available in the bond market, dividends paid by stocks became less attractive and stock prices declined relative to earnings. Although owning a small number of shares of a corporation's stock would produce a relatively low return, however, anyone who could buy a majority of a firm's shares would own the company. In many cases, the value of the company's assets was far greater than the combined value of all the shares. This led to a situation where corporations and even wealthy individuals would offer to buy all the shares of a corporation's stock even though the management of the company opposed this acquisition. This is known as a hostile takeover. During the 1974-1985 period, there were 243 contested attempts at such buy-outs. About half were successful. Whether successful or not, these battles often lead to the selling of parts of the targeted corporation, and the restructuring of what remains. During this process, many employees at all levels find they are out of a job (Chastain, 1985; Simic, 1986).

For those who are successful at a corporate buyout, hostile or friendly, there can be huge profits. Metromedia stock, to give a concrete example, was bought out in 1984 for $1.6 billion. The sale of Metromedia's television stations then brought in $2 billion. The mobile phone and paging services realized $1.6 billion more, with another $1 billion coming from other sales of corporate assets (Davidson, 1987).

If there is much turbulence experienced by employees of small businesses, then, there is equal turbulence among the employees of major corporations. One major — and still unanswered — question is whether the current wave of corporate mergers, combined with significant reductions in the layers of middle management, will in any way reduce the attractiveness of the internal labor markets of major corporations. There is certainly a deep awareness of the problem among corporate employees. In 1984, the management literature had four times as many articles and books on termination as in 1981 (Latack and Dozier, 1986).

There is some evidence that when managers leave a large corporation they tend not to go to another. Dyer, for example, found that when middle managers lost positions in larger firms they did not usually find similar positions elsewhere. Studying a sample of unemployed, middle-aged managers from the Forty Plus Club of Southern California (a self-help group for unemployed professionals and executives), he found that 53 percent had previously been employed by corporations of 1000 or more employees, but only 19 percent found new employment with such firms. Significantly, almost three-fourths of those who supplied salary data reported a decrease in income in their new positions (Dyer, 1973). More recently, one of the authors (Chapman) has noted the same pattern of displaced managers and professionals moving to smaller firms. A high proportion, in fact, go into business for themselves rather than move to another major corporation.

Productivity Pressures Result In Even More Layoffs

Most firms today, and particularly large ones, have programs designed to achieve greater productivity. Productivity, however, can be unemployment spelled backwards. The ability to produce more goods with fewer people may make the entire economy more efficient in the long run, but in the short run it can mean letting workers go (more typically it involves not hiring at least some of those who might otherwise have been hired).

The Fortune 500 (the 500 largest manufacturing corporations in the U.S.) have managed to increase their sales per employee (net of inflation) by 11.5 percent over the last 10 years. Chrysler, for example, used to produce 10 cars per worker per year; today it produces 15 (Nulty, 1984). Yet, over this same period the number of workers employed by these large firms dropped by 10 percent, during a time when the total number of employed Americans was increasing by 18 percent.

This unrelenting pressure to produce more profit with fewer workers is having dramatic effects. In 1987 the Fortune 500 employed 11 percent of the nation's workforce, a smaller proportion than in 1954 (the first year Fortune Magazine gathered data on them). After-tax profits of the Fortune 500, however, were 66 percent of all corporate profits in 1987; they were only 39 percent in 1954 (Guzzardi, 1988).

Many new and small businesses, particularly in the retail trade and service sectors, have absorbed a high proportion of those who might in years past have found jobs with larger manufacturing firms. Small firms typically have flexible work rules and are free of rigid corporate policy guidelines. They can be more creative in the problem-solving necessary to meet new challenges. Employment in a small business, however, also often brings less income than a similar position with a major corporation. This is especially true for the less educated. In individual cases, of course, a given small business position may pay well and provide much opportunity for advancement. Training is apt to be more personal and more tailored to the individual, and the whole environment can be less intimidating than that found in a large corporation. Some workers, as a result, have a strong preference for smaller firms. Nonetheless, particularly at a time of high real interest rates (which raise costs), small business employment can mean lower income, fewer fringe benefits and less opportunity for advancement because of a lower profit margin and a smaller and less differentiated internal labor market.

The Shift To A "Service" Economy Will Dramatically Reduce Manufacturing Jobs

For some years now, various authors have been describing (or predicting) the emergence of a "service economy" for the United States and, eventually, for the rest of the developed world. Daniel Bell's *The Coming of Post-Industrial Society* (Bell, 1973) is a thoughtful book on this topic. Alvin Toffler's *The Third Wave* (Toffler, 1981) is a popular work in this same genre. These books describe a society in which the number of persons working in manufacturing has, like the number working on farms, fallen sharply. Most workers are engaged in providing a service, not producing some material product.

One problem with discussions of this topic is a certain ambiguity in the term "service industry." Some authors are referring to everything except the goods-producing sector of the economy (that is, to everything except agriculture, manufacturing, mining and construction). Others prefer to distinguish between the goods-producing sector, wholesale and retail trade, government employment, and other services. "Other services" would then include such areas as finance, insurance, real estate, business services (programming consultants, for example, or an accounting firm), medical services of all kinds, non-government educational services, utilities, transportation, and so on.

For our purposes we will use the latter approach, since it allows us to see more clearly how the set of available jobs is changing, particularly since the pattern of employment in the different non-goods producing sectors varies significantly.

TABLE THREE

Non-Agricultural Payroll Employment by Major Industry Division

Year	Goods-producing (%)	Trade (%)	Other Service (%)	Government (%)	Total (%)
1950	41	21	25	13	100
1955	41	21	25	14	100
1960	38	21	26	15	100
1965	36	21	26	17	100
1970	33	21	28	18	100
1975	29	22	29	19	100
1980	28	22	31	18	100
1985	25	24	34	17	100
1990	24	24	36	16	100
1995	22	25	37	16	100
2000	21	25	39	15	100

Source: Bureau of Labor Statistics. Details may not add to totals due to rounding. Figures for the years after 1985 are projections.

Table Three gives the proportion of non-agricultural payroll employment found in each major industry division during the postwar period. Employment in the goods-producing sector has been falling steadily for the past 30 years. This decline was particularly rapid during the 1974-1975 recession.

Employment in wholesale and retail trade, which until 1980 provided a steady one-fifth of total employment, has more recently experienced some growth. It is important to observe that this growth is largely due to the expansion of only two types of retail operation: eating and drinking places, which grew 87 percent between 1973 and 1985, and food stores. With these exceptions, the proportion of workers in the trade sector has been generally stable. It should also be noted that the retail industry employs a disproportionately large share of part-time workers, women, young workers, persons with below-average earnings, the self-employed, and unpaid family workers. Although the number of persons working in this sector has gone up substantially, average weekly hours worked fell 11 percent during the 1973-1985 period (Urquhart, 1984; Haugen, 1986).

A Diverse And Growing Service Sector

The private service sector has clearly played a major role in absorbing the increasing number of individuals seeking work in recent years. Today a full third of employed Americans are working in this sector, and this proportion is expected to continue growing at a steady rate in the years ahead. An examination of the nature of service sector jobs is, therefore, an important step in understanding how the set of jobs available in the American economy has changed.

In examining the employment opportunities in the service sector, one is struck by their diversity. A famous surgeon examining the results from a CAT scanner (a highly technical and expensive "super X-ray") is working in the service sector. So is someone employed in a barber shop or playing with children in a day care center. So is an individual who provides seminars, on a consulting basis, to local businesses.

Some service sector firms are capital intensive (that is, they use much expensive equipment per worker). Railroad transportation and television broadcasting would be examples. Other service sector jobs, like elementary education services, typically require much less investment in equipment. Some service industries are labor intensive (hotels, for example, or medical services), employing many workers to produce each unit of output. Other segments of the service sector exhibit the reverse pattern, needing few workers per unit of output. Gas and electric utilities would be examples of these (Kutscher and Mark, 1983). The job opportunities in the service sector are thus very diverse. The pay for these jobs is equally wide-ranging.

Accurate data on the service sector is somewhat more scarce than is information on the other sectors of the economy. Collecting information on service jobs is difficult because, particularly in the non-capital intensive segments, so many small companies are involved. These small businesses enter and exit the field with great rapidity. Smaller companies are more likely than large corporations to ignore government requests for information. Smaller firms are also usually privately owned. Unlike large firms whose stock is publicly traded, they are not required by the government to publish financial and other data.

In addition, a significant segment of service sector positions are in "easy entry" occupations with low wages and high turnover, which again makes accurate and timely data collection difficult. There is also far more part-time employment (21 percent) in the service area than in the goods-producing sector (4.5 percent). This, too, adds to data collection problems (Plewes, 1982). The challenges are even greater when trying to collect information on the self-employed, and especially on those who work alone. Anyone with a business card and a telephone can become a consultant, for example. Some even skip the business card.

We have already noted that information about those services which are provided by American companies to firms and governments of other nations is frequently incomplete and inaccurate. There is a parallel (though smaller) degree of uncertainty in the data collected on the service sector of the American economy, for the reasons just reviewed. What is beyond doubt, however, is that the service sector provides a very diverse collection of jobs (from bank president to trash collector), with many small enterprises, much self-employment, and many minimum wage jobs.

Although the service sector is growing rapidly, not all parts of the service sector are growing at the same rate. Business services is the fastest growing division of this sector of the labor market, and indeed of the entire economy. This category includes temporary help agencies, computer and data processing services, medical service firms, mailing and reproduction services, advertising and management consulting (Howe, 1986). Many of the jobs being created in these firms are well paid, and demand specialized skills.

This is an important point. Many people believe the increasing number of service sector jobs are largely unskilled. This is not true. Much of the growth is in professional and managerial positions. Between 1972 and 1987, occupations with high proportions of college-educated workers grew, while those with few college-educated workers declined (Howe, 1988).

The Impact Of New Technologies

One important unknown for the future of the service sector will be the effect of foreign trade and technological change. On the one hand, American firms may well offer more services to other countries. This could, as we have already noted, help to make up for the jobs lost in manufacturing as a result of import competition. The apparel industry in New York City, for example, was once the city's largest export industry. Today New York's largest export industry is legal services. The nature of the available jobs is, of course, significantly different (Ginzberg and Vojta, 1981).

On the other hand, technology may make it practical to do some service sector jobs more cheaply overseas, just as it is already possible to manufacture many goods more cheaply in other countries. Anderson (1982) reports that satellite communications have now made it possible to do routine typing and word processing work in low-wage, English-speaking countries. Such work can be done in Barbados (an island in the Caribbean), for example, and transmitted by satellite back to the United States when completed.

Technically, there's no reason an employer in Des Moines can't have a secretary in Jamaica. American computer software companies are already employing programmers in

India. Data processing companies regularly have written documents converted into machine-readable form in Korea, Taiwan, Hong Kong and the Phillipines, where labor is cheaper. These materials (charge card slips, for example) can be flown in and processed. The resulting computer-compatible information is then either beamed back by satellite or flown back on computer tape (Executive Office of the President, 1982). Thus, even service sector jobs can be lost to foreign competition. Although such job loss may not be large, developments here are worth watching.

Competition For Government Jobs Increase

Statistics on government employment are sometimes combined with data on service employment in the private sector. Unlike the private service sector, however, the proportion of employment with federal, state and local governments is not increasing, so it is more useful to look at these figures separately.

Table Three shows that the proportion of total employment provided by government peaked about 1975, and then dropped; this drop is projected to continue. Most such jobs, it should be noted, are provided by state and local government units; federal civilian employment has been relatively low and quite stable during the postwar period.

Although this downward trend in the proportion of jobs available in government has been much less discussed than the drop in manufacturing employment, the change in trend is equally important. Instead of absorbing an increasing proportion of new workers, government employment is now not even holding its own, which puts additional pressures on the private service sector to provide jobs for all those seeking them.

It is important to note that the goods-producing and government sectors of the economy have traditionally provided a high proportion of "good jobs" (that is, positions which offer reasonable wages, a high level of job security, fringe benefits such as health insurance and pension plans, opportunities for advancement with seniority, and particularly opportunities to learn on the job and advance for those with relatively low levels of formal education). When both goods-producing and government employment grow more slowly than the rest of the economy, such jobs become relatively scarce. Pay in the trade sectors is often low, and income from service sector jobs varies widely (Cooper, 1987). This makes the competition for the "good jobs" which remain in government and manufacturing that much more intense.

Even for some of those who have managed to find or keep well-paid jobs in manufacturing, there is significant pressure on income. Real income in several industries, such as steel or meat processing, is falling (sometimes absolutely because of "give-backs," though more often because pay increases are less than inflation). Some new employees coming in under "two-tier" contracts are paid lower wages than other employees with the same jobs.

Displaced Workers Face Lower Living Standards

The transition to a service economy has given rise to the problem of the "displaced worker," the employee whose firm has either closed or permanently reduced its work force, and who must now find new employment. Many such workers, though of course not all, had jobs in manufacturing.

Displaced workers, particularly those who have worked for the same company for many years, face severe problems. A large proportion suffer a significant and permanent loss of income. Workers who lose jobs are much more likely to experience a longer period of unemployment than are those who quit or are newly entering the labor force. After finally obtaining new jobs, displaced workers typically work fewer hours than in their former jobs, and at lower pay.

Older workers have particularly difficult problems. Despite all the men aged 25 to 54 who were out of work during the 1981-1982 recession, these men still had a 25 percent better chance of finding a job than did men aged 55 and over (Rones, 1984). We have observed many "outplaced" workers over 55 try to find new employment, fail, and then either retire early or begin their own consulting or other businesses.

Even when finding new jobs, the involuntarily unemployed often face additional and serious readjustment problems. Langerman, Byerly and Root, who interviewed such workers and their spouses in Iowa, found them experiencing lower wages, less responsibility, bad hours and more physical work in their new jobs. Spouses reported health problems of various sorts (headaches, sleeplessness, backaches, high blood pressure), as well as drinking problems. There were frequent disagreements about money. There was also a tendency to contract their social lives. Some considered moving, but various personal and economic considerations (such as the problem of selling a house in a depressed housing market) often made this impractical (Langerman, Byerly and Root, 1982).

Two Boston economists who studied the employment histories of workers who lost their jobs when New England's old mill-based economy declined found that most such displaced workers experienced permanently lowered income (Anderson, 1982). The Downriver Community Conference, recognized for its exemplary service to workers displaced by plant closings in the area south of Detroit, reports that these workers had previously earned an average wage of over $9 an hour. Program participants were able to earn $8.20 on reemployment, many after receiving new training. Those who did not participate but were able to find new jobs on their own averaged only $5.72 or $6.86 an hour, depending on which comparison group was used. These figures do not include declines in fringe benefits. Although the workers in this study were mostly middle-aged men with families and solid work histories, only half of those from the plants in the comparison groups were reemployed during the first two years after losing their jobs (Smith and Kulik, 1983).

Although much of the research on displaced workers focuses on men, women workers also suffer greatly from the financial, social and emotional effects of unemployment (Nowak and Snyder, 1983).

Longer Periods Of Unemployment, Particularly For Older Workers

Some displaced workers are having a very difficult time accepting what has happened to them. There are reports of men who come every morning to their closed plants. At noon they open their lunch buckets. Then, at the hour they used to quit work, they go home.

Others cannot adjust at all. "One Akron rubber worker lost his job and watched his life shrivel. His wife divorced him and took the kid away. On the day his divorce became final, the man drove to her business and waited for her to leave work. Then he drew his car alongside hers and blew his brains out with a deer rifle. It's a tale told in whispers in the city's blue- collar bars and union halls" (Manning and McCormick, 1984: 55). It is such individual experiences of pain and loss that lie behind the general statistics we have been reviewing.

Workers who experienced no unemployment during 1981 had median family incomes of $26,600. For those who did experience some unemployment, however, this figure falls to $18,500 (Terry, 1983). It is important to note that Terry also finds unemployment associated with significantly lower incomes even after a person is reemployed.

The proportion of men who have jobs or are seeking them continues to decline even as the proportion of women at work rises, a trend which is related to the difficulties experienced by older men who lose their jobs and are unable to find new employment.

Rones (1983) reports that the older a male worker becomes, the less likely he is to quit a job and look for a new one. When older workers do become unemployed, however, the period of unemployment is likely to be a long one, and many eventually give up and withdraw from the labor force altogether. The probability of an older worker giving up the search for employment is three times what it is for a younger person. Further, even if the older worker finds a new job, it is typically at a much lower wage.

Gordus, Jarley and Ferman (1981), in a review of studies of plant closings, found that most of the workers displaced by these closings were of above-average age, since earlier layoffs had been by seniority. Educational levels were also typically low, since older workers were educated when it was common to leave school at much earlier ages than is the case today. Although blue collar workers usually take the first job offer they receive, those over 45 had significantly higher unemployment rates, which suggests that they were often unable to generate any offers. Many who did find jobs experienced large income declines. There was also a pattern of workers taking a new job and then losing it after a short period.

In mid-1983, about one in four unemployed workers had been looking for a new job for more than six months (Norwood, 1984). Between 1970 and 1982, the unemployment rate rose by 83 percent; the average duration of unemployment went up by 88 percent. This suggests that the number of unemployed individuals did not increase substantially. Instead, those who became unemployed stayed unemployed for a significantly longer period (Podgursky, 1984).

As the weeks go on, many of these individuals give up and stop looking. They are then no longer counted as unemployed by the Department of Labor, but instead as "discouraged workers" who are no longer part of the labor force. Specifically, about half of the men and 70 percent of the women who leave unemployment after experiencing it for 27 weeks or more do not find jobs, but simply give up (Garfinkle, 1977).

Because of national concern about the problem of displaced workers, the Bureau of Labor Statistics studied individuals who became unemployed because their jobs were abolished or their employers shut down between January, 1979 and January, 1984. Of the 5.1 million of these workers who had been at their jobs for at least three years before losing them, only 60 percent were reemployed in January 1984. The more skilled the person's occupation, the greater the likelihood of reemployment. About 25 percent were still looking for work; the rest had left the labor force.

Some 3.5 million of these persons filed for and collected Unemployment Insurance; nearly half of them were still unemployed when the payments ran out. The probability of reemployment declined significantly with age. It was 70 percent for those aged 20-24, but only 41 percent for those 55-64. Those who did manage to find new full-time jobs were often earning substantially less than they had previously (Flaim and Sehgal, 1985). A follow-up survey, done a year later, found that about half of the unemployed had now found jobs. Those with continuing difficulties were blacks, blue-collar workers and persons formerly employed in manufacturing (Devens, 1986; see also Horvath, 1987).

New Workers Find It Harder To "Break In" — Earn Less Even When Employed

The difficulties of older workers are paralleled by those of inexperienced youth who are making initial attempts to find employment. Higher unemployment and rapid turnover make it harder to "break in." Levin (1983) cites a study which found that a one percentage point rise in adult male unemployment is associated with a four to six percent increase in the proportion of 16-19 year old males who are unemployed.

This initial unemployment can have severe consequences. One research project, using data from the National Longitudinal Study of the high school senior class of 1972, found that those young people who did not attend college moved back and forth between a variety of jobs. The key to whether one of them was employed or unemployed in 1976 was not the quality of job held in 1973, but whether the person had *any* job in 1973. Unemployment, again, has a tendency to become chronic (Griffin, Kalleberg and Alexander, 1981). As job opportunities for high school graduates have declined, the number of young workers who may fall into a pattern of chronic unemployment has increased. In the 1979-1987 period, the increase in unemployment among 25-54 year old male high school graduates was twice as large as the rise in the overall unemployment rate (Howe, 1988).

The jobs available to high school graduates have changed dramatically. Employment in retail trade and services now provides 48 percent of jobs for young male high school graduates; it was 30 percent in 1968. In 1968, on the other hand, 57 percent of male high school graduates under 20 worked in high-paid sectors of the economy such as manufacturing; in 1986 it was only 36 percent. As a result, male high school graduates now earn 28 percent less than comparable males a decade ago. This has had a dramatic effect on their ability to successfully begin families. Among families headed by a person under 25, the poverty rate for white families doubled from 1973 to 1985, from 12 percent to 25 percent (Grant Commission, 1988). This situation has also had a severe impact on the status of young children. Two-fifths of all young families with children had incomes at or below half of the poverty level in 1986 (Congressional Budget Office, 1988). In the early 1970s, nearly

60 percent of 20-24 year old men earned enough to keep a family of three above the poverty level; by 1984, this figure had fallen to 42 percent (Berlin and Sum, 1988). One out of four children who are part of intact (married-couple) families would be poor if they were reliant only on their fathers' income.

Minority And Older Workers

The transition to a service economy has been hard on minority workers, many of whom have weak educational backgrounds. In addition, the black middle class is losing one of its sources of stable employment. Historically, a high proportion of black college graduates have taken government jobs. As job opportunities in government decline, opportunities for both new employment and promotion lessen (Freeman, 1981).

Older workers, as has already been noted, often bear a disproportionate share of the burden when plants close and corporations downsize. Between 1950 and 1960, labor force participation rates for men aged 55, 60 and 63 remained essentially steady. Between 1968 and 1980, however, their participation rates fell by 8, 13 and 27 percent respectively (Burkhauser and Turner, 1982). Some of this drop was due to voluntary early retirement, but surely not all. Many older workers want new employment but are unable to find it. There are a variety of reasons for this failure. One study which obtained responses from readers of the Harvard Business Review found that, presented with a description of exactly the same problems involving a younger worker in one case and an older worker in another, respondents perceived the older employee to be more inflexible and resistant to change. Because of this, the respondents said they would make much less effort to discuss needed changes in performance with an older worker. Yet, when asked directly about policies for older workers, these same respondents favored more affirmative action!

These findings, and the regularity with which older workers report difficulty in finding new employment, suggest that age discrimination may be the most pervasive form of discrimination remaining in the American labor market. Lower levels of formal education, not a problem when these workers were young, can be a real hindrance today. The perception of older workers as less trainable and less manageable, when combined with fears of increased and disproportionate drains on health insurance and pension funds, can be a potent barrier to their reemployment (Rosen and Jerdee, 1977).

Weakening Union Influences

Plant closings, permanent layoffs and other structural changes have led to significant reductions in union membership. The number of workers belonging to unions declined by an average of 817,000 a year between 1979 and 1983, and 361,000 a year between 1983 and 1985. By 1986 unions represented only 17.5 percent of all wage and salary workers, down from 23.0 percent in 1980 (N.A., 1987). Even those who remain members of unions often find themselves in new situations. Employee stock ownership plans, like quality circles and bonuses based on corporate profit levels, have created major changes in traditional union-management relationships.

One particularly important result of less unionization will be to contribute to a growing gap between the incomes of workers at the high and low ends of the pay scale. One goal of unions has been to reduce the variation in earnings across establishments (Freeman, 1978). Unions consistently attempt to negotiate a master contract covering all the employers in a given industry, so there is little or no pay differential from one employer to another. Unions also work to raise the pay of unskilled workers. Thus union contracts have reduced the variation in wages, both between firms and within them, including the gap between blue collar and white collar workers.

Foreign competition, however, has tended to undercut these master contracts, since foreign workers are obviously not a party to such agreements. As unions weaken, it is likely that the range of salaries and wages, both between different firms and within them, will increase. This will be particularly true in the service sector. Not only are fewer service sector workers unionized, but even those unions which do exist are often less influential, since it is difficult to negotiate a master contract with a multitude of small employers facing non-union competition.

The Growing Demand For Educated Workers

As we have seen, government and goods-producing employment have not kept up with the growth of the economy. Instead, growth has been concentrated in foodstores and the bar and restaurant segments of the retail trade sector (where pay is often low) and in the service sector (where jobs have a wide range of pay and benefits, and well-paid jobs usually require college degrees). Does this imply a decline in the overall proportion of well-paying jobs?

Probably not. While the jobs being lost are often in the higher-paying industries, many of the new jobs being created are in the higher-paying occupations (Secretary of Labor's Task Force on Economic Adjustment and Worker Dislocation, 1986). These new, demanding and well-paying service jobs are being eagerly filled by a surplus of college graduates, something we will discuss in the next chapter.

Rosenthal (1985) reports that he took the 416 detailed occupations covered by the Current Population Survey, ranked them by pay, and split them into three groups, with an equal number of occupations in each group. He then compared the proportion of workers in each group in 1973 and 1982, and found little change. The pay levels in all three groups, net of inflation, went down a bit, especially in the bottom two-thirds. One can speculate that this might be because of lower pay for the same occupations in smaller firms or different industries, though this is not certain. There is a further discussion of this issue in McMahon and Tschetter (1986). The most reasonable interpretation of the available information is that pay is becoming more closely linked to skills and education. Those who seek employment in the 1980s must, therefore, realize that they are dealing with a labor market which has changed significantly since the earlier part of the postwar period. It is not just that there are too few jobs for the large numbers of persons seeking employment, though that is certainly a major problem. It is also that the jobs which remain are less secure, and either pay less or demand higher levels of education and training. This means there is competition for all jobs because of high unemployment, and because the number of college graduates has expanded even more quickly than the number of jobs requiring a college degree There is particularly fierce competition for well-paid jobs that most people can fill, because of their increasing scarcity. This is true now, and will be true in the future. The occupations where the most rapid growth is projected require above-average math, language and reasoning skills. More than half the new jobs created over the 1984-2000 period will require education beyond high school; a third will require a college degree (Hudson Institute, 1987).

For Many, Family Income Is Going Down

Because of all the changes we have been discussing, a significant number of Americans have recently experienced, or are now experiencing, downward mobility. This is particularly true in the bottom half of the income structure, and is very different from the experience of the 1950s and 1960s. During the 1950s median real family income rose by $4200; during the 1960s, by $5300. In the 1970s, however, despite 3.2 million wives joining the work force, median family income net of inflation rose by less than $100 (Sternlieb and Hughes, 1982; all figures are in constant 1980 dollars).

Even those who remain in unionized occupations have been receiving only very small pay increases in recent years. In 1986, major collective bargaining settlements provided record low wage and compensation adjustments. Such record lows have been common for some years. In fact, although 1.7 million workers negotiated pay increases under union contracts in 1986, another half million received no increase and a quarter million accepted pay cuts (Lacombe and Borum, 1987).

Increased foreign trade has been fallen particularly hard on unionized blue collar workers. In the economy as a whole, one job in five is held by a college graduate. Only one job in every seven lost because of foreign trade, however, requires a college degree. It is the blue collar jobs typically held by less educated workers which have been most vulnerable to increased trade (Office of Technology Assessment, 1988).

Downward mobility is not confined to blue collar workers, however. A similar fate may lie in store for those who are turned out of professional positions and are unable to find something new at comparable pay. Paula Leventman has documented the experience of scientists, engineers and computer professionals who lost their jobs with firms in the route 128 area around Boston during the 1970 economic downturn. Some never were reemployed, particularly among the group over 45, and more than a quarter ended up in jobs well below their previous level of pay and responsibility. Much bitterness, disillusionment and resentment were found among this group (Leventman, 1981). We have noted the apparent contradiction in the pattern of simultaneous worker movement from higher-paying industries to lower, while at the same time many better-paid occupations are growing. This is but one example of the up and down pattern of income which is typical of the new economy. Some individuals and families are doing much better financially; others much worse. One way to get a clearer idea of what is happening is to examine the trend of individual income regardless of industry or occupation.

TABLE FOUR

Median Weekly Earnings of
Male Wage and Salary Workers Aged 25 and Over

Year	Current Dollars	Constant 1987 Dollars	Year	Current Dollars	Constant 1987 Dollars
1973	203	519	1981	371	464
1974	219	505	1982	393	463
1975	235	496	1983	406	463
1976	250	499	1984	422	462
1977	272	510	1985	442	467
1978	293	510	1986	462	479
1979	314	492	1987	477	477
1980	339	468			

Source: Bureau of Labor Statistics. Consumer Price Index used is that for Urban Wage Earners and Clerical Workers.

Because of the large number of women and young persons who newly entered the labor force in recent years (a group which one would expect to have lower incomes since they have less seniority and experience), it is useful to examine what has happened to the income of adult males. Table Four gives the median usual weekly earnings of men aged 25 and over who are working full-time. These figures are not affected by the lower earnings of women and younger workers, nor by the lowered earnings of men who are unemployed or working only part-time.

The general pattern is downward, with a decline of about eight percent over the 1973-1987 period, but it is not an even pattern. There was a large movement down during the high inflation of 1978-1981, and a leveling off with some recovery in recent years. The net effect is certainly not an income collapse, but it is a loss. Associated with this loss is a different pattern of family incomes (discussed in Chapter Three) and much movement, in individual incomes, both up and down.

The Fastest And Slowest Growing Jobs

The Department of Labor has done a detailed projection of the occupations which will grow most rapidly as the U.S. economy moves toward the year 2000. We include two tables of data here, taken from Kutscher (1988).

TABLE FIVE

Fastest Growing Occupations, 1986-2000
(Numbers in thousands)

Occupation	Employment		Change in employment, 1986-2000		Percent of projected job growth 1986-2000
	1986	Projected 2000	Number	Percent	
Legal assistants	61	125	64	103.7	0.3
Medical assistants	132	251	119	90.4	.6
Physical therapists	61	115	53	87.5	.2
Physical and corrective therapy assistants and aides	36	65	29	81.6	.1
Data processing equipment repairers	69	125	56	80.4	.3
Homemaker-home health aides	138	249	111	80.1	.5
Podiatrists	13	23	10	77.2	0
Computer systems analysts	331	582	251	75.6	1.2
Medical record technicians	40	70	30	75.0	.1
Employment interviewers	75	129	54	71.2	.3
Computer programmers	479	813	335	69.9	1.6
Radiologic technologists and technicians	115	190	75	64.7	.3
Dental hygienists	87	141	54	62.6	.3
Dental assistants	155	244	88	57.0	.4
Physicians assistants	26	41	15	56.7	.1
Operations research analysts	38	59	21	54.1	.1
Occupational therapists	29	45	15	52.2	1

TABLE FIVE (Continued)

Fastest Growing Occupations, 1986-2000
(Numbers in thousands)

Occupation	Employment		Change in employment, 1986-2000		Percent of projected job growth
	1986	Projected 2000	Number	Percent	1986-2000
Peripheral electronic data processing equipment operators	46	70	24	50.8	.1
Data entry keyers, composing	29	43	15	50.8	.1
Optometrists	37	55	18	49.2	.1

Notice how many of the growing occupations are found in trade and services, particularly business and health services. Many of these jobs require specialized training beyond high school. Notice also the concentration of declining occupations in manufacturing, and particularly in assembly line work. Many of these jobs could be filled by high school graduates. There are also a number of clerical occupations (stenographers, statistical clerks, central officer operators) where fewer people are needed because much of the work is now done by computers or computer- controlled equipment. These jobs, too, typically do not require any training beyond high school. More and more, post-high school training is becoming essential for well-paid employment.

TABLE SIX

Fastest Declining Occupations, 1986-2000
(Numbers in thousands)

Occupation	Employment		Change in employment, 1986-2000	
	1986	Projected 2000	Number	Percent
Electrical and electronics assemblers	249	116	133	53.7
Electronic semiconductor processors	29	14	15	51.1
Railroad conductors and yardmasters	29	17	12	40.9
Railroad brake, signal, and switch operators	42	25	17	39.9
Gas and petroleum plant and system occupations	31	20	11	34.3

TABLE SIX *(Continued)*

Fastest Declining Occupations, 1986-2000
(Numbers in thousands)

Occupation	Employment Projected		Change in employment, 1986-2000	
	1986	2000	Number	Percent
Industrial truck and tractor operators	426	283	143	33.6
Shoe sewing-machine operators and tenders	27	18	9	32.1
Station installers and repairers, telephone	58	40	18	31.8
Chemical equipment controllers, operators, and tenders	73	52	21	29.7
Chemical plant and system operators	33	23	10	29.6
Stenographers	178	128	50	28.2
Farmers	1,182	850	332	28.1
Statistical clerks	71	52	19	26.4
Textile draw-out and winding machine operators and tenders	219	164	55	25.2
Central office and PBX installers and repairers	74	57	17	23.1
Farm workers	940	750	190	20.3
Coil winders, tapers, and finishers	34	28	6	18.5
Central office operators	42	34	8	17.9
Directory assistance operators	32	27	5	17.7
Compositors, typesetters, and arrangers, precision	30	25	5	17.1

Growth In The 225 Most Popular Jobs

Table Seven summarizes data on the growth of 225 of the most popular jobs in our economy (White, 1988). About two-thirds of all U.S. workers are employed in one of them. The average growth expected to the year 2000 for all occupations is 19 percent. This average, however, conceals wide differences from occupation to occupation. Run your eye down the "Percent change, 1986-2000" column in Table Seven. You will see some occupations that will grow far more than average, and others that will actually decline.

The 225 occupations covered by this table are grouped into 18 clusters. This allows you to look both at a specific occupation, and at related occupations requiring similar skills, or found in other settings.

The U.S. Department of Labor publishes two reference books with more detailed information on each of the occupations in this table. Both the *Occupational Outlook Handbook* and *Occupational Projections and Training Data* can be found in most libraries. The *Occupational Outlook Handbook* provides particularly helpful and readable information on each of the jobs covered in Table Seven. Another excellent source of information is *The American Almanac of Jobs and Salaries* (Wright, 1984).

TABLE SEVEN

Job Outlook in 225 Most Popular Jobs, 1986-2000

Ocupational Cluster Occupation	Employed 1986	% Change 1986-2000	# Change 1986-2000
Managerial and management-related occupations			
Accountants and auditors	945,000	40	376,000
Construction and building inspectors	50,000	11	15,400
Cost estimators	157,000	20	31,000
Education administrators	288,000	13	37,000
Employment interviewers	75,000	71	54,000
Financial managers	638,000	24	154,000
General managers and top executives	2,383,000	24	582,000
Health service managers	274,000	56	153,000
Hotel managers and assistants	78,000	50	39,000
Inspectors and compliance officers, except construction	125,000	13	17,000
Management analysts and consultants	126,000	31	40,000
Marketing, advertising, and public relations managers	323,000	32	105,000
Personnel, training, and labor relations specialists and managers	381,000	24	91,000
Property and real estate managers	128,000	39	50,000
Purchasing agents and managers	418,000	8	35,000
Restaurant and food service managers	470,000	28	133,000
Underwriters	99,000	34	34,000
Wholesale and retail buyers	192,000	9	17,000
Ocupational Cluster **Occupation**	**Employed** **1986**	**% Change** **1986-2000**	**# Change** **1986-2000**
Engineers, Surveyors, and Architects			
Engineers	1,371,000	32	444,000
Aerospace engineers	53,000	11	5,800

TABLE SEVEN *(continued)*

Job Outlook in 225 Most Popular Jobs, 1986-2000

Ocupational Cluster Occupation	Employed 1986	% Change 1986-2000	# Change 1986-2000
Chemical engineers	52,000	16	8,100
Civil engineers	199,000	25	50,000
Electrical and electronics engineers	401,000	48	192,000
Industrial engineers	117,000	30	35,000
Mechanical engineering	233,000	33	76,000
Metallurgical, ceramic, and materials engineers	18,000	25	4,500
Mining engineers	5,200	0	Less than 500
Nuclear engineers	14,000	1	Less than 500
Petroleum engineers	22,000	8	1,700

Ocupational Cluster Occupation	Employed 1986	% Change 1986-2000	# Change 1986-2000
Architects and surveyors			
Architects	84,000	30	25,000
Landscape architects	18,000	38	7,000
Surveyors	94,000	20	19,000

Ocupational Cluster Occupation	Employed 1986	% Change 1986-2000	# Change 1986-2000
Natural, Computer, and Mathematical Scientists			
Actuaries	9,400	48	4,500
Computer systems analysts	331,000	76	251,000
Mathematicians	20,000	24	4,800
Operations research analysts	38,000	54	21,000
Statisticians	18,000	24	4,400
Agricultural scientists	28,000	22	6,300
Biological scientists	61,000	23	14,000
Foresters and conservation	24,000	10	2,300
Chemists	86,000	11	9,800
Geologists and geophysicists	44,000	13	5,800
Meteorologists	5,600	29	1,600
Physicists and astronomers	22,000	17	3,700

TABLE SEVEN *(continued)*

Job Outlook in 225 Most Popular Jobs, 1986-2000

Ocupational Cluster Occupation	Employed 1986	% Change 1986-2000	# Change 1986-2000
Lawyers, Social scientists, Social workers, and religious workers			
Lawyers	527,000	36	191,000
Economists	37,000	34	13,000
Psychologists	110,000	34	37,000
Sociologists		(estimates not available)	
Urban and regional planners	20,000	19	4,000
Human services workers	88,000	38	34,000
Social workers	365,000	33	120,000
Recreation workers	164,000	20	33,000
Protestant ministers	429,000	(estimates not available)	
Rabbis	6,500	(estimates not available)	
Roman Catholic priests	57,000	(estimates not available)	

Ocupational Cluster Occupation	Employed 1986	% Change 1986-2000	# Change 1986-2000
Teachers, Librarians and Counselors			
Adult and vocational educational teachers	427,000	19	82,000
Archivists and curators	8,300	22	1,800
College and university faculty	754,000	-4	-32,000
Counselors	123,000	21	25,000
Kindergarten and elementary school teachers	1,527,000	20	299,000
Librarians	136,000	13	18,000
Secondary school teachers	1,128,000	13	152,000

Ocupational Cluster Occupation	Employed 1986	% Change 1986-2000	# Change 1986-2000
Health Practitioners			
Chiropractors	32,000	(estimates not available)	
Dentists	151,000	30	45,000
Optometrists	37,000	49	18,000
Physicians	491,000	38	188,000
Podiatrists	13,000	77	10,000
Veterinarians	37,000	46	17,000

TABLE SEVEN (continued)

Job Outlook in 225 Most Popular Jobs, 1986-2000

Ocupational Cluster Occupation	Employed 1986	% Change 1986-2000	# Change 1986-2000
Health Assessing and Treating Occupations			
Dietitians and nutritionists	40,000	34	14,000
Occupational therapists	29,000	52	15,000
Pharmacists	151,000	24	36,000
Physicial therapists	61,000	87	53,000
Physician assistants	26,000	57	15,000
Recreational therapists	29,000	49	14,000
Registered nurses	1,406,000	44	612,000
Respiratory therapists	56,000	34	19,000
Speech-language pathologists and audiologists	45,000	34	15,000

Ocupational Cluster Occupation	Employed 1986	% Change 1986-2000	# Change 1986-2000
Writers, Artists and Entertainers			
Public Relations specialists	87,000	40	35,000
Radio and television announcers and newscasters	61,000	24	15,000
Reporters and correspondents	75,000	18	13,000
Writers and editors	214,000	34	73,000
Designers	259,000	32	84,000
Photographers and camera operators	109,000	33	37,000
Visual artists	176,000	34	59,000
Actors, directors and producers	73,000	34	24,000
Dancers and choreographers	14,000	31	4,300
Musicians	189,000	23	42,000

Ocupational Cluster Occupation	Employed 1986	% Change 1986-2000	# Change 1986-2000
Technician Occupations			
Clinical laboratory technologists and technicians	239,000	24	57,000
Dental hygienists	87,000	63	54,000
Dispensing opticians	50,000	46	23,000
EEG technologists and technicians	5,900	42	2,500
EKG technicians	18,000	16	2,900
Emergency medical technicians	65,000	15	9,800

TABLE SEVEN (continued)

Job Outlook in 225 Most Popular Jobs, 1986-2000

Ocupational Cluster Occupation	Employed 1986	% Change 1986-2000	# Change 1986-2000
Licensed practical nurses	631,000	38	238,000
Medical record technicians	40,000	75	30,000
Nuclear medicine technologists	9,700	23	2,200
Radiologic technologists	115,000	65	75,000
Surgicial technicians	37,000	33	12,000
Air traffic controllers	26,000	8	2.100
Broadcast technicians	27,000	20	5,400
Computer programmers	479,000	70	335,000
Drafters	348,000	2	5,500
Engineering technicians	689,000	35	245,000
Legal assistants	61,000	104	64,000
Library technicians	51,000	13	6,600
Science technicians	227,000	15	35,000
Tool programmers, numerical control	8,800	15	1,300

Ocupational Cluster Occupation	Employed 1986	% Change 1986-2000	# Change 1986-2000
Marketing and Sales Occupations (*excludes self-employed workers)			
Cashiers	2,165,000	27	575,000
Counter and rental clerks	178,000	34	60,000
Insurance sales workers	463,000	22	102,000
Manufacturers' sales workers	*543,000	3	18,000
Real estate agents and brokers	376,000	44	166,000
Retail sales workers	*4,266,000	32	1,345,000
Securities and financial services sales representatives	197,000	42	82,000
Services sales representatives	*419,000	56	237,000
Travel agents	105,00	46	49,000
Wholesale trade sales workers	*1,217,000	33	405,000

Ocupational Cluster Occupation	Employed 1986	% Change 1986-2000	# Change 1986-2000
Administrative Support Occupations, including Clerical			
Bank tellers	539,000	13	71,000
Bookkeepers and accounting clerks	2,116,000	4	92,000

TABLE SEVEN *(continued)*

Job Outlook in 225 Most Popular Jobs, 1986-2000

Ocupational Cluster Occupation	Employed 1986	% Change 1986-2000	# Change 1986-2000
Clerical supervisors and managers	956,000	21	205,000
Computer and peripheral equipment operators	309,000	48	148,000
Data entry keyers	400,000	-16	-66,000
File clerks	242,000	13	32,000
General office clerks	2,361,000	20	462,000
Insurance claims and policy processing occupations	388,000	11	42,000
Postal clerks and mail carriers	639,000	6	40,000
Receptionists and information clerks	682,000	41	282,000
Reservation and transportation ticket agents and travel clerks	122,000	20	24,000
Secretaries	3,234,000	13	424,000
Statistical clerks	71,000	-26	-19,000
Stenographers	178,000	-28	-50,000
Stock clerks	1,813,000	11	202,000
Teachers aides	648,000	19	125,000
Telephone operators	353,000	11	38,000
Traffic, shipping and receiving clerks	548,000	7	38,000
Typists and word processors	1,002,000	-14	-140,000

Ocupational Cluster Occupation	Employed 1986	% Change 1986-2000	# Change 1986-2000
Service Occupations			
Correction officers	176,000	34	60,000
Firefighting occupations	279,000	17	47,000
Guards	794,000	48	383,000
Police, detectives, and special agents	489,000	18	87,000
Chefs, cooks and other kitchen workers	2,563,000	34	864,000
Food and beverage service workers	4,204,000	39	1,628,000
Dental assistants	155,000	57	88,000
Medical assistants	132,000	90	119,000
Nursing aides and psychiatric aides	1,312,000	33	437,000
Barbers	80,000	1	800
Childcare workers	589,000	20	118,000
Cosmetologists and related workers	595,000	18	107,000
Flight attendants	80,000	32	26,000
Homemaker-home health aides	197,000	71	139,000

Job Outlook in 225 Most Popular Jobs, 1986-2000

Ocupational Cluster Occupation	Employed 1986	% Change 1986-2000	# Change 1986-2000
Janitors and cleaners	2,676,000	23	604,000
Private household workers	981,000	-3	-26,000

Ocupational Cluster Occupation	Employed 1986	% Change 1986-2000	# Change 1986-2000
Agriculture, Forestry, Fishing and related occupations			
Farm operators and managers	1,336,000	-21	- 285,000
Timber cutting and logging occupations	103,000	-7	- 6,900

Ocupational Cluster Occupation	Employed 1986	% Change 1986-2000	# Change 1986-2000
Mechanics, Installers and Repairers			
Aircraft mechanics and engine specialists	107,000	20	22,000
Automotive body repairs	214,000	12	25,000
Automotive mechanics	748,000	8	60,000
Commercial and industrial electronic equipment repairers	81,000	28	23,000
Communications equipment mechanics	109,000	-21	-23,000
Computer service technicians	69,000	80	56,000
Diesel mechanics	263,000	24	63,000
Electronic home entertainment equipment repairers	49,000	20	9,900
Elevator installers and repairers	15,000	22	3,400
Farm equipment mechanics	52,000	4	1,900
General maintenance mechanics	1,039,000	22	232,000
Heating, air-conditioning and refrigeration mechanics	222,000	22	50,000
Home appliance and power tool repairers	76,000	10	7,700
Industrial machinery repairers	421,000	6	26,000
Line installers and cable splicers	227,000	0	Less than 500
Millwrights	86,000	8	7,200
Mobile heavy equipment mechanics	102,000	24	25,000
Motorcycle, boat and small engine mechanics	49,000	21	10,000
Musical instrument repairers and tuners	8,100	7	600
Office machine and cash register servicers	56,000	40	22,000

TABLE SEVEN (continued)

Job Outlook in 225 Most Popular Jobs, 1986-2000

Ocupational Cluster Occupation	Employed 1986	% Change 1986-2000	# Change 1986-2000
Telephone installers and repairers	58,000	-32	-18,000
Vending machine servicers and repairers	27,000	12	3,100

Ocupational Cluster Occupation	Employed 1986	% Change 1986-2000	# Change 1986-2000
Construction Trades and Extractive Occupations			
Bricklayers and stonemasons	161,000	16	26,000
Carpenters	1,010,000	18	182,000
Carpet installers	66,000	26	17,000
Cement masons and terrazzo workers	118,000	21	24,000
Drywall workers and lathers	154,000	24	37,000
Electricians	556,000	16	89,000
Glaziers	47,000	19	9,100
Insulation workers	62,000	22	13,000
Painters and paperhangers	412,000	22	90,000
Plasterers	28,000	12	3,300
Plumbers and pipefitters	402,000	17	69,000
Roofers	142,000	28	39,000
Roustabouts	56,000	-7	-4,200
Sheet-metal workers	93,000	22	20,000
Structural and reinforcing metal workers	86,000	20	17,000
Tilesetters	32,000	25	7,800

Ocupational Cluster Occupation	Employed 1986	% Change 1986-2000	# Change 1986-2000
Production Occupations			
Apparel workers	1,081,000	-9	97,000
Bindery workers	83,000	22	18,000
Blue-collar worker supervisors	1,823,000	8	144,000
Boilermakers	30,000	5	1,600
Butchers and meatcutters	248,000	4	11,000
Compositors and typesetters	96,000	9	8,300
Dental laboratory technicians	46,000	39	18,000
Electric powerplant operators and power distributors and dispatchers	45,000	11	4,900

Job Outlook in 225 Most Popular Jobs, 1986-2000

Ocupational Cluster Occupation	Employed 1986	% Change 1986-2000	# Change 1986-2000
Inspectors, testers and graders	694,000	0	-2,600
Jewelers	36,000	22	8,100
Lithographic and photoengraving	77,000	25	19,000
Machinists	378,000	-1	-5,500
Metalworking and plastic-working machine operators	1,298,000	-5	-60,000
Numerical-control machine-tool operators	56,000	7	3,700
Ophthalmic laboratory technicians	24,000	27	6,400
Painting and coating machine operators	100,000	1	1,400
Photographic process workers	56,000	29	16,000
Precision assemblers	351,000	-1	-2,700
Printing press operators	222,000	18	40,000
Shoe and leatherworkers and repairers	35,000	-17	-5,900
Stationary engineers	41,000	5	1,900
Textile machinery operators	309,000	-22	-67,000
Tool-and-die makers	160,000	5	8,300
Upholsterers	74,000	10	7,600
Water and wastewater treatment plant operators	74,000	15	11,000
Welders, cutters and welding machine operators	414,000	1	4,600
Woodworking occupations	351,000	12	42,000
Ocupational Cluster Occupation	**Employed** 1986	**% Change** 1986-2000	**# Change** 1986-2000
Transportation and Material Moving Occupations			
Aircraft pilots	76,000	29	22,000
Busdrivers	478,000	16	77,000
Material moving equipment operators	998,000	-9	-93,000
Truckdrivers	2,463,000	21	505,000
Ocupational Cluster Occupation	**Employed** 1986	**% Change** 1986-2000	**# Change** 1986-2000
Handlers, Equipment Cleaners, Helpers and Laborers			
Construction trade helpers	519,000	13	68,000

Labor Market Changes Affect Society

The sectoral changes in employment discussed in this chapter are not only economic issues. They also involve major social changes. As jobs move and individual incomes rise or fall, the status of the family and all of its members rises or falls too. When more and more women work, the role of women changes, raising children becomes difficult and the nature of family life shifts significantly. As college educated women seek professional careers while proportionately fewer less educated women seek paid employment, the economic significance of a college degree changes. When persons with college degrees fail to find professional employment and instead take lower level jobs, they compete for these jobs with those who have less education, increasing the unemployment rates of the less educated. All these changes create a very different society from the one we knew in the first quarter century after the end of World War II. In Chapter Three, we will look at some of these changes more closely.

Notes✦✦✦

Regarding Table Four, readers unfamiliar with the distinction should note that, whereas the mean is the arithmetic average (the mean of 3,4,8,9 and 21 is 3+4+8+9+21 divided by 5, or 9), the median is the middle number of the distribution (in this case, 8). The median is ordinarily used when very large or very small numbers make the mean untypical of the group. A few millionaires can make a small town's average income quite high, for example, even though most people in the town have only moderate incomes. In such a situation the median income is a much better measure of what is typical.

CHAPTER THREE
A Different Culture
Is Emerging

America's changing employment patterns have led to many related social and economic changes. In this chapter we will discuss three: a changed pattern of family income, a new role for women in the labor force and in the family, and a more competitive situation for those who have earned college degrees.

The Rich Get Richer

We have already noted that the real income of adult males has declined over the last decade. The effect of this change has, however, been counterbalanced (and often more than counterbalanced) by the entry of many wives into the labor force. Further, although average male incomes have declined, the incomes of some men have risen while those of others have dropped because of forced moves to lower paid employment.

The net effect of all these trends has been to significantly change the mix of family incomes. The number of affluent families has increased substantially. Unfortunately, the number of poor families has also edged up. In 1986 the richest fifth of the nation's families received nearly 44 percent of the country's total money income, a larger share than has been typical during the rest of the postwar period. This is 9.5 times as much as the poorest fifth received. The ratio was 7.5 to one just 10 years ago (Steinberg, 1983).

TABLE EIGHT

Total Family Income in Constant 1986 Dollars

Income	1970 (%)	1975 (%)	1980 (%)	1986 (%)
Under $20,000	31.8	32.6	33.4	31.8
$20,000-34,999	34.5	32.4	30.9	27.9
$35,000 and Up	33.7	35.1	35.6	40.3
Median Income	$27,862	$27,949	$27,974	$29,458

Source: Bureau of the Census. Details may not add to totals due to rounding.

The changing pattern of family income distribution can be seen in Table Eight. Although median family income moved within a narrow range during the 1970s, this fact conceals the changes which were taking place in the overall shape of the family income distribution. In 1970, about a third of the nation's families were in each of the income categories given. By 1986, however, the middle proportion had dropped substantially, while the proportion of upper income families went up by the same amount. The bottom third stayed the same. However, the lowest-income part of this third (families with incomes below $10,000) increased.

Fewer "Traditional" Families

We see here the result of many cross-currents of change, both those we have been discussing and some we have not. The family structure itself has changed during this period. Today's "family" is not the same as the "family" of 1970. The average family now includes fewer children, more single parent families, more elderly, and more childless couples.

Between 1970 and 1985, the proportion of married couples among the country's 86.8 million households fell from 71 percent to 58 percent. There has been a 90 percent increase in the number of people living alone over this same period. The median age at which women marry is over 23, the highest in U.S. history. Average household size has dropped from 3.1 to 2.7 (Beckwith, 1985).

These demographic changes cushion the effects of lower individual incomes (because fewer dollars are needed by smaller families to maintain the same standard of living). Note, however, that it is difficult to determine the order of causality. Are people having fewer children so they can work, or working because they have no desire for children?

The trend toward increasing extremes of family income, and an increasing gap between those who are affluent and those who are not, is projected to continue in the years ahead. Hunter (1984) cites projections made by Data Resources, Inc. According to these data, the number of U.S. households earning $30,000 or more (in constant 1982 dollars) should almost double, from 24.6 million in 1980 to 43.9 million in 1995, as their share of total household income rises from 30 percent in 1980 to 42 percent in 1995.

There are two fundamental reasons why this pattern is projected to continue. The first is the increased income of the two-career family. The second is the movement of the baby-boom group into the prime earning years (ages 35-50). Families which are doing well, and especially those with two professional incomes, will experience growing affluence. Less educated and less successful households, however, will be experiencing declining incomes.

For The First Time, Over 50 Percent Of All Women Work Outside The Home

Women played a major part in the social and economic changes which transformed both the labor market and society. They are now regularly providing a high proportion of family income, and filling many of the new jobs being created in this country. It is difficult to imagine the recent strong growth in the service sector occurring without an increased group of women workers seeking and obtaining these positions.

Table Nine shows that the pattern of increasing female employment has been constant throughout the postwar era, with a particularly rapid increase during 1975-1980. Census data suggests that this pattern of consistent increase goes back at least to 1890, when 18 percent of the nation's women aged 14 and over worked outside the home. This proportion increased slowly from 1890 to 1930. It rose more rapidly after 1930, with the beginning of the Great Depression.

The recent growth in female labor force participation has been strong enough to more than cancel the drop in male labor force participation. As a result, the employed proportion of the civilian adult population has risen to an all-time high. About 60 percent of the married-couple families in 1940 reported the husband as the sole wage-earner. This was true of less than 25 percent of such families in 1981 (Legrande, 1983). Equally important, women are now moving toward year-round, full-time, uninterrupted work patterns (Shank, 1988). By 1978, for the first time in American History, half of America's adult women were working or actively seeking work outside the home. More and more, women are continuing to work after childbirth. Since 1980, the number of children with mothers in the labor force has increased by over 2.5 million. Children under 6 were 90% of this increase. By 1984, 56 percent of all children below the age of 18 had mothers who were either employed or looking for work (Hayghe, 1984). In 1970, only 24 percent of the women with children one year old or younger were in the labor force. By 1984, this figure had almost doubled, to 47 percent. By 1987, over half of the families with children under six had an employed mother, and more than 70 percent of the women in the prime working years (25-54) were in the labor force.

TABLE NINE

Female Civilian Labor Force Participation Rate

Year	Participation Rate (%)
1950	33.9
1955	35.7
1960	37.7
1965	39.3
1970	43.3
1975	46.3
1980	51.5
1985	54.5
1990	57.4
1995	59.8
2000	61.5

Source: Bureau of Labor Statistics. Figures after 1985 are estimates.

Closely related to this rise in the number of married women working outside the home is the fall in the number of children per family. In 1970, the average child had 2.4 siblings under the age of 18. By 1979, this had fallen to an average of only 1.6 siblings (Fuchs, 1983). We are clearly witnessing a trend toward postponing both marriage and child-bearing to a later age. Young women who are delaying marriage until their late twenties have a particularly high labor force participation rate.

Why Are More Women Working?

Clearly, there is no simple answer to this question. It is, as we have seen, not a new trend. At least three major, interacting factors are involved.

First, many women are more conscious of a need to achieve something in the world beyond the home as well as within it. And, now that so many women have jobs, they are receiving more social support in their efforts to fulfill this need. This is not to imply that such a transition is always easy, however. Lillian Rubin has vividly described the movement from work within the home to work outside of it, and the problems involved in making this change, in her book *Women of a Certain Age* (Rubin, 1981).

Second, there is the drawing power of the income which can be earned. There has been a large increase in the number of women receiving college degrees, and income grows with level of education. Women with college educations who work full-time have median weekly earnings which are 46 percent higher than the earnings of women with only high school diplomas (Bureau of Labor Statistics, 1982). So it is not surprising that the higher her level of education, the more likely a woman works outside the home. During 1982, women with 4 or more years of college experienced a 5.1 percent gain in real income, while women with lower educational levels had no gain, and men experienced a decline (Bureau of the Census, 1983). Since college-educated women tend to marry college-educated men, this female income pattern is one contributor toward an increasing gap between well- off families and poorer families.

Finally, there is the press of need. As the real income of adult males dropped, many women sought paid employment to maintain family living standards. The labor force participation rate of husbands, which was 91 percent in 1955, is now only 79 percent. This drop is largely due to a dramatic decline in labor force participation by husbands aged 55 and over (Hayghe and Haugen, 1987). At least some of this decline is attributable to male job loss followed by failure to find new employment.

Economic pressures are even stronger when, usually because of divorce, a woman must support herself and her children in a single parent family. Between 1957 and 1987, the proportion of divorced and not remarried women in the adult population rose from 3.0 to 11.8 percent (Shank,.1988). Since divorcees have historically had the highest labor force participation rates of any group of women, a high divorce rate is an important factor in the growing number of women working outside the home.

Many divorced individuals remarry, of course, but some do not. Since 1940, the number of married couples has nearly doubled, but the number of families maintained by women has almost tripled (Waldman, 1983). Many of these female-headed families live in or near poverty.

Women Earn Less, But The Gap Is Narrowing

Although the proportion of women working outside the home has risen dramatically, their experience in the labor market is still markedly different from that of men. Rytina (1983) reports that if the 1981 annual earnings of women working full time are compared to those of men, women earned only 60 percent of what men earned. If weekly earnings are compared, women earned 65 percent of what men earned. (There are several technical reasons for this difference; annual data include all jobs held during the year, overtime, and the earnings of the self-employed, while the weekly figures do not.) The earnings of women working full-time have been rising faster than inflation, however, and also faster than the earnings of men working full-time. By 1987, women were receiving over 70 percent of the weekly earnings of men.

The Occupational Segregation Of Women

Although the gap is narrowing, women still consistently earn less than men, at least on average. A review of the jobs typically held by women reveals that women are concentrated in a relatively small number of occupational categories, most of which do not pay particularly well (Rytina, 1982). This concentration holds true even for professionals. Nearly half of female professionals are either nurses or noncollege teachers (Rytina and Bianchi, 1984).

As the percentage of female workers in an occupation goes up, the earnings of both sexes in that occupation goes down (Quester and Olson, 1978). One study found each percentage point female associated with $42 less in median annual earnings (Reskin and Hartmann, 1986). Similarly, profitable and high-paying firms more often hire men, while those offering lower pay are more likely to hire women (Blau, 1977).

One unfortunate effect of the downturn in manufacturing employment in such high-paying industries as steel and auto has been a loss of employment by women who entered such jobs during the 1970s. The steel industry employed 14,500 women in production and maintenance in 1980; by 1985, employment had fallen below 3,000. Similarly, female membership in the United Auto Workers fell by one-third between 1981 and 1984 (Wilson, 1985).

A little-noted but important aspect of segregation by sex is the degree to which workers are segregated in individual businesses. Even occupations which are routinely held by both men and women are rarely held by both sexes in the same firm. Some restaurants have waitresses, for example, and some have waiters, but few have both. Accountants in one business will be largely male; in another, largely female. Individual employers apparently see some jobs as appropriate for women and others for men, and rarely mix them — even when an employer down the street is doing the exact opposite (Bielby and Baron, 1986). Family demands also play a role in holding down women's earnings. Service sector jobs, which attract many women and are more likely to have flexible hours, are also more likely to be located near residential areas. Many of these positions have relatively low pay. Employers of "back office" workers sometimes prefer to locate in suburban areas to attract dependable, educated women workers who wish to avoid the time, costs and distance from family involved in commuting to downtown employment.

There is much such commuting. About twice as many people commute daily from one suburb to another as go from a suburb to a central city. Suburban jobs, however, typically pay less than downtown or industrial area jobs (Fuchs, 1983). Higher incomes are associated with commuting beyond one's immediate neighborhood (Westcott, 1979).

Women Are Less Stable — A Self-Fulfilling Prophecy?

For a variety of reasons similarly rooted in family and child care requirements, women are more likely to move in and out of the labor force at various times during their adult lives. As a result, at most ages men have worked at least 50 percent more years with their current employers than have women of the same age (Fuchs, 1983). This has seriously negative consequences for a woman's salary. The longer a woman has been with the same employer, the more likely she is to be promoted and the less likely she is to experience downward mobility (Felmlee, 1982). One Census Bureau study estimates that, if women had the same experience, work interruptions and education as men, the gap between male and female earnings would be reduced 15 percent (N.A., 1985).

The average man now enters or reenters the labor force 3 times during his lifetime, and spends 38.5 years working or looking for work. Women enter or reenter 4.5 times, and spend 27.7 years in the labor force (Smith, 1982). As women continue to move into full-time, year-round jobs, however, these figures will change, and the work patterns of the two sexes will become more similar.

The perception that women are not fully committed to the labor market can act as a self-fulfilling prophecy. Employers, not expecting women to stay, may channel them to jobs requiring a lower training investment and providing fewer opportunities for advancement. Such unattractive jobs may then provide less motivation for a woman to remain with that employer, thus confirming the employer's expectations.

Women Start With Higher Pay But Lose Out In The Long Run

The labor force experience of women — what it means to a woman to "have a job" — clearly differs significantly from that of men. These differences hold even when comparing men and women who work full time. Men employed full time work more hours and are more likely to be in higher-paying occupations (management and administration, professional/technical jobs, and craft work), while women work fewer hours and are more often found in lower paid clerical and service jobs (Mellor and Stamas, 1982).

One study which followed a group of high school graduates from 1957 to 1975 found that women often found first jobs with higher statuses than those initially held by young men. This pattern reversed by mid-life, however. Sewell and Hauser (1980) also found women almost excluded from both the top and bottom of the occupational prestige hierarchy. They found them losing average standing over the years in the middle, in contrast to men, who began lower but moved up. Consistent with this finding, Mellor and Stamas (1982) report that the average weekly earnings of women peak at a much younger age than those of men. Women do find their jobs more quickly than men, however, and hence remain unemployed for shorter periods when seeking employment (Terry, 1983).

Training plays an important role in determining pay and promotion. Hoffman (1981) reports that the average on the job training period for white men is 2.25 years, compared to less than one year for women and blacks. Although more than a quarter of the white men in his study were receiving such training, fewer than 14 percent of the white women were (and only 9 percent of the blacks, male or female).

A study by Bridges and Berk (1978) found that the jobs typically held by women are structured differently from those usually held by men. They surveyed white collar employees and first-line supervisors, all of whom worked full-time and year-round in 20 Chicago firms. They classified 305 jobs as female (the incumbents were 99 percent women) and 105 jobs as male (the incumbents were 67 percent men). The difference in mean incomes between the two groups of jobs was $2250, only $180 less than the overall average difference between the incomes of individual men and women.

What was particularly striking in this study was the way that the "rules of the game" seemed to be different in the two sets of jobs. In the women's jobs a woman might be promoted, become more free from detailed rules and regulations, do less repetitive work, and attain more seniority. None of this translated into higher income, however. Qualifications and work skills just didn't lead to increased salary, as they did in the men's jobs. It is these kinds of structural differences which have led to demands for pay based on "comparable worth."

Many Women Expect To Work And Earn More

One major question about the structure of the American labor market in the years to come is whether this segregation of most women into a small number of occupations which have flat income patterns and low pay will continue. Women are organizing to try to eliminate such practices. With equal pay for equal work mandated by law, women's groups are working to open all jobs to qualified women. They are also questioning the low pay offered women (and, theoretically, men, should any apply) when they take traditional women's jobs. Since women's lower incomes are due far more to occupational segregation than to unequal pay for the same work, this is an issue with the potential to produce significant social and economic effects.

Despite resistance, some changes in the pattern of women's employment are appearing. Between 1970 and 1980, the proportion of managers who were women rose from 18 to 31 percent. During these same years, the number of occupations dominated by men declined. Today there are at least some women in almost every occupation. The reverse, however, is not true. Although women are entering jobs formerly held almost entirely by men, men are only rarely entering occupations traditionally held by women (Rytina and Bianchi, 1984).

Concentration in lower-paying service industry positions did act somewhat to women's advantage during the 1981-82 recession, which hit the male-dominated manufacturing sector with particular force. Nineteen eighty-two was the first year since 1947 (when such data were first collected) that the unemployment rate for men was higher than that for women (Nilsen, 1984). This change may be a permanent one. One study has projected the female unemployment rate as intermittently below that for males well into the 1990s (DeBoer and Seeborg, 1984).

In one attack on the problem of unequal earnings caused by occupational segregation, women have filed suits demanding comparable pay for work of comparable worth. It is not enough, they argue, to make it illegal to pay men and women different salaries when they do the same job. So long as there are "women's jobs" with different pay scales, equal pay alone will have little effect on women's incomes. That the few men doing these jobs are also receiving low pay does not mean there is true equality of opportunity.

What is being challenged is the practice of, for example, a given firm paying accounting clerks (largely women) less than shipping and receiving clerks (largely men) even when both jobs demand essentially the same skills and level of responsibility. If the demands of the job are comparable, women argue, then the pay should also be comparable.

If court suits can restructure such pay patterns in government employment (where suits are easier to win because of open records laws and legal requirements for equal treatment), it will be difficult for private enterprise to avoid similar concessions (Bunzel, 1982). At least 18 states have considered comparable worth pay scales, as have many local governments. Some states, including Minnesota, Iowa, Wisconsin, New Mexico, Washington State, New York and Connecticut have begun to make equalizing payments. So have the cities of Chicago, Los Angeles and San Francisco. If this movement eventually spreads to private industry, the potential results could be revolutionary (Nelson, 1984; Lamar, 1984; Beck, Borger and Weathers, 1984; Koziara, 1985; Killingsworth, 1985).

Whether or not such changes occur (and there is much vocal opposition to the comparable worth concept), in the years ahead women will be entering the work force with different attitudes and goals than has typically been the case in the past. Regan and Roland (1982) report that twice as many women among college seniors they surveyed (compared to a similar group surveyed 10 years previously) expected work to constitute their most important life satisfaction. These women viewed education, not as an end in itself, but primarily as a way to obtain the knowledge and skills needed for employment. A parallel change in occupational choice is occurring. Women are now almost as likely as men to aspire to professional positions other than nurse or teacher. What is striking is that this change in attitude is occurring just as the demand for nurses and elementary teachers is growing rapidly, a pattern which may lead to major shortages in these areas.

It is not likely that younger, well educated women will easily accept the traditional, restricted patterns of employment and promotion previously offered them. Data from the National Longitudinal survey indicate that women who attend college are more likely to plan on working at age 35. These plans are important. A young woman who, at an early age, decides that she will be working at age 35 ends up earning almost 30 percent more than those who do not have such plans (Shaw and Shapiro, 1987).

On the other hand, if only college educated women continue to make progress while other women do not, the gap between the sexes may narrow while the gap between the social classes widens. Nearly half of the women who, when young, had no plans to be working at age 35 ended up with jobs at that age anyway. They paid a significant financial penalty for their lack of planning and skill acquisition.

In any case, one must be realistic about the fact that patterns of sexual segregation in employment are very deeply ingrained. One psychiatrist who surveyed 170 individuals involved in sex-change operations found that every person who changed from female to male earned more after the change!

The Unemployment Overhang — Competition For Possible Openings

The many changes in the American labor market — more women seeking employment, increased foreign competition, the movement out of government and manufacturing employment — have had both direct and indirect effects on American society.

For one thing, a chronically high level of unemployment means there is a large pool of unemployed individuals eager to take any well-paid job. This "unemployment overhang" then influences the tenor of labor-management negotiations for those workers who are employed. In 1984, wage settlements concluded under major collective bargaining agreements reached an historic low of 2.4 percent (Lacombe and Conley, 1985). Yet there were only 62 strikes during 1984, the lowest figure since 1947. This pattern of low wage settlements has continued. The sight of hundreds of workers lined up, hoping to apply for a few industrial openings, brings home to all factory workers how easily their jobs could be filled by others.

So does the ease with which a corporation such as Greyhound can threaten to replace its entire striking workforce. When the news media reported Greyhound's announcement that it might have to replace all of its 12,700 unionized employees if they did not accept a pay cut, the company received 65,000 unsolicited applications for these well-paid jobs which did not require a high level of formal education. It could have replaced all its striking workers five times over and still turned away hundreds (Flax, 1984)

More College Grads Push Out Those With Less Education

At the same time that such jobs have declined, the number of persons who have a high level of formal education has increased (Young, 1985). In 1970, only 14 percent of working adults (aged 25 to 64) had a college degree. By 1987, this proportion had almost doubled, to over 25 percent.

Part of this increase occurred because so many of the large baby boom group graduated from college during the 1970s. Equally important, well educated women are much more likely to seek employment than are those with less education. Although only 45 percent of adult women who are not high school graduates are in the labor force, the figure is 80 percent for women with college degrees. In recent years the first figure has been falling and the second rising, as educated women seek jobs and uneducated women do not. Women now represent 40 percent of all adult workers with four or more years of college, compared to 32 percent in 1970.

This pattern of drawing well-educated women into the labor force while leaving the majority of poorly educated women out has created a labor force which is much more highly educated than the adult population as a whole. It has also significantly increased the competition for professional and managerial jobs.

Although the number of adult workers with college degrees went rapidly from one in seven to one in four, the number of positions requiring a college education did not grow anywhere nearly as quickly. As a result, an increased number of persons with college degrees are now working at jobs which do not require advanced educations. In 1970, 65 percent of all 25 to 64-year-old college graduates were working in professional or technical positions. By 1982, this had fallen to 54 percent. College graduates today are much more likely to be working in lower level sales, clerical, service, and blue collar jobs than was the case in the past. Although some of these jobs have become more complex and now require workers with more education, the major reason for this "underemployment" is the inability of college graduates to find the more challenging jobs for which they assumed their educations were preparing them.

There has been a noticeable increase in the number of persons with college degrees working as managers. What is apparently happening is that lower level management positions, previously held by those with high school diplomas, are now being filled by persons with college degrees.

College Grads May Experience Underemployment, But Not Much Unemployment

The rate of unemployment for both men and women varies inversely as a function of education. The more education a person has, the lower the level of unemployment (Young, 1985). In March of 1987, adult unemployment rates (for those aged 25 to 64) were 11 percent for those who did not complete high school, 6 percent for high school graduates, 5 percent for those with one to three years of college, and less than 3 percent for college graduates. The college educated are, then, rarely unemployed. The burden of unemployment falls most heavily on those with lower levels of formal education

The problem of the educated is not unemployment, but underemployment. During the 1970s, the proportion of sales and clerical workers (of both sexes) who were college graduates almost doubled. At the same time, the percentage without high school diplomas fell by more than half (Young, 1981).

The increase in the number of college graduates seeking employment has been much faster than the increase in the number of professional and technical jobs. In the middle 1960s there were about a half million bachelor's degrees being awarded per year. By the early 1980s this had almost doubled. While the labor force grew 31 percent between 1970 and 1980, the college graduate labor force increased by 85 percent.

What happened was that three trends came together at the same time. A larger proportion of students went to college, the number of students was itself larger because of the baby boom, and then a higher proportion of the women who received degrees entered the labor market. The number of college graduates who were working or looking for work shot up so fast that, for the first time in American history, we experienced a high rate of underemployment.

It is important to note, however, that the labor market is now eating into this surplus by generating more and more jobs requiring educated workers. A few years ago it was expected that, for the 15 million college graduates expected to enter the labor force during the 1980s (about 60 percent of these being new graduates, and the rest degreed persons reentering the work force), there would be only 12-13 million openings in jobs requiring college training. This would leave an annual average deficit of about 300,000 college level positions. More than one college graduate in five would be unable to find employment in a job requiring college training. These individuals were expected to join the estimated 3.8 million college graduates who, in 1980, experienced either unemployment or employment in lower level positions (Sargent, 1982).

More recent projections, as we have noted, show those occupations requiring the most education to have the most rapid growth rates. As a result, the balance between the supply and demand for college graduates is now expected to narrow considerably during the 1990s (Kutscher, 1987; Silvestri and

Lukasiewicz, 1987). There will still be a surplus of college graduates, but it will be down from 300,000 to 100,000 per year. Because of slightly smaller graduating classes, this means that only one graduate in 20 will face underemployment.

This situation will lessen the intense competition among college graduates for challenging and well-paid jobs. It will not have much effect, however, on those who have some college training but no degree. Most workers who attended but did not graduate from college have been accepting positions similar to those of high school graduates (Young, 1984). Although a college degree does not guarantee a professional, managerial or technical job, it is clear that such a position will be more and more difficult to obtain *without* a completed degree. This does not mean that all such "surplus" education is wasted. Even apart from the humanizing value of education, and the fact that some who are working at less demanding jobs choose to do so for any number of reasons, data from the Panel Study of Income Dynamics also suggest an eventual economic payoff. This long-term study of income patterns found that having more education than a job requires had a positive influence on the pay received. The economic returns to education in lower level jobs are not as large as in more advanced positions, but there are significant returns nonetheless (Duncan and Hoffman, 1981).

Despite these eventual benefits, there is little doubt that underemployment can be frustrating for many individuals, with markedly negative personal and social results. Job satisfaction surveys have consistently found that the combination of high levels of schooling with low pay produces serious job dissatisfaction (Levitan and Johnson, 1982).

Those in the baby boom generation may find that not only does a college degree lead to less income than they expected, but that their income may remain permanently lower as the years pass. They will be competing with many others of the same age throughout their working lives for a limited number of well paid positions. Those who entered the labor force during the depression years of the 1930's had a similar experience. Their incomes were consistently lower than other age groups even after the depression was over (Freeman, 1979). Of course, such a differential is relative. Those of the same age without advanced educations earn even less.

As a proportion of the college educated find that they have to seek lower level employment, they in turn increase the competition faced by those without college degrees. The person looking for work today therefore faces a difficult challenge regardless of his or her level of education. The number of individuals trying to obtain available positions has increased at every level.

More People Are Unemployed, And For Longer Periods

Labor market changes have a geographic dimension. Jobs are being created and disappearing with great rapidity; the rate of change varies from place to place. A few years ago, the Northeast and West Coast states had particularly high unemployment. Now unemployment is concentrated in the country's mid-section and Gulf Coast. The future geographic pattern of employment and unemployment is hard to predict (Devens, 1988). Those who are in the right place at the right time have an obvious advantage. Others will have greater difficulties.

There are many new entrants to the labor market, and much movement from job to job. Almost 30 percent of all American workers have been with their present employer for one year or less. Although movement from one employer to another declines with age, there is substantial turnover at all age levels (Horvath, 1982). Indeed, America stands out sharply when compared to other industrialized countries, where employment is much more stable (Boyer, 1984).

Most of us, as children, played musical chairs. We circled the chairs while the music played, and sat down when it stopped. Since the number of chairs was always one less than the number of children, someone was always "out." Another chair was then pulled away, and the game went on.

The American labor market today resembles a huge game of musical chairs. There are many job openings, but an even larger number of workers are seeking these openings. Some — the unemployed — are always left out.

One study found that there have typically been five or more people seeking work for every available job opening. A careful analysis of this data leads to the conclusion that jobs which come open remain unfilled for about 5-15 days (Abraham,

1983). To find work, an unemployed person must somehow manage to be at the right place at the right time.

The average length of time spent unemployed has been rising consistently since the late 1960s. Not only is the length of any given spell of unemployment getting longer, but many people experience several periods of unemployment in the same year. Figures on the average duration of unemployment therefore understate the total time spent looking for work each year (Bowers, 1980). During 1986, for example, about a third of the unemployed had more than one period of unemployment during the year.

Unemployment tends to breed more unemployment. Data from the Panel Study of Income Dynamics on male heads of household aged 25 to 54 in 1972, with at least five years experience in the labor force (presumably a stable group), show that, over the 1968-1976 period, nothing explained the probability of being unemployed as much as the length of time the worker had held his present job. Even a worker who changed jobs five years ago had 2.6 times the probability of experiencing unemployment of a worker who had been in his present job for more than five years (DiPrete, 1981).

And there is lot of unemployment. During 1983, the peak unemployment rate for any one month was 10.4 percent, a high figure compared to most of the postwar period. However, at some point during the year over 20 percent of the 118 million persons who were in the labor force experienced a period of unemployment. The level of unemployment declined during the early 1980s. By 1986, this figure had fallen to 16 percent, the lowest level since 1979. This still represents one out of every six workers.

The monthly unemployment rate, in other words, gives only the number of persons who are seeking work at any one time during that month. As the days and months go on, however, some find jobs and others become unemployed, so a much larger group is unemployed at some time during any given year.

Given the problems caused by all this unemployment, what can be done about it?

Retraining Appears To Be A Limited Solution

During the 1960s, when a much smaller proportion of the population was unable to find work, it was commonly accepted that one effective approach to lowering unemployment was to provide job training. Most of this training was designed to move the unemployed into job openings for which they were not otherwise qualified.

Such training programs were usually too short to prepare an untrained individual for a highly skilled position. However, they could at least help him or her to get a foot in the door, and begin learning on the job. Other programs were offered to those who had already obtained entry level work, to upgrade their skills and move them on to more advanced positions. This, in turn, opened their jobs for the unemployed who had little or no prior experience.

How useful would such programs be today, particularly if offered on a wide scale?

For an individual person, of course, a practical course of training which builds on his or her natural aptitudes might make sense. But how general a solution is this, given the changing structure of the labor market, and the changing mix of available jobs?

Today, there is no large pool of jobs (at any pay) that remain open because no one has the skills to fill them. True shortages of qualified workers are found in few industries. Some such shortages exist in an occasional engineering specialty, or among the most highly skilled blue collar positions, but they involve only small numbers of openings (Kuttner, 1983).

Despite the publicity given to job possibilities in "high technology," jobs in these industries contributed only 7.9 percent of the employment growth during the 1972-1982 period. During 1982-1995, the Department of Labor projects that high technology industries will account for only eight or nine percent of expected employment growth. Furthermore, this growth will be concentrated in a small number of areas, with about 40 percent found in only five states: California, New York, Texas, New Jersey and Massachusetts (Riche, Hecker and Burgan, 1983). Retraining for employment in high technology clearly will not be a solution for the large number of workers displaced by automation, foreign competition, declining government

employment and the other structural changes which we have
been reviewing.

Retraining alone may be an outdated answer to high
unemployment. The problem today is not that large numbers of
jobs are sitting open, if only there were people trained to fill
them. The problem today is too few jobs, and an even greater
shortage of positions offering good pay and opportunities for
advancement for those without college degrees. Offering short
training programs in computer programming or other similar
skills will have little effect on the basic forces which have
brought about these fundamental changes in the structure of our
economy and our society. The danger is that such training
programs will lead to even greater frustration, as participants
leave them and then discover there is still a high level of
competition for jobs using their new skills, and salary offers of
half the pay they earned before receiving this new training.

What Solutions Exist For National Policy?

Over the long run, the problems outlined in this
chapter must be addressed on the structural level. Many such
structural changes are being proposed. The decisions on which
programs to adopt will be made through the political process. A
detailed discussion of this subject is beyond the scope of this
book. We mention one or two possibilities merely to show some
of the issues involved.

Robert Reich has argued that the solution to our
economic problems lies in a more conscious industrial policy,
integrating such decisions as tax rules, research and
development grants, credit subsidies and import restrictions. All
of these government actions would be integrated in such a way
that the total effect would be to maintain productivity growth
and enhance real income (Reich, 1983).

The critics of this approach doubt that government has
the wisdom to make such decisions, or the political will to carry
them out in the face of demands from those who might be hurt
by them.

Wassily Leontief, the nobel laureate in economics, has
a different perspective. He reports that a projection of what will
happen to the Austrian economy as new technology is

introduced shows high levels of unemployment developing despite a substantial increase in output. With the work week reduced to 35 hours, however, unemployment remains quite low, with few other negative effects. Leontief suggests that the United States look carefully at whether the unemployment/work week relationship might be similar in this country (Leontief, 1982).

European unions have pushed hard for work week reductions to make jobs available to more workers. France has already reduced the work week to 39 hours, with a commitment to move toward 35. Some British unions have also made the first move to 39 hours. After a seven week strike, most German plants are going to a 38.5 hour week, with some reducing the work week even more.

European unions demanded that these reductions in working time not lead to any reduction in weekly pay, however. It is not clear how this will affect costs, prices and the competitive position of European industry. Unless matched by productivity increases, an increase in hourly wages could raise costs, lower sales, and ultimately be counter-productive. An increase in productivity may occur, however, since employers are free, under the agreement, to schedule weekend shifts and long workdays without paying overtime, so long as the average work week over the year is 38.5 hours. The West German Federal Institute for Labor estimates that 40,000 new jobs will result from this work week reduction.

The question of what structural changes would be most successful in increasing employment clearly raises a series of complex and controversial issues. These issues will be complicated by cost pressures which are already apparent. We suspect that rapidly rising costs for health insurance, as well as the burden of early retirement payments, will cause employers to seriously reconsider the whole question of fringe benefits in the near future, for example.

We expect rapid change in the labor market to continue in the years immediately ahead. International ownership is already adding a whole new dimension to employee-employer relationships, and could weaken employee loyalty. Downsizings and layoffs in major corporations have already seriously weakened the sense of an "implied contract" guaranteeing employment in return for loyalty to the corporation. The next serious recession may weaken this contract irretrievably.

The Best Solution May Be To Learn Better Job Seeking Skills

Until key economic policy decisions are made and have had time to produce results, individuals and institutions will have to adapt to the present situation as best they can. What this means, practically, is that people need to know how to find the best job they can in as efficient a manner as possible, so they can cope with unemployment when and if it occurs.

A first step toward this goal lies in an awareness of what past research shows about the job search process. Unfortunately, these research findings are little known. Teachers rarely discuss them in traditional school courses, either at the high school or college level. Nor is there any indication that they have much effect on national policy.

One purpose of this book is to present some of the information which could help fill this void. As we have tried to make clear in Part I, the need for this information is much greater than it used to be. People today need to develop what has become an essential adult survival skill: the ability to define an employment goal and then reach that goal in as short a time as possible, despite a shortage of openings and a high level of competition. In Part II, we want to pull together what is known about the job search process, and draw out the implications of these findings for both the unemployed person and those who are trying to help them.

Notes♦♦♦

The study of persons involved in sex-change operations, and the employment results, was reported in the January 25, 1982 issue of Business Week (pages 12-13).

Much of the data in this chapter comes from news releases of the Bureau of Labor Statistics. We have generally not cited specific releases because they are not usually available in libraries. Readers who want to be added to the mailing list for these news reports should write the Bureau of Labor Statistics, U.S. Department of Labor, Washington, DC 20212

PART TWO
Job Search Skills

Because of the structural changes in the labor market discussed in Part One, there is far more competition for job openings today than there was in the past. Given this high level of competition, how a job search is conducted can make a significant difference in how long it takes to find new employment. When there are many job openings and few people looking for work, even a poorly organized effort will usually produce some job offers. A lack of strategy and organization under today's highly competitive conditions, however, can lead to an unnecessarily prolonged job search. The resulting discouragement can lead some unemployed individuals to give up altogether, and withdraw from the labor market.

The adoption of an efficient job search strategy requires some knowledge of how the labor market operates. The first aim of Part Two is therefore to summarize the available research on the process of finding employment. The second aim is to explore the practical implications of these findings for those who are assisting others to find work as quickly and efficiently as possible.

Chapter Four provides an overview. It pulls together the findings of several major studies which examined how Americans typically obtain employment. As the process by which employer and employee come together is reviewed, the lack of information on both sides of the transaction becomes apparent. The American labor market is a place of both considerable movement and many errors, with the structure of opportunity often far from clear. There are productive employees and unproductive employees, good jobs and bad jobs, and much uncertainty about which is which. Chapter Four also discusses the difference between the primary and secondary labor markets, and some recent research on the usefulness (and ambiguity) of this distinction.

After the overview in Chapter Four, the remaining chapters look in more detail at specific aspects of the job search process. Chapter Five reviews the problem of occupational choice. The real issue for most people, Chapter Five argues, is not a permanent occupational commitment, but finding an employment goal that makes sense for now.

Once an occupational goal has been set, the next step is to meet with individuals who have the authority to hire for that kind of position — in other words, to "get an interview." There are a variety of methods by which interviews are obtained, and Chapters Six, Seven and Eight discuss them in detail.

Chapter Six explores the approach which leads to the most job satisfaction and the longest job tenure: learning of a job possibility from an acquaintance or contact. One can then approach the potential employer with at least some advance information about not only the job itself, but also the quality of life in this particular workplace.

Chapter Seven deals with the second major method by which those looking for work obtain interviews, a direct approach to employers. Many job openings can be found by methodically going to appropriate firms, asking at each if there are any openings. In effect, going to one employer after another amounts to a sampling procedure. Job openings come up intermittently among the total population of employers. Since they are not reported to any central location, however, no one knows where all of these openings are at any one time. One way to find them is to continually sample employers until one turns up. In addition, there is always the possibility that an employer will create a position for a promising applicant.

The use of labor market intermediaries is the third possibility open to someone trying to obtain a job interview. Their use is discussed in Chapter Eight. These intermediaries present somewhat of a paradox. Working with them would seem, at first glance, to be the most direct and efficient method of finding employment. A closer examination, however, shows they have access to only a small proportion of the available job openings. In addition, they are often trying to match the most difficult to place applicants with the most difficult to fill jobs, and necessarily having a hard time doing it.

However the opening is found, the unemployed person eventually ends up meeting with a potential employer in a selection interview. Chapter Nine reviews the research on interviewing, and also looks at some general findings on establishing rapport and making a good first impression.

The information reviewed in Parts One and Two makes it clear that the process of obtaining employment can be difficult. Many people will need help finding a new job if they are to do so within a reasonable period. Finding openings, interviewing and seeking offers can go on for months and even years when these tasks are not being done properly.

Although some people navigate their way through these difficulties with little trouble, others become discouraged and some even stop trying. Part Three discusses the information, training and support needed by those who are having trouble finding employment, and practical ways to provide such assistance.

CHAPTER FOUR
How People Actually Find Jobs

At any given time there are a large number of persons looking for work, and a smaller (but still large) number of job openings. Since 30 percent of all jobs come open during a one year period, over 30 million job openings must occur each year. Because any given opening will typically be filled within one to three weeks, the number of openings on any one day is, of course, much smaller.

How do people find these openings? What job search behavior typically leads to the offer of a new position? How, in other words, does the labor market function?

There are several major studies which have shed considerable light on these questions. The purpose of this chapter is to review their principal findings. Together, they provide a good overview of how employers and those looking for work come together. The job search strategies we recommend are based on these studies.

Then, in the chapters which follow, more detail will be added about each major approach to the job search process.

A Major Study Found Two Job Search Methods To Be Most Important

The first major source of information on how Americans find work is a national survey, done at the request of the Department of Labor, as a supplement to the Current Population Survey.

The Bureau of the Census takes the Current Population Survey each month. The primary purpose of this survey is to determine the monthly unemployment rate. (Many people erroneously believe that the unemployment rate is determined by the number of persons receiving unemployment compensation. This is not true. Less than half the unemployed receive these payments, and there is no connection between their numbers and the official unemployment rate.)

A sample of about 60,000 households, typically containing about 100,000 adults, is contacted each month by the Current Population Survey. A large sample is used because the data must be valid for individual states as well as for the entire country. Although the major purpose of this survey is to learn the employment status of each household member who is at least 16 years old, supplementary questions are also regularly added. The data from each month's CPS enlarge our understanding of how the labor market operates, and provide a clearer picture of the typical work patterns of American households (Bregger, 1984).

In January of 1973, a series of questions was asked of those respondents to the Current Population Survey for that month who had begun their current job sometime during the past year (1972). Among other things, people were asked how they had gone about their searches for employment, and which search methods led to their present jobs.

The survey results revealed that over a third of those who had begun their new jobs within the past year had not, strictly speaking, had to search for the position. Some had returned to jobs which they formerly held. Others were offered jobs with no effort on their part (it was the employer who approached them). Another group entered family businesses.

TABLE TEN

Job Search Method Used to Find Current Job

	%		%
Applied directly to employer	34.9	Used private employment agency	5.6
Asked friends:		Used state employment service	5.1
About jobs where they work	12.4	Used school placement office	3.0
About jobs elsewhere	5.5	Took civil service test	2.1
Asked relatives		Used union hiring hall	1.5
About jobs where they work	6.1	Asked teacher or professor	1.4
About jobs elsewhere	2.2	Other	6.7
Answered newspaper ads		Total	100.0
Local	12.2		
Nonlocal	1.3		

'Source: U.S. Department of Labor- 1975

Of the individuals who did have to search for work, the majority found their present positions by using one of two methods. One group heard of a job possibility from a friend or relative. The other went from one employer to another looking for openings, and applying for whatever possibilities turned up. Smaller numbers of applicants found jobs by using a labor market intermediary (the want ads, state employment service offices, private employment agencies, or similar persons or institutions which attempt to compile lists of job openings or serve as brokers in the employment process). Table Ten lists the methods which led to success for at least one percent of those who looked for and found employment during 1972.

Most of those seeking employment kept their searches close to home. Over 60 percent of the men and 85 percent of the women traveled 25 miles or less to look for work. They usually accepted the first job offer they received. Only one person in three turned down even one job offer.

Over half the group found a job less than five weeks after beginning the search. (Note that the average unemployment rate during 1972 was 5.9 percent; it declined during the year, reaching 5.1 percent by December. When unemployment is higher, the average search period will be longer.) The number of hours spent looking for work was low. About two-thirds of the group spent five hours or less per week on their job search activities. (U.S. Department of Labor, 1975)

Taken together, these findings suggest a job search process which is not very wide-ranging, not very thorough, and not very intense.

The Camil Study Verifies Major Findings

A second major study was done in the last half of 1974 by Camil Associates, a consulting group working under contract to the Department of Labor. Unlike the Current Population Survey, which is based on a nationwide sample of households, this study was limited to a set of 20 cities with populations between 100,000 and 250,000. Several separate surveys were taken. First, a sample of employers paying unemployment insurance (UI) taxes was drawn, thereby including nearly all local employers except for a few exempt non-profit and government agencies. Then a sample of the employees recently hired by these employers was studied. Findings from this group were contrasted with a second group of employees hired by those employers who used the local employment service office to find workers, and with a third sample of workers who had sought help from the employment service, whether or not they found jobs as a result.

TABLE ELEVEN

Job Search Method Through Which Job Was Obtained (Camil Study)

	%
Asked friends/relatives	30.7
Direct application to employer	29.8
Answered ad	16.6
Used private agency	5.6
Used employment service	5.6
Asked business associates	3.3
Used school placement office	3.0
Used labor union	1.4
Other	4.0
Total	100.0

Source: U.S. Department of Labor, 1976

This study is different in several ways from the one discussed previously: sampling employers provided an alternate method of reaching workers who had recently found employment; the nature of the sample eliminated civil service applicants; the study was limited to middle-sized cities; and unemployment at the time (1974) was increasing rather than falling. Despite these differences in context and research method, the results are consistent with what was discovered by the Current Population Survey. As Table Eleven shows, most new employees said they obtained their jobs through informal methods. Either they heard of an opening from friends or relatives, or they went directly to employers, rather than using a broker or intermediary.

The Camil study also found that, because so many employers were small, only seven percent had personnel departments. At almost all small businesses (82 percent of the firms in the sample had 25 or fewer employees), the owner or manager did the hiring personally. Informal methods of filling vacancies predominated at these small firms. This is an important finding, given the major increase in the numbers of small businesses since 1974.

Major employers had, as one would expect, more openings per employer. Smaller employers as a group, however, had a large number of positions available. Over 70 percent of the establishments surveyed had at least one opening during the six month period of the study (U.S. Department of Labor, 1976).

Two important questions are unanswered by these and similar studies. First, is there any difference in the jobs obtained by different search methods? And, second, what determines whether employers inform any of the labor market intermediaries that they have an opening?

Most firms can fill a large proportion of their openings from the two groups of job applicants who regularly approach them. The first group come recommended by friends, relatives and present employees. The second come in on their own initiative. Why, then, do employers list a job in the want ads, use search firms or employment agencies, or contact the local employment service office when they can easily choose employees from those who apply or are referred to them?

Other Job Search Methods Found To Be Limited

These questions were examined by a major research project which studied the openings listed in two of the three largest labor market intermediaries. The research was done between June 1974 and May 1975, and was directed by one of the authors (Johnson). The findings were reported in *The Public Employment Service and Help Wanted Ads: A Bifocal View of the Labor Market*. During the study year, researchers examined over 200,000 want ads from 19 newspapers in a sample of 12 cities. Employment service listings for 30 communities within these same 12 metropolitan areas were also reviewed.

Private employment agencies, the third major intermediary, should ideally have been included in this research. However, information about these agencies is not easily available. They are private businesses, and their job listings are proprietary information.

Although they were not formally included in the research, informal interviews were arranged at several employment agencies. The information from these interviews helped to fit their operations into the general picture which emerged from examining the other two intermediaries.

The view of the labor market which emerged from this study is consistent with the findings of the Camil study and the Current Population Survey. Neither employment service lists nor the want ads contained more than a small fraction of the jobs available in any of the localities studied. More important, this small fraction was far from a random sample. Certain categories of jobs predominated; others were largely absent.

The Want Ads Include Mostly Hard-To-Fill Job Openings

Openings for a variety of professional jobs (engineering or accounting positions, for example), as well as clerical or sales openings, are regularly advertised in local newspapers, particularly in the Sunday editions. Want ads in the daily editions contain more listings for service occupations (domestic help or restaurant work, for example). Although the Sunday want ads have more positions listed at one time than the daily papers, more new openings (jobs not previously advertised) appear on weekdays, since the daily paper comes out six times a week.

The openings which appear in the want ads are concentrated on the two ends of the skill/experience spectrum, with a relative scarcity of jobs in the middle. At one extreme are advertisements for accounting, nursing, engineering and other professional positions which require high levels of training, and some years of experience. Some of these openings are located in other cities. Employers who want to fill these positions know that few persons seeking employment have the needed skills, so they advertise widely to get even a few applicants.

At the other end of the spectrum are openings for jobs which the Labor Department classifies as "low-pay, low-status." These jobs typically account for 15 percent of the total employment in a given community. However, such openings (for domestic employees, fast food restaurant workers, janitors, and so on) make up a fourth of the new want ad listings.

Employment Service Tends To List Few Of The Better Jobs

Similar patterns were found in an examination of the openings listed with local employment service offices. Here again some job titles appear frequently, and others are rarely seen. Openings for accounting clerks, janitors and porters, clerk-typists and truck drivers, for example, are more likely to be listed with the employment service than put into the want ads. Other positions (teacher, for example, or retail sales worker) are found only infrequently in either source.

There was an even heavier predominance of low-pay, low- status jobs in the employment service listings than in the want ads. Such positions made up about 40 percent of the openings listed with the job service, almost triple their proportion in the labor market. There were also some positions with high skill demands, but these were rarely filled. Many of these openings were presumably listed by firms with federal contracts, since they are required by law to notify the employment service of all openings generated by these contracts. Other listings for highly-skilled jobs come from employers who are also giving their openings to several private employment agencies and advertising them in one or more newspapers. When people with rare skills are needed, employers broadcast news of the opening widely, hoping to attract at least a few qualified applicants.

The employment service lists, then, contain a mixture of two groups of job openings: a stock of demanding jobs which the employment service rarely fills, and a flow of semi-skilled and unskilled service and blue collar openings which are typically filled shortly after being received.

Many "middle" jobs exist in any community. These positions offer reasonable pay and some chance for advancement but do not require advanced or specialized technical training. These positions are disproportionately absent from employment service lists, as they are from the want ads.

Private Employment Agency Operations

Private employment agencies account for about 20 percent of the job openings listed in the want ads. These notices often tell surprisingly little about the nature or location of the openings they are advertising. Unlike ads placed by employers, employment agencies usually write their ads to attract the largest possible number of qualified applicants to the agency's office. Interviews with agency personnel suggest that the purpose of this advertising is not so much to fill the listed jobs as it is to find persons with good qualifications who will be easy to market to employers.

The reason for wanting to draw in as many qualified applicants as possible is that most people who find jobs through private employment agencies are not placed in positions which were first listed with the agency by an employer. It is more a process of persons with marketable skills being placed with employers as the result of phone calls made by the agency, which contacts employer after employer trying to find an appropriate opening. As is true for those recommended by friends and relatives and those coming in on their own initiative, the employer need not take any action to be informed of such prospective employees. The first contact is made by the agency.

Conclusion: Only "Left Over" Jobs Get Advertised

After reviewing their findings, the authors of this study concluded that openings listed with the employment service and in the want ads are, to a large extent, the leftovers. The jobs in these listings are disproportionately at the two extreme ends of the skill/experience/pay spectrum, with the jobs in the middle of the spectrum in short supply. This suggests that the total set of job openings first undergoes "a picking off and filtering process through other formal and informal channels that are preferred by employers. As a whole, the announcement of a job in either or both mechanisms represents a last-resort employer recruitment method." (U.S. Department of Labor, 1978: 90). This pattern has been summarized in the recruitment/job search model on the following page (U.S. Department of Labor, 1978: 8).

Recruitment/Job Search Model

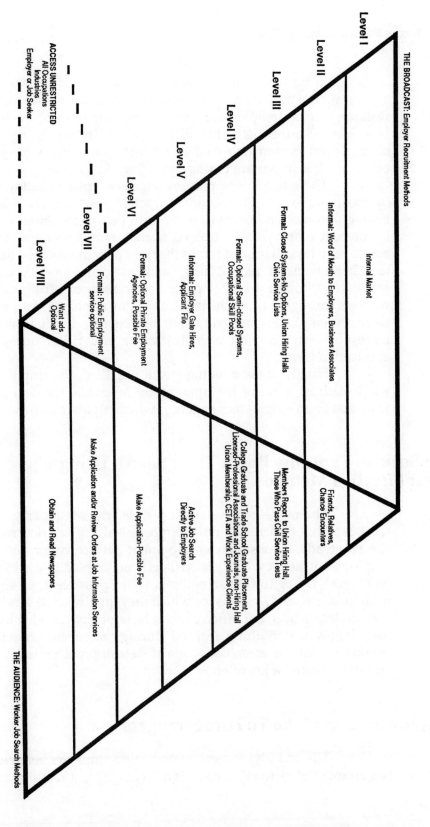

THE BROADCAST: Employer Recruitment Methods

Level I

Internal Market

Level II

Informal: Word of Mouth to Employers, Business Associates

Friends, Relatives, Chance Encounters

Level III

Formal: Closed Systems-No Options, Union Hiring Halls, Civic Service Lists

Members Report to Union Hiring Hall, Those Who Pass Civil Service Tests

Level IV

Formal: Optional Semi-closed Systems, Occupational Skill Pools

College Graduate and Trade School Graduate Placement, Licensed-Professional Associations and Journals, non-Hiring Hall Union Membership, CETA and Work Experience Clients

Level V

Informal: Employer Gate Hires, Applicant File

Active Job Search Directly to Employers

Level VI

Formal: Optional Private Employment Agencies, Possible Fee

Make Application-Possible Fee

Level VII

Formal: Public Employment service optional

Make Application and/or Review Orders at Job Information Services

Level VIII

Want ads Optional

Obtain and Read Newspapers

ACCESS UNRESTRICTED
All Occupations
Industries
Employer or Job Seeker

THE AUDIENCE: Worker Job Search Methods

What is striking about this finding is that the easiest and most obvious job search methods (reading the want ads, or walking into an employment service or employment agency office) are also the methods which are least likely to bring the unemployed person into contact with the most desirable job openings. It is important to understand why this is so.

There is a hiring pattern which is typically followed by most employers. First, many attractive positions are filled through promotion from within, or with people recommended by present employees or trusted friends and associates. The employer who still has not found the right person may then turn to other means of recruitment, such as hiring new college graduates through a school placement center, or hiring craft workers through a union hiring hall. If this approach does not work, the employer can next turn to the pool of individuals who have come in on their own initiative and filled out job application forms.

Finally, if the opening is still not filled, the employer will broadcast news of the opening to the public through the want ads or an employment agency, whether public or private.

Job Seekers Typically Begin Their Search Using The Least Effective Methods

The model suggests that people who are looking for work search for openings in the opposite order. They first read the want ads, or visit an employment service office or an employment agency. They also begin making calls on local employers, trying to find something. When possible, they sign up with any closed systems for which they qualify (civil service lists, college placement offices, union hiring halls). In addition, they follow up anything learned during conversations with friends or relatives. Eventually, one of these approaches leads to an interview and a job offer.

Employers Don't Like To Hire Strangers

The underlying motivation behind employer behavior is a simple but powerful need. Employers favor a recruitment process which gives them maximum knowledge about anyone they are going to hire.

Hence where practical an employer will recall a former employee or promote a present one. This enables the employer to deal with someone whose characteristics are known. If this is not possible, the next best step is to turn to a friend, relative or current employee who can be trusted to recommend a good candidate. A school placement office which has referred acceptable applicants in the past, or an employment agency which has done the same, might be a next resort. Those who come in looking for work, if they make a good impression, may also be considered. Here less is known, but at least these are applicants who have expressed a desire to work at this particular business.

Only when all else fails will the employer announce an opening publicly in the want ads or some similar medium. This action usually produces a deluge of applicants, many unqualified, with unknown personal and work-related characteristics.

The employer, in other words, broadcasts word of the opening only as widely as is necessary to find a qualified applicant. If the employer fails to find someone when trying a narrow but trustworthy pool, then the next larger (and next less trustworthy) source of applicants must be used.

Stephen Mangum, in a study using this model, surveyed a stratified sample of 65 firms in the Salt Lake City area. His findings were consistent with the model. The internal labor market (promotion from within the firm) was particularly important for jobs at higher skill levels. In general, the higher the level of skill and responsibility involved, the less likely the employer was to list the position with the local employment service office or advertise it in the paper.

Informal, word of mouth contacts were important in filling jobs on all levels. As one would expect, it was the larger corporations which more often filled openings through personnel offices, although even here management positions were likely to be filled without any participation by personnel officials.

There are those who believe that formal personnel procedures do more harm than good even at the lower levels. Bowes (1987) argues that large corporations would do better if they formalized the informal recommendation process. He also recommends using more temporary workers, consultants and college interns as a way to see what people are really like before deciding who to hire.

Looking over both the model and the results of his survey, Mangum concluded that the most effective role for the employment service might be teaching the unemployed how to find work on their own instead of sending them to interview for the small set of openings of which the service is informed (Mangum, 1982). This is a theme to which we will return later.

American Workers Move Early And Often

American workers change jobs frequently. They leave one employer for another at a much higher rate than is common in other parts of the developed world (Norwood, 1983). The frontier tradition of picking up and moving on, always hoping for a better opportunity, is part of the American way. American employers also have far more freedom to hire and fire, move plants from place to place, and create or dissolve subsidiaries than is typical in other countries.

We have already noted that almost 30 percent of the American work force has been with their present employers for one year or less. Other data suggest that it is not just employer change which goes on at a rapid rate. Occupational change is almost as brisk. One government survey found that 9.5 percent of the work force changed occupations over a one year period, with close to half of all workers reporting they had been employed in their present occupations for less than five years (Rytina, 1982).

Much of this employer and occupational change takes place out of a desire for higher income. Bradley Schiller, in a study based on social security records, found a pattern of workers taking their first "permanent" job with a small employer, and then moving on to a larger employer for better pay. Specifically, he compared the employers of male workers in their first steady job (held for all or part of at least four consecutive calendar quarters) with their employers nine years later.

Schiller found that two-thirds of these workers got their first jobs in small businesses, compared to only 11 percent who found initial employment in firms with 1000 or more workers. In neither case could the first choice really be called permanent. Only 1.2 percent were with the same employer nine years later. However, almost three times as many of these young workers moved from small firms to large ones as went in the opposite direction. Small firms, the study concluded, often do the socializing and training for large corporations (Schiller, 1983).

Not all those who make such transfers are able, of course, to survive in the atmosphere of the large corporation. Many will move again, and return to a smaller organization.

Job Seekers Find A Confusing Labor Market

We thus have several anomalies. The constant movement of workers from job to job creates many openings, but employers avoid broadcasting word of these openings too widely, lest they be deluged with applicants. Most people do not know the locations of most openings, and no one has anything even close to a complete list. Labor market intermediaries (who sometimes do claim to know of many openings) really know of relatively few, and the jobs on their lists are disproportionately drawn from the extreme ends of the skill/experience spectrum. In a country where people regularly move from job to job and occupation to occupation, job search skills are of great importance. Yet neither schools, colleges nor any other institution routinely provides instruction or training in how the labor market works and how best to move within it.

Even at individual firms, things are not as they seem. One would expect a corporation's personnel office to know of openings within the firm. Often this is not so. One study which surveyed 38 businesses located in a midwestern community found that, in 12 of the 38 cases, at least three people would have to be contacted at each firm to have a complete picture of employee turnover and vacancies. The personnel office was often aware of openings only after they had been filled (Ferber and Ford, 1965). And these were not huge organizations; most had only 51 to 300 employees. In really large corporations an even higher proportion of openings may be known, not to personnel officials, but only to managers scattered throughout the organization.

It is small wonder that many people seeking employment feel they are in an Alice in Wonderland situation, with nothing working as they expect it to. Friends and relatives can be approached, but many know of no appropriate openings, and others make suggestions which turn out to be dead ends. One can always go methodically from employer to employer. This consumes a lot of time, however, and can involve filling out endless application forms which are then "kept on file" but rarely consulted. When intermediaries are approached, the jobs they list are often poor ones, or demand skills and experience which few have.

Under these circumstances the process of obtaining new employment can easily become a frustrating, time-consuming, inherently discouraging experience. There are jobs out there, but how does one find them?

Searching While Still Employed Results In Lower Wages

Kahn and Low compared the results obtained when looking for work while still employed to what happens when a person quits one job to seek another. They discovered that (even taking lost wages into account) those who left their old jobs first did better. Using data for young males taken from the National Longitudinal Survey, they found that those who were unemployed, and therefore had more time available to conduct a thorough search, obtained 10 percent higher wage offers than those who tried to continue working at their old jobs while seeking another (Kahn and Low, 1982).

Given the demands of the American labor market, trying to find an acceptable job opening is clearly a difficult and time- consuming process. There are still a few employers who look on an unemployed applicant with suspicion, as if unemployment inherently carried a stigma. The reality, however, is that finding suitable new employment is often just too complicated and time-consuming to do well while also employed at another full- time job.

A Job Search Is An Information Search

Looking over the findings reviewed so far, the critical element in the job search process is information about where job openings can be found, and about the nature of these openings. A job search involves, essentially, a search for information. Obtaining this information usually takes much time and effort.

The employer faces a parallel problem. He or she must find, among thousands of potential candidates, a few people who can both do the job and have the necessary personal attributes. The employer wants applicants who are trustworthy, dependable, and able to work smoothly with the firm's personnel and customers.

Often neither employer nor applicant have good information about each other, and hence both approach the hiring process warily. Each tries to get information from trusted friends and colleagues first whenever possible. This mutual wariness can create an uncomfortable atmosphere and make a candid exchange during the job interview difficult — the exact opposite of what both parties to the process need.

Good Jobs Are Hard To Get, But Worth It

When discussing the kinds of jobs available to those seeking employment, social scientists often distinguish between primary and secondary labor markets. Jobs in the former category are typically with large firms. They are often unionized, pay well, have good fringe benefits, provide some measure of job security and offer on the job training and opportunities for advancement. They are, in other words, what the average person refers to as "good jobs."

Secondary labor market positions, on the other hand, often provide only short term employment, pay low wages with few or no fringe benefits, neither require nor provide much training and are more often found in small, less profitable businesses. These jobs are often taken by young people with little formal education who are just breaking into the labor market, or by minorities or others who are unable to obtain more desirable positions.

This primary/secondary distinction is often useful. Many jobs do have characteristics which are close to these two ideal types, and there is no doubt that the major concern of many of those seeking work is finding and obtaining a "good job." However, the characteristics of these two sets of jobs do not correlate as highly as was at first thought. As Hodson and Kaufman (1982) point out, for example, major multinational firms do not always provide primary labor market opportunities. These corporations sometimes hire large numbers of workers at the minimum wage, give them little on the job training, and provide few opportunities for advancement. The jobs of other employees of the same corporation might, however, have far more primary characteristics.

Labor market segmentation certainly exists, but it is not easy to predict just how this segmentation will be structured. Each industry, firm and job must be examined separately to determine its characteristics.

The theory behind the primary/secondary distinction presumes that once a worker takes a secondary labor market job in a peripheral industry, he or she will have difficulty moving to a better job in a higher-paying, higher-profit "core" industry. Jacobs (1983) used data from the National Longitudinal Survey to follow workers from job to job. He did not find this pattern. The simple blue collar/white collar dichotomy was a much better predictor of who would move, and to what new job he or she would go, than whether the worker was in a core or peripheral industry. Jacobs concluded that the primary/secondary distinction could not be made simply from a job's location in either the core or peripheral sectors of the economy. Howell and Reese (1986), on the other hand, studied the mobility patterns of workers from six southern states. They found that the entry level job did play a strong role in keeping workers in either the core or peripheral sector. This was particularly true for women.

Two studies in which Marged Sugarman has participated may help explain what is happening. The first involved using computerized hiring and employment data (submitted by employers along with their unemployment insurance tax payments) to describe California's labor market (Hardiman and Sugarman, 1979) This study found much movement from job to job by a segment of the state's workforce. California has about 6 million nonagricultural, private sector jobs. During the period from April to June, 1976, there were 1.6 million hires by California employers. Many of these newly hired workers were clearly working in the secondary labor market. About 15 percent earned less than $100 at their new jobs during that three month period (a group classified as "short-time workers"). Another 52 percent were temporary workers, holding their jobs for no more than two consecutive quarters. Of the remainder of the new hires (the 33 percent classified as "permanent"), three out of five earned less than $3.50 an hour.

The labor market which emerges from these figures is one in which many workers are steadily employed, but with a large minority moving rapidly from one low wage job to another. These mobile workers experience intermittent periods of unemployment, full time work, and part time work.

Low wages and high turnover are associated. As a study by one of the authors (Johnson) concluded, "high turnover is one important dimension of the secondary labor market because it is often caused by low status and low wages. Such jobs are more easily obtained and as quickly abandoned. "Good" jobs generally take longer to get because they are either in protected markets or become available at the ports of entry into internal markets. Characteristically, obtaining such jobs requires a deliberate choice, and above all, persistence of effort." (Johnson, 1982: 68)

Another study looked into the means by which the structure of the labor market leads many workers to remain stable although, at the same time, a large minority move from job to job (Sugarman, 1978). A group of 52 Northern California firms was contacted. In 49 of the 52 cases, employers reported that they thought of their workforces as composed of two groups. The first was a core staff of full-time, year-round employees. The remaining employees were intermittent, part-time, or seasonal workers who performed more routine tasks.

On the one hand, employers said they needed to maintain a stable, core workforce which knew how to handle the essential tasks of the business. At the same time, they had to increase or decrease the size of their workforces as they experienced seasonal or economic variations in the demand for their products.

As business slackened, they laid off peripheral staff, usually in order of reverse seniority (last hired, first fired). These positions usually required little firm-specific knowledge. Workers could be discharged when no longer needed; others could easily be hired again when business improved. Turnover of core staff, on the other hand, would be much more disruptive. Employers expressed a willingness to go to great lengths to keep experienced workers on the payroll. As Sugarman points out, this suggests that job opening frequency and job quality are inversely related. More attractive jobs come open infrequently. Less attractive jobs come open much more often.

Finding Opportunity

Variation in the structure of opportunity exists not only between industries, but also between one firm and another in the same industry, and even within a given firm. Students of the labor market have found a wide variety of patterns in different industries and parts of industries.

Kaufman and Spilerman (1982) suggest, for example, that the age patterns typical of a given occupation or industry may provide one key to the structure of opportunity there. The mean age of managers in computer manufacturing was 39, for example, while in apparel manufacturing it was 47. The first area had been expanding, the latter contracting. Secondary labor market jobs, on the other hand, often have a U-shaped age distribution. Many younger workers start in these positions, few remain there in their middle years, and older workers often return before retirement.

Training is another key to opportunity. The source of the training needed to do a job varies from occupation to occupation. College training is the obvious route to being a teacher, lawyer or doctor. Many health technicians are trained by community colleges. Private vocational schools typically prepare hairdressers, barbers and licensed practical nurses. Many typists, bookkeepers, clerks, drafters and auto mechanics obtain their skills from high school vocational courses. On the job training is more important for legal assistants, actors, upholsterers, editors and reporters. Training given by the firm or agency before the job begins is common for police officers, insurance and real estate sales people, telephone installers and bus drivers. The armed forces provide preparatory instruction and work experience for many aircraft engine mechanics and data processing equipment repairers (Carey and Eck, 1984).

The importance of formal education varies not only by occupation, but by firm size. As corporations become larger and more bureaucratized, the employee's ability to communicate in writing becomes more important, and formal education is more closely related to job title and earnings (Stolzenberg, 1978). The effect of formal education on earnings was 2.6 times as great in corporations with over 500 workers than in smaller firms.

The earnings of American workers usually start at a low level, then rise, plateau, and finally decline before retirement (Spilerman, 1977). Age structures, however, vary widely by industry, and the worker whose main goal is maximizing income should leave some jobs early, and others only after a much longer period

There is a general tendency for a simultaneous change of both occupation and industry to lead to lower earnings, at least in the short term. This is not the case if a worker changes jobs with either the occupation or the industry remaining the same. Where a job leads financially is also closely related to the age of the person obtaining it.

The structure of opportunity within the labor market varies in a number of other ways. Small towns differ from large ones. The employment service office in a small town, for example, may list a much larger proportion of the area's job openings than in a large city. Similarly, the hiring process can differ significantly from one sector of the economy to another. Getting a job in a steel plant, a grocery store, a United Fund agency or the U.S. Postal Service can be surprisingly different experiences.

The owners of small firms usually hire personally. The number of openings at any one small firm is generally small. Approaching such firms presents a different job search challenge than dealing with large employers who have more openings but also personnel offices and many more steps in the hiring process (forms, screening interviews, and so on) In addition, some jobs are limited to those who have obtained required licenses or are members of certain unions or professional organizations, or who hold specific college degrees. Sometimes there are exceptions to these requirements under certain circumstances, however. The labor market is characterized by extraordinarily varied patterns, with individual industries and occupations having different traditions and employment practices.

Practical Implications

There are, beyond doubt, both "good jobs" and "just jobs," high-paying industries and low-paying industries, dead-end positions and high-potential positions. There is also a clear over-all pattern of those with less education experiencing an earlier peak in earnings, and an earlier decline. The level of formal education is becoming more closely linked to pay and opportunity.

Beyond this, however, it is hard to generalize. There is no substitute for reviewing the condition of a particular industry, checking out the status of a particular job in the operating pattern of a specific employer, and asking about the job's opportunity structure within that pattern. Although some jobs are obviously attractive and others are not, there are many positions which turn out to be significantly different from what they seem at first.

The job search process, again, inevitably involves much searching for needed information. A high quality of decision- making is more likely to occur when the decisions are based on accurate and complete information. This is true whether deciding where to apply, what to stress in the interview, or what position to seek in the first place.

Making a reasonable and practical choice of the job to be sought is the critical first step. This first step is sometimes surprisingly difficult. At one extreme are the people who say, "I'll take anything." Unfortunately, they often end with nothing, since they have made no statement to the employer of what they can do, would like to do, or have the training to do.

At the other extreme are those who lock in so tightly on a narrowly defined employment objective that they lose all flexibility. They are often blind to reasonable alternatives which may come up during the job search process. They have no sense of how their skills could be transferred to different settings.

Both extremes can be destructive. The latter case is a particular problem when a person has previously worked in an occupation for which there is now little or no demand.

At root, the job choice process involves a search for a good match between the needs and abilities of the person seeking employment and the needs of employers in the local labor market. How such a match can best be made will be discussed in the next chapter.

Notes✦✦✦

Job mobility is highest during late adolescence and early adulthood. This is also the period when drug use is likely to be most common. Kandel and Yamaguchi (1987) report that drug use is associated with job turnover, and discuss this relationship.

CHAPTER FIVE
Deciding On A Job Objective

Occupational choices are often made almost by accident. An opportunity comes along, an offer of employment is made and accepted, and the individual goes to work. Little consideration is given to alternatives.

At the other end of the spectrum is the person for whom the process of choosing an occupation is excruciatingly difficult. For some it is a problem of too many options, each with its own attractions. Others fear they have no attractive choices, and there is little they can do which will lift them above minimum wage employment.

Although the major focus of this book is on the process of finding employment, we cannot completely neglect the issue of occupational choice. The design of an effective set of job search strategies presupposes that the person looking for work has first decided which job to seek, or at least narrowed the possibilities down to a small number of options.

More than anything else, we believe a wisely chosen employment goal will have three characteristics. The work itself will be performed without undue stress or difficulty. The pay, benefits, and working conditions (fellow workers, supervisors, physical environment, hours) will be acceptable. And job openings will be available in the local labor market. When these three conditions are present, attempting to find and interview for a position is a realistic and practical goal.

One Life, One Occupation?

Trying to make an occupational choice is a challenge at any age. When dealing with the young, however, many parents and counselors ask even more. Youth are often asked to make a "career choice." Underlying this demand is the implicit picture of a one-time decision leading to specialized training, and then a lifetime sequence of jobs (or self-employment) centered around a particular profession: law, medicine, accounting, construction management, marketing, electrical work, journalism or whatever. With this picture in mind we are forever asking children, "What are you going to be when you grow up?"

This "one life, one occupation" model is deeply ingrained. High school students see an occupational choice as a major life turning point, a once-and-for-all commitment to a lifetime work role. Adolescents understandably view this decision as overwhelmingly important, since it has the potential for determining either lifetime success and happiness, or lifetime failure and sorrow. Given such a perception, it becomes desperately important to have interests, since interests might at least suggest an occupational choice (Hedin, Wolfe, Fruetel and Bush, 1977).

People Change Occupations Frequently, Often With No Apparent Plan

It is striking that this view is so common among adolescents, and the adults from whom they have absorbed it, when the reality is so different. The 1970 census gathered information on both current occupation, and occupation in 1965, 5 years previously. Over 32 percent of the adult population had changed occupations over that five year period (Sommers and Eck, 1977). Unfortunately, this question was omitted from the 1980 census, so we do not have more recent (and directly comparative) data. Current surveys, however, continue to show a high rate of occupational change. Sehgal (1984) found over seven percent of employed adults (age 25 or over) changing occupations in a single year.

Some of these occupational changes are logical progressions (teacher to principal, or salesperson to sales manager, for example). With so much change in such a short time, however, it is unlikely that all or even most are such neat "next steps," particularly given the pattern of downward mobility which is so common in today's economy.

As one would expect, younger workers change their occupations more frequently than older workers. It is equally unsurprising that professions requiring advanced education have lower change rates than occupations which are more easily entered. Physicians, for example, had a five percent occupational change rate over the 1965-1970 period, while for dishwashers it was 43 percent. Occupations requiring a considerable investment of time and money are obviously not as quickly abandoned as those which are more easily entered. Despite such variations, however, adult occupational change is common to the point of being almost routine.

Age And Other Factors Affect Career Changes

Harold Wilensky collected work histories from 678 white males holding lower middle and upper working class jobs in the Detroit area. He found that less than a third had employment patterns which, for even half of their working lives, could be construed as orderly careers. Although there were a few whose sequence of jobs seemed to follow an orderly pattern, this was not true for most of these workers. After reviewing the data, Wilensky concluded that, "a vast majority of the labor force is going nowhere in an unordered way or can expect a worklife of thoroughly-unpredictable ups and downs." (Wilensky, 1961: 526)

A logical, ordered career is found primarily among a subset of the upper middle class. Even when it is found, however, there is some question whether such occupational stability is necessarily healthy. Several adult developmental psychologists have carefully examined the changing role of work during the adult years. They believe occupational change is not only normal but may even be necessary for sound adult growth and development. Accurate self-knowledge comes slowly. Because of this, it is unrealistic to expect most people to make wise and permanent occupational choices in their early twenties. It is not only common but normal to reconsider occupational roles during the thirties and forties, even in the absence of economic pressure to do so.

The presence or absence of an occupational dream or vision, whether one has a mentor, the degree to which childhood work-role fantasies are modified or abandoned, changing motivations for work, learning to deal with the emptiness of success and the inevitability of failure, and slowly fitting one's talents into a satisfying niche constitute a lifetime's effort for most people, not a one-time decision (Levinson, 1978; Gould, 1978). How these factors work out varies by social class (Farrell and Rosenberg, 1981). In his or her mid-thirties or early forties a working class individual often peaks in income, for example, and may then begin a slow downward slide, particularly if he or she has health problems. At this same age, many upper middle class professionals experience a significant upward movement in income. Others, however, may face the trauma of unexpected unemployment because of a corporate merger or reorganization, and their lives may then follow quite different patterns. At fifty, things change again. Mobility decreases, and the focus of attention shifts to preparation for retirement (Katchadourian, 1987).

For most of the population, then, permanent occupational choice need not and probably should not be the major issue when new employment must be sought. There is no one role with which a person must identify so deeply as to "be" an electrician, or reporter, or drug store manager until retirement. The more common pattern is to hold a series of jobs, some logically related and some not, during one's working life.

Not all moves, of course, are equally common. Matthew (1985) reports that few people go from manual to nonmanual occupations. There is also little movement from professional to other white-collar occupations, or from the crafts to other manual occupations. Managers, on the other hand, often go to or come from sales positions, and clerks frequently become managers (and vice versa).

Siegelman (1983) argues that a healthy occupational change is one which allows some previously undeveloped aspect of the self to emerge. While there is always some risk in changing employment, reasonable risk is healthy. It raises self-esteem. Avoiding all risk, on the other hand, lowers self-esteem.

Given these facts, it would be far better to ask children, "When you finish your present stretch of schooling, what are you going to do first?" This question would at least implicitly let them know that the process of finding an appropriate occupation takes place over many years. It is a process of much trail, and much error. In most cases the Pennsylvania Dutch are right: "Ve get too soon old, und too late schmart." But better late than never.

The Immediate Question: Which Job Is Best?

Whether an adult is unemployed or unhappily employed, the question of what job to seek next is the critical one. This is true whether he or she stays with the new occupation for one year or 20. The decision is important, not because it is necessarily a lifetime choice, but because it will play a major role in determining the quality of life for the next few years. It will also help determine the options that will be available when the next such decision must be made.

At root, making a wise job choice is essentially a value-guided matching process. The question is: given a reasonable level of experience and self-knowledge, and enough information on what jobs are available, which job or jobs are realistic goals?

Many young persons seeking employment are fuzzy on the answers to these essential questions. They have not explicitly identified their strongest personality traits and natural aptitudes, and they know little about what jobs are available. As workers grow older and become more knowledgeable, they experience success and failure at a variety of tasks, learn new skills, and observe others work at a range of jobs. Their occupational decisions are now based on more and better information.

Despite this growth in knowledge, however, it is also true that American society is characterized by a large number of occupational opportunities. New technologies are invented. New needs are created by changing world conditions. Individuals found businesses to fill these needs, and jobs are created.

Even experienced workers may be unaware of many employment possibilities in unfamiliar industries or settings. Making a good occupational choice is always challenging. Both the human personality and the American labor market are complex, so it is always a question of how deeply one wishes to probe.

Self-knowledge can involve a simple five-minute review: I can drive a truck and have a commercial license, but can't do heavy lifting because of my back. Alternatively, it can be the result of weeks of reflecting on one's interests, values, natural aptitudes, personality traits, skills learned in school, past employment, and so on. Good friends and previous employers can be consulted in an attempt to exhaustively review one's gifts and characteristics.

Similarly, knowledge of the labor market can be simply the observation of some obvious patterns: because of their port facilities, both Houston and San Francisco are major wholesaling centers with many trucking firms, so there is likely to be strong demand for diesel mechanics. Or it can involve a thorough analysis of what job titles are found in what industries at what salaries, with what levels of job creation and change expected over the next decade.

As a practical matter, even a basic knowledge of the labor market requires an understanding of several important institutional and structural variables. "Examples are the relative advantage of working for small, medium, and large employers; the paths that lead out of secondary market entrapment in various fields; prevailing practices in hiring and upgrading in different occupations and industries; the trade-offs between starting wage, fringe benefits, and chances for upgrading; back doors into job preserves (e.g., 'helpers' jobs into apprenticeships, clerical into professional, temporary or part- time into permanent); long-range civil service strategies; and other types of such mapping information... " (Johnson, 1982: 72)

Examine Past Accomplishments For Key Skills

A variety of books on job choice and job finding have become popular during the past decade, as unemployment has risen (Bolles, annual editions; Crystal and Bolles, 1974; Germann and Arnold, 1980; Haldane, 1975; Moore, 1976; Wegmann and Chapman, 1987). These works suggest that a person who needs to seek a new job should first look carefully at his or her past accomplishments as a way to identify the strongest and most enjoyed skills and personality traits. With these findings in mind, one can then undertake a serious review of several jobs which seem to demand these skills and personal characteristics. Although the process of gathering detailed information about different occupations and their demands may be time-consuming, these authors argue, it will pay off in greater happiness and productivity.

The heart of this approach lies in a careful review of the personal characteristics which have been the key to past successes. To find them, a person begins by listing those things he or she has done most successfully in the past. This can involve writing an autobiography, or simply making a list of accomplishments. Each achievement is then examined. The interests, natural aptitudes and personality traits that consistently show through are summarized. Friends and relatives are consulted as a "reality check," to be sure this analysis is realistic. Acquired skills, work experience and special knowledges are reviewed. One or more jobs are identified which seem to be a good match to the picture which emerges from this review. The person then begins interviewing those who have such jobs to see whether the match would indeed be a good one, and whether it is practical to seek any of these positions.

For those who are willing to undertake the effort, the results of such personal analysis and labor market research can be very worthwhile. A fair amount of time must be devoted to such efforts, however. This type of activity is usually easier for those with some advanced education. The process demands a willingness to undertake self-examination, and enough vocabulary to distinguish between a variety of personality characteristics and skill areas. It requires a willingness to approach people whom one does not know for information, as well as some facility at making and keeping appointments, writing thank you notes, dealing with secretaries, using library resources, and so on. The process can be adapted to less educated or lower income populations by a skilled counselor or group leader. One approach to doing this is outlined by Farr (1988a).

In addition to these approaches, which have become popular in the last decade or so, there are also a range of more traditional vocational interest tests available. The selection of instruments has been expanded by computerized, interactive programs that branch off in different directions depending on how one answers questions on personal interests, values and so on. These inventories and computer programs are undoubtedly helpful to some individuals. This is, however, an art which is still in its infancy.

There Is No Central Source of Job Openings

Whatever the problems associated with examining the human personality, it might be expected that the easy part of searching for a good person-job match would be reviewing the local labor market. The opposite is often true. Detailed information on most local labor markets is surprisingly difficult to find.

There is a common assumption among those looking for work that some government agency requires all employers to list any unfilled job openings, along with their pay and demands. Many people, when visiting their local employment service office, are disappointed when they are referred to only one or two openings. These openings may not even be the type of job they seek. Some will fill out their application forms and then go home to sit patiently by the phone. They assume the government has some way to inform employers about their availability for work. In fact, of course, nothing of the kind is happening.

There is no such central agency, and no such clearing house. Employers are free to recruit as they wish, with only minimal prohibitions by the Equal Employment Opportunities Act against blatant discrimination. Laws mandating that employment information be given to the government are minimal. The information which is collected is used to produce statewide or national statistics. One cannot look at such figures and learn that it is to a particular employer one should go to have the best chance of finding a job opening of a given kind.

McKee and Froeschle (1985) present one approach to using government data to get as clear a picture as possible, after which one has to interview employers to fill in the missing pieces. The State Occupational Information Coordinating Committees (SOICCs) are trying to coordinate this kind of information and make it more available. There is limited funding for such efforts, however. Therefore, most people have to rely on what they can learn from friends and acquaintances.

A Job Seeker's Life Situation Often Justifies Compromises

The life situation of a person looking for work is always a key factor in any job choice. A single parent, for example, may have such an overwhelming need for a job which is both nearby and provides health insurance that extensive self-analysis is really beside the point. There may, as a practical matter, be such a limited number of jobs providing these benefits that the choice between them will soon boil down to which one can be obtained. Similarly, for some persons facing multiple barriers to employment, obtaining *any* job can be a triumph. Someone who has just retired with a pension after 30 years of military service, on the other hand, might be willing and able to take the necessary time for both intensive self-analysis and extensive labor market review to find something which is as close to a "best fit" as possible.

The point of all this is not that the fit does not matter. Clearly it does. But there is a hierarchy of needs, and survival sometimes has to come first. "The ambience of the work place; the size of the firm, its location, hours and shifts, its products or services; and even such amenities as what clothes are worn, the availability of a telephone for personal use, the existence of a cafeteria, a bowling team, all impact on job satisfaction, on need, and therefore on choice for search. To a woman with children, hours, distance from home, and wages sufficient to compensate for additional costs incurred by working may be far more critical than the tasks she will perform. To the father of a young family, the medical coverage in the fringe benefits can be a make-or-break consideration. The possibilities for future stability, upgrading, and incorporation into a protected position in an internal market structure, a trade union, or a Civil Service system may critically influence the trade-off decisions made by job seekers in planning or targeting their search strategies. The financial situation of the job seeker may pose the most serious determinant of all — the degree of urgency for immediate income." (Johnson, 1982: 76- 77)

For many persons, then, the most immediate need is for detailed local labor market information, so desirable options will not be overlooked Given the importance of this employment goal, it is natural to ask where help in obtaining the needed information can be obtained.

Helpful Advice Is Hard To Find

The tragedy is that help is surprisingly hard to come by. The person who says, "Take me to a guidance counselor," will usually be sent to a school building to meet with a people-oriented individual trained in a School of Education or Department of Psychology. This counselor may be prepared to administer interest inventories, discuss "career maturity" or just listen sympathetically. However, he or she will often know surprisingly little about which job titles are found at what employers, the typical local pay for a given job, or the level of competition to be expected when seeking a specific blue collar or service industry position.

The request, "Take me to a local labor market expert," on the other hand, would likely produce a blank stare. At best it would lead to a conversation with a statistician in the back room of the local employment service office. This person can supply statistics on total employment by industrial sector, or by size of firm. He or she may even be able to provide a list of the jobs most often listed with the employment service but not filled. Here too, however, there will be less detailed information than one needs to answer the practical questions about exactly what is now available within a given geographic area, at what pay, and with which specific employers. Yet these are the facts which are needed to begin an efficient job search.

Many People Are Unhappy With Their Jobs, And A Good Match Is Hard To Get

Marvin Rozen has observed that his fellow economists generally have not been sufficiently appreciative of how flawed the process of matching people and jobs is in practice (Rozen, 1982). We totally agree. Data from the 1977 Quality of Employment Survey suggest that many Americans would prefer to be in a different job. The proportion who wish they were in a different position varies by sector of the economy.

Dissatisfaction ranges from a high of 63 percent in the private sector to a low of 46 percent of those working for private, nonprofit institutions (Mirvis and Hackett, 1983). Even the lowest of these figures is almost half the workforce!

House argues that high stress levels are likely to result from a lack of fit between the person and his or her environment, with the level of stress related to the probability of coronary heart disease. If this is true, the fit between each person and his or her job can be significant not only for immediate health, but ultimately for longevity (House, 1974). Therefore, data suggesting widespread job dissatisfaction and frequent person/job mismatches must be taken seriously.

Chesney and her colleagues have recently demonstrated that the same job characteristics which will raise the blood pressures of hard-driving, competitive "Type A" personalities will lower the blood pressures of more sensitive and introverted "Type B" persons. Similarly, what upsets a "Type B" person was found to please and challenge a "Type A" (Chesney, et. al., 1981). A job which is healthy for one person can be unhealthily stressful for another.

In a parallel study, Morse (1975) found a higher sense of competence among workers who were well matched with the degree of complexity and ambiguity (as opposed to predictability) in their jobs, compared to those who were poorly matched. It was the fit to the worker's personality that counted, not the job's characteristics.

So the person/job match is important, but difficult to make well, partly because of ignorance about both elements of the match. Self-knowledge comes slowly. As someone said, "I don't know who discovered water, but it wasn't a fish." We are too close to ourselves to see many of our own traits clearly.

Depending on personality, social class background and educational level, people are more or less comfortable undertaking intense self-examination. Yet there is no other practical way to make explicit the particular combination of natural aptitudes, training, experience, personality traits, interests, values and needs that make a person better at one job than another. This effort requires time and motivation; chief among the motivations is a belief that desirable employment alternatives exist, and are realistically available. Help from someone who knows the person well (and is willing to be honest) is also usually needed to keep the self-examination process accurate and realistic.

Even then, this knowledge will not lead to an optimal job choice unless it is balanced by an equivalent depth of understanding of the labor market. What jobs are available? What skills do they demand? What are the differences in atmosphere between the various firms in which these jobs are located? What levels of stress would this job cause, given a particular set of personality characteristics? What are the trade-offs between immediate pay, fringe benefits, on-the-job training, potential for advancement and so on? Given the level of competition for a particular job, and an individual's age, education and experience, what is the practical likelihood that such a position will be offered? Is this firm, and this industry, likely to grow or decline in the years ahead? Given these facts, what is a reasonable projected income after five years of experience?

A person can gather this information, but doing so is time-consuming and expensive (in foregone income if nothing else). Personal characteristics such as research ability, articulateness, level of education, initiative and so on play a major role in determining how much information is obtained by any given individual. There is no one place to which a person can go to get answers to all these questions. The pieces of the puzzle must be stitched together from a wide variety of sources, printed and personal.

What Could Be Done?

Local labor market information, in usable form, does not have to be this difficult to obtain. The present situation can be improved, and this improvement can come on many levels. Summer jobs offer the young a variety of opportunities to see what different work situations are like. Wise parental guidance can lead an adolescent to work one summer in a store, one summer in an office, one summer outdoors, and so on. Such a pattern may not maximize summer income, but there is a good chance it will maximize learning.

School districts could offer their students much more specific information about the local economy in social science courses. Such information would provide a natural starting point from which to look at particular occupations. Much of the data gathered by the employment service, the chamber of commerce, local universities, research bureaus and other similar sources is free for the asking. It needs to be synthesized and put into teachable form, which school districts are well equipped to do once they take the subject seriously.

Later in this volume we will discuss how labor market information for a particular city could be effectively communicated to the public by local employment service offices. Providing this information would fill a major void.

The Importance Of Local Labor Market Information

Anyone who is attempting to assist others to find employment will want to obtain as much detailed, practical information about the local labor market as possible. If people who are looking for work can be briefed on the local economy in general, they will then need to gather only those specifics which particularly concern them. Among the general information that would be helpful are a review of the major local employers and their needs, the key economic role of smaller firms, the easiest jobs to obtain, common jobs which are more difficult to find but which have higher pay and more chance for advancement, lists of employers and the person to see at each firm, areas where growth is most likely in the year ahead, occupations where demand is greatest, the firms which offer the best training possibilities, ways to combine work and training, and so on.

The time needed to gather all this information will vary, of course, as a function of city size. In any city, however, enough detailed information is available to provide a large head start on setting a sound and informed employment goal, as well as useful help in making realistic longer-term plans.

Moving From Job Choice To Job Search

Once the decision to seek a specific job has been made, a short interim period of organizing for the job search process often follows. It takes time to prepare a resume, locate potential references and obtain their cooperation, check addresses and phone numbers, list specific employers to be approached, and so on.

At this point, then, the focus moves from choosing the job to getting it. The next major step in the job search process is meeting with someone who has the authority to make a hiring decision. It is to the process of obtaining such interviews that we now turn.

Notes✦✦✦

Many would probably use the phrase "career choice" where we have preferred "occupational choice." The modern usage of the word "career" has given the word a developmental sense, however, and we think it is useful to preserve this meaning. Leeman (1984) argues that the word career is properly used to refer to a lifelong sequence of work, educational and leisure experiences. In this sense one can develop a career, or change career direction, but one cannot choose or change a career. Occupations can, of course, be chosen and changed.

Those wishing to read more on the person/job match might start with Frederick Herzberg's classic article, "One More Time: How Do You Motivate Employees?" Although such factors as pay, working conditions, status, security and so on must be favorable to avoid job dissatisfaction, Herzberg argues, they will not in themselves motivate a worker toward higher productivity. The critical growth or motivation factors are intrinsic to the job itself: achievement, the nature of the work, responsibility, a sense of growth, and so on (Herzberg, 1968).

Miller and Matson (1977) have written an intriguing book entitled *The Truth About You*. They argue that each person has a dominant motivational pattern or thrust which comes from the particular way that interests, abilities and personality traits combine in a specific individual. This motivational pattern determines, essentially, the kinds of things each person was made to do. If work is consistent with this fundamental motivational thrust, then it will be satisfying; if not, work will be frustrating and a source of constant irritation.

The process of self-examination, followed by a review of the available options, is expanded from jobs and work to all areas of life in Bolles (1978).

There are a variety of sources of occupational information. Although they rarely contain detailed local information, they do provide a good start in identifying what must be learned about the situation in a particular city or area. The Department of Labor's *Occupational Outlook Handbook* is a standard source. Wright (1984) has produced an excellent (though more white-collar oriented) volume with similar information, *The American Almanac of Jobs and Salaries*. This book also contains an impressive collection of state and local information.

Some important thoughts on interpreting average salaries will be found in "Average Salaries...And Why They're Not So Average" (N.A., 1981). As this article points out, average salaries can be misleading; the range of salaries is equally important. Accountants, for example, have higher average earnings than technicians. The top 10 percent of engineering technicians, however, earn more than 80 percent of all accountants. The best in any field (or the best located) may earn far more than the average for that occupation.

Finally, a job is a set of tasks, and each task requires a set of skills. When examining a job, the essential approach is to get below the job title and look carefully at what a person with that job title actually does all day. One major reason that people can change occupations successfully is that, however different the job titles and even the job descriptions, the skills required are largely the same. One of the first to approach this kind of analysis in an organized way was Sidney Fine (Fine and Wiley, 1971).

CHAPTER SIX
The Number One Job Search Method: Getting Interviews From People You Know

Once an individual has decided what job he or she will seek, the actual job search process begins. In this and succeeding chapters we will look in detail at that process.

Many skills are needed to handle all the tasks which the job search process involves. The person who is looking for work must be able to locate actual or potential openings; deal with whatever written documents are required (letters of application or recommendation, resumes, application forms); prepare for one or more interviews; and survive reference checks which may involve contacts with previous employers and personal references, credit or police record checks, and possibly bonding eligibility certification. If any one of these steps is performed badly, the employer is likely to reject an application and instead consider other candidates.

Sometimes the fear of embarrassment or failure occurring during one of these steps can be enough to close off whole areas of employment. Some inner city residents have intermittent work histories, for example. Other individuals have problems reading and writing. They may be so put off by formal application forms that they do not even bother to apply at personnel offices or government civil service centers. Similarly, applicants with criminal records may avoid interviews where discussion of their past offenses might lead to embarrassment or rejection. A major task of group job search programs (discussed in Chapter Ten) is to help participants overcome these fears and learn how to handle such situations successfully.

There is little evidence that employment interviews are effective at separating those who will do well at a job from those who will not. Nonetheless, few employers will consider hiring someone without an interview. Obtaining an appointment with the person who does the hiring is therefore the first major step for anyone looking for work.

Roadblocks Often Screen Job Seekers Out

The effort needed to obtain an employment interview and a job offer can vary tremendously from setting to setting. At one extreme is the federal government. To obtain a civil service position, an applicant must deal with multiple and detailed forms, required job postings which must remain active for stated lengths of time, examinations, multiple interviews, the construction of lists of eligible applicants, and mandatory procedures for choosing candidates from these lists. At the other extreme is the young person who applies for an unskilled, minimum wage job early in the morning, and goes to work that same day. In this case the interview may consist of a glance which determines that the applicant seems physically capable of doing the work, a quick question or two, an announcement of the hourly wage, and instructions where to report.

Between these two extremes are a wide range of interview settings and demands. The size of the firm, the type of job being sought, the level of competition for the position, and many other variables influence what happens as someone who wants a job meets with the person who hires. In a few cases, when applicants are scarce, the employer will eagerly interview any who apply. In most cases, however, the person looking for work will quickly run into gatekeepers. These persons protect the employer's time. They see to it that he or she interviews only a few of those applying for openings (presumably those most qualified or most needed).

How this gatekeeper system functions will vary. A small employer may instruct his or her secretary to have job applicants leave a name and phone number. They will be contacted if and when there is an opening. Large employers have personnel offices which supervise a multi-level screening process. The supervisor who makes the final decision will interview only two or three candidates sent by personnel. The other applicants are rejected long before these interviews take place. Those who try to bypass personnel by calling the supervisor directly often have trouble getting through. Secretaries, on learning that the person calling is looking for work, will usually reply that all job applicants must first go through the personnel department.

The Three Basic Ways To Get Interviews

The person looking for work finds, therefore, that his or her first major challenge, after having decided what type of employment to seek, is getting through the gatekeepers and in to see those who hire. Although there are many ways a person can approach the problem of obtaining interviews, we will divide these search methods into three broad groups or categories, devoting one chapter to the discussion of each.

First, a person looking for work can try to locate a job possibility through personal contacts. In conversations with friends, relatives and acquaintances, he or she may hear about a current or possible opening at a particular firm or agency. This chapter will summarize what research and experience has taught us about this informal, word of mouth approach to getting interviews.

A second general approach, discussed in the next chapter, involves going methodically from one employer to another. The person seeking work does not know if there is an opening available or not. He or she simply applies to each employer until an interview is obtained. This method, the making of what people in sales call "cold calls," will be discussed in Chapter Seven. The final alternative is to use a labor market intermediary. Included in this category are employment agencies, the want ads, the state employment service, or any other agency or institution which lists job openings or acts as a broker in the hiring process). The research on this approach is summarized in Chapter Eight.

Large And Small Employers Use Different Procedures

When approaching a firm in order to seek an interview, it makes a big difference whether the company is large enough to have a personnel office. If so, the hiring procedures will vary significantly from what is done by small employers.

There are some in-between gradations: the medium-sized employer who, instead of having a personnel office, regularly uses an employment agency, for example. Ordinarily, though, the experience of applying for work at small firms where the owners or managers hire personally will be consistently and significantly different from dealing with the executives, supervisors and personnel offices of major corporations.

Dealing with a small employer is typically a much more direct and personal experience. The small firm either needs help or it doesn't. One person, usually the owner or manager, will make the decision when or whether to hire someone. There is an intense concern with cash flow in most small businesses. A new employee must contribute quickly to profitability if the firm is going to meet its next payroll.

In larger firms, the problem of meeting the next payroll is ordinarily less immediate. A major corporation can hire an attractive professional or technical applicant first and then find him or her something to do. A good person will always be useful.

The personnel office adds a new dimension to the hiring process in the large firm. The role of this office varies widely from corporation to corporation, however. It might or might not screen every candidate. Some new employees may be routinely recruited by supervisors and then sent to personnel to fill out paperwork. Even if the personnel office is supposed to do all preliminary screening, an individual supervisor may occasionally decide to hire a person who comes to his or her attention and makes a good impression. Sometimes the personnel office objects to this vigorously; sometimes not.

Some personnel officials can make hiring decisions themselves, particularly for lower level positions. The newly-hired workers are then directed to report to their supervisors. More commonly, the personnel office will only screen applicants. One or more who appear qualified will then be sent to the supervisor, who makes the final decision. Personnel employees sometimes routinely interview everyone who applies, whether there are openings or not. Alternatively, they may first review the firm's needs and the current application forms before deciding who should be interviewed.

Employers Prefer Hiring Referrals — And Get Better People

Despite the complexity and bureaucratization of the hiring process in large corporations, there are also some important similarities to what happens in smaller businesses. A significant proportion of those hired by all businesses, large and small, come to the employer's attention through personal referrals. Managers, owners and personnel officials all have a clear preference for hiring those recommended by persons they know, particularly when the referral comes from a present employee. Ullman (1966) reports findings from a series of interviews with the personnel managers of 80 companies in the Chicago area. He found that 85 percent of those expressing a preference favored hiring through informal channels. They used other methods only when these channels failed. These personnel officials were convinced that they obtained much better employees this way.

This preference creates an obvious conflict with ideals of affirmative action and equal employment opportunity. The natural tendency of a word of mouth process is to exclude individuals from impoverished and minority groups. Without friends, relatives, and neighbors with good jobs there is no one to pass on word of job openings and possibilities. Hence equal employment opportunity regulations require wide advertising of job openings.

Research, however, indicates that employees hired through personal referrals are more stable. Employers who prefer referrals are not necessarily trying to discriminate. Several studies have categorized employees by how they were hired, and then related the hiring method to how long the employees remained on the job. Ullman (1966) reports data from two large companies which kept such records. At the first, after one year, only 12 percent of those hired through the want ads were still with the firm. Twice as high a proportion, 25 percent, were still working from the group hired through referrals. At the second firm, 26 percent of those hired through want ads were still employed, compared to 72 percent of the employees hired by referral.

Gannon (1971) found a similar pattern in data kept by a large New York bank. Only 27 percent of those referred by the bank's employees left before completing a full year, compared to approximately 40 percent of those hired through want ads or sent by an employment agency.

Decker and Cornelius (1979) reviewed the personnel records of 2466 employees of an insurance company, a bank, and a professional abstracting service. In each case, the lowest quit rates were found among those who had been hired through referral by other employees. The highest quit rates were among those sent by an employment agency (for the bank), or those hired through the want ads (for the insurance company and the abstracting service).

The importance of personal referrals in the hiring process is worth some reflection. The workings of this process explain many of the problems and tensions experienced when looking for new employment.

Rees (1966) draws a useful analogy between hiring a new worker and buying a used car. Since all new cars of the same make and model are essentially the same, it makes sense to check with as many new car dealers as possible to get the lowest price. Used cars, on the other hand, are very different from each other. When buying a used car it is more important to know as much as possible about the characteristics of a given car than it is to check prices with a large number of dealers. It is not irrational to pay a premium price for a friend's car if one has detailed and trustworthy information about its history and characteristics, even though one could buy another car more cheaply from a stranger.

Similarly, when buying stock it makes no difference which stock exchange is used; 100 shares of IBM are the same no matter where purchased. Buying a house for investment purposes, on the other hand, presents the investor with a very different situation. In this case it can be much more important to have detailed and accurate information about the neighborhood, the condition of a particular house, any recent damage incurred, chronic plumbing or electrical problems, and so on. It makes much more sense to spend one's time thoroughly checking out a few houses than gathering a little information about a large number of them.

The labor market, Rees argues, resembles the used car market or the housing market much more than it does the new car market or the stock market. An employer can hire with less fear of error if he or she deals with a few applicants about whom there is trustworthy information. This is essentially what happens when present employees make referrals. The alternative is to collect hundreds of applications from persons about whom little is known with certainty, which is the usual result of placing a want ad.

It is understandable, therefore, that employers prefer applicants recommended by present employees and other trusted sources, despite the problems this raises for equal employment opportunity. Many potential employees (some of whom would do fine work) are missed by this approach. Nonetheless, employers often consider this a lesser evil compared to taking the risk of hiring an unknown individual who later proves to be inadequate, undependable or dishonest.

The applicant, too, obtains benefits from the referral process. The person making the referral can usually provide some helpful information about the job's demands, the quality of life in the workplace, pay, chances for advancement, and so on. The applicant, like the employer, is better off with detailed knowledge of a few good employment possibilities. This is more useful than a list of hundreds of miscellaneous job opportunities with little information beyond the job title and the name of the employer, which is about all one learns from many want ads.

Job Seekers Need To Evaluate The Work Environment

When considering the value of detailed information about employers, it is important to have a sense of how much variation there really is in the quality of life in different companies. Shrank (1979) describes a working life which began when he dropped out of grammar school to work in a furniture factory during the depression. After holding an exceptionally wide variety of jobs in various factories, unions, management and government, he eventually finished a PhD and worked for the Ford Foundation. Reflecting on his wide experience, he argues that many scholars miss the humanity and community which characterize the workplace.

The quality of worklife — the degree of humanity and community in a particular firm — can vary greatly, however. Several excellent books (Terkel, 1972, for example, or Kanter and Stein, 1979) provide detailed accounts of working environments which vary from the bland, creamy existence of an insurance office to the conflicts and tensions among engineers faking data on a major defense contract.

Even positions which look the same or have the same job title can turn out to be surprisingly different, as many people learn in their first few jobs. Glueck (1974) observed the job search behavior of university students. He noticed that it was those with the widest prior work experience who sought the most interviews, made the most site visits, and received the most job offers. They seemed to realize how different firms are, and looked carefully behind job titles to see what the job really involved. Less experienced students apparently assumed that one job was the same as another, and did not bother to do as much checking.

Because working conditions vary so widely, it is understandable that those hired by referral, particularly when the referral comes from a present employee, have a major advantage. They enter the workplace with more information about its characteristics. They are, as a result, more likely to remain. They begin with a clearer idea of what they're getting into. They also have a social advantage if whoever referred them introduces them to others and helps them make a smooth transition to their new work setting.

One question this raises is whether employers, realizing the variation in understanding among new employees, should do more for those who come in without this information. New employees might stay longer if they were initially given more detailed information about both their new jobs and the corporate culture. Wanous (1978) reports that six experimental studies of programs designed to provide a "realistic job preview" for new hires all report a favorable effect on employee retention.

Checking Out The Job First Results In More Satisfaction

What will make a particular set of working conditions attractive to a given person is not always easy to predict. One of us (Johnson) dealt some years ago with the graduate of a government-sponsored program for key punch operators. He was a young black man, and had been assigned to the program by mistake. He finished the training, however, and was placed with a major insurance company. He found himself working for low pay in a large room with hundreds of women doing similar clerical tasks. Everyone involved assumed he would quickly leave the position. His case was even brought up to the Lieutenant Governor's employment committee as an example of the organizational problems of the federally sponsored training.

About six months later, the young man had a day off and stopped by to say hello. To everyone's amazement, he had not only stayed with the job but loved it. He had received a small raise and was even being considered for a supervisory position.

Talking to him made it clear that this position was unlike any other job he had ever had. He could now go to work with his good clothes on, tell his friends he was employed in a major downtown building, and invite his girl friend to join him for lunch in a pleasant cafeteria setting. Far from being disgusted with the job, he was proud of it. He saw it as a "real job" of a kind he had never experienced before. This was far more important to him than the low pay, so he had stayed with the position long enough to get a raise and learn there were opportunities for advancement.

Given the diverse needs and backgrounds of those looking for work, what makes a job attractive can be surprisingly varied. Easy access to a telephone during breaks, day care facilities, location on a convenient bus line, or any of a thousand considerations may be important to one person but of no significance to another.

Nearly half of all employment turnover is concentrated in the first year a new hire spends with an organization. It is a reasonable assumption that many people discover during that first year that they have taken jobs which do not meet their expectations.

Given the difficulties of finding a new position, it obviously helps to gather as much information as possible on the demands of a position and the climate of an organization before accepting a job. Women with children might be less likely to move from job to job, for example, if they located convenient child care facilities first. Similarly, it would help a great deal if they knew the employer's attitude toward work schedule flexibility before accepting a job. Although this takes some time and assertiveness, it can have a large payoff. Ullman and Gutteridge (1974) report that university graduates who put more effort into researching potential employers before accepting offers of employment were more likely to stay with those employers, and were also more satisfied and better paid.

Better Job Leads From Acquaintances Than Friends

The quality and quantity of information which each party to the employment process has about the other is clearly essential. This makes it important to understand the dynamics of the job referral process.

It would be natural to assume that referrals and information about job openings come primarily from those friends and relatives who are most intimately acquainted with the unemployed, and most concerned about them. These close friends and relatives would also be in the best position to pass on detailed information about the applicant to employers.

Surprisingly, research suggests the exact opposite is true. Mark Granovetter, a sociologist, studied professional, managerial and technical workers who had changed jobs within the past year. The subjects of this study were residents of Newton, a Boston suburb. They were asked if they had obtained their new jobs with the help of a friend or relative. Many replied that they had heard about the opening from someone who was more accurately described as an acquaintance.

Further questioning revealed that in more than a fourth of the cases the information which led to their new positions came from someone who was normally seen once a year or less. Yet more than 80 percent of these contacts did more than simply inform the unemployed individual about a possible job opening. They also "put in a good word" to the employer, recommending the applicant be hired. Acquaintances were more likely to do this than were close friends! Granovetter summarized this phenomenon in the phrase "the strength of weak ties" (Granovetter 1973, 1974).

A follow-up study done some years later confirmed this finding. Lin, Ensel and Vaughn (1981) contacted a random sample of 399 men aged 20 to 64 in the Albany-Schenectady-Troy area of New York State. They asked these men how they obtained their current jobs. This study was not limited to those with professional, technical and managerial positions, as was Granovetter's. The findings, however, were similar. The mean income of those who heard about their new jobs from someone they did not know well was $2500 a year above the income of those who got their information from a close friend or relative.

These researchers also discovered that the status level of the contact was a major factor in that person's ability to tell the applicant about a job opening. They concluded that the use of "weak ties" helped to reach these high status contacts, many of whom were connected with the firm which eventually offered the applicant a position.

One implication of these findings is that individuals who are regularly in touch with large numbers of people, even if they do not know them well, may have good access to information about job openings. This is particularly true if these contacts are highly placed.

Membership in business and social groups provides a natural opportunity for such contacts. These organizations can be an important element in finding new employment opportunities, and in explaining employment inequalities.

Another follow-up study of Granovetter's findings was done by Bridges and Villemez (1986). They gathered data from a survey of employed adults in the Chicago area. They also confirmed the strength of weak ties, but only for men. They argue that what is really important is a broad range of labor market contacts, and that this comes from a continuous and successful work history.

Such a work history creates many relationships, and this means that there are many people from whom information about jobs can be obtained. Organizational memberships can play a similar function. McPherson and Smith-Lovin (1982) obtained information from a representative sample of Nebraska adults on the groups to which they belonged. They found that the organizations joined by men were, on average, three times the size of women's organizations. Even limiting the data to professional organizations, they found the groups to which women belonged averaging 200 fewer members per group than those to which men belonged. The hours per month spent by men attending organizational meetings was essentially the same as the time committed to such activities by women. However, men went to meetings of groups involving 600 other people while women were members of groups totaling fewer than 185. Women clearly had fewer potential contacts.

In another study, these same authors located 815 groups where a sample of adults from 10 Nebraska communities met face-to-face. They found almost half of these groups exclusively made up of women. As a result, the typical woman's membership in the voluntary groups in this study generated contact with 29 others, less than four of whom were men. Men, on the other hand, typically met with 37 others, about 8 of whom were women (McPherson and Smith-Lovin, 1986). This segregation by sex had the natural effect of cutting both men and women off from some informal communications networks. Since business networks are often male dominated, this tends to cut women off from the unplanned, "lucky" receipt of information that may lead to desirable employment.

Employers Will "Interview" Even When There Are No Openings

To understand how informal contacts lead to jobs, it is important to note some additional findings from Granovetter's research. First, there are some job openings which should probably be called "quasi jobs." No official opening has been defined, but someone with the authority to hire knows of problems or opportunities, and is open to hiring the right person should he or she come along. This can be true for jobs at any level. The employer may have seen work backing up in the storeroom and considered hiring another stocker, or may be seriously thinking of computerizing the company's finances.

It should be noted that there are also a significant number of people who are quasi job seekers. They have taken no explicit action to find a new position, but would be willing to discuss one if someone brought it up.

Only A Few People Know Of An Opening

Second, information about a job opening does not seem to travel very far. Hypothetically, one might imagine that Mike would hear from Tom who heard from John who heard from Mary who heard from her boss about a job opening at Universal Widget. In practice, this doesn't happen. In 39 percent of Granovetter's cases the applicant heard of the job possibility directly from the employer. In another 45 percent of the cases, there was only one link in the communications chain (that is, the information went from the employer to someone else to the applicant). This leaves only 16 percent of the cases for chains of two or three; there were no chains of four or more.

This finding is consistent with the other studies already reviewed, which found employers broadcasting word of their openings only as far as necessary. As a result, relatively few people know about any given job opening. Unemployed individuals therefore need to talk to as many acquaintances as possible about their job search activities until they find one who has heard of something.

Jobs From Referrals Are Better, Pay More

Granovetter found that jobs obtained through word of mouth information and personal referral are, on average, both more highly paid and more often newly-created than jobs found by other means. This, too, is consistent with other research findings. Dyer (1972), for example, studied members of the Forty Plus Club of Southern California, a self-help group for unemployed managers and professionals over 40 years of age. He found that getting information from either business acquaintances or relatives and friends consistently led to good jobs. Sending unsolicited resumes or making "cold calls," on the other hand, led more often to lower paying jobs.

The importance of personal contacts is also highlighted in some findings reported by Corcoran, Datcher and Duncan (1980), summarizing data from the eleventh wave of the Panel Study of Income Dynamics. This is a continuing research project, begun in 1968, involving more than 5000 American families. About half of the young adults in the study had heard of their current job through a friend or relative. Similarly, about half knew someone who worked for their current employer before accepting a job there. Many of the referring individuals also put in a "good word" for the applicant. About four tenths of the men and a third of the women reported that another person helped them get their current job.

There is no question that person to person exchanges of information are regularly found at the heart of the employment process. As an electrical engineer once summed it up for Richard Bolles, "paper is an insulating material." Although forms and resumes play a part in finding employment, it is personal contacts, information from friends and acquaintances, and good personal impressions that play the major role, especially in obtaining desirable and well-paid positions.

The Power of Networking

Because of this, several authors (Djeddah, 1978, for example, or Haldane, Haldane and Martin, 1980) suggest that job applicants at all levels meet with executives and other supervisors with the power to hire. The purpose of these meetings is not necessarily to obtain immediate employment. Instead, the idea is to ask these highly placed individuals for suggestions about people the applicants should be meeting, and to request any information the executives may have about job openings or possibilities.

Even casual acquaintances will often help set up such appointments, and one introduction will often lead to another. Through these "remembrance and referral" interviews, the unemployed person can, in effect, tap into the informal communications channels where information about job openings can be found.

Consciously trying to penetrate informal communications networks has, in recent years, come to be popularly known as "networking." What this process does, in effect, is turn what would otherwise be a more spontaneous, unplanned series of chance meetings into a deliberate process. Someone who is good at this can build up a corps of people who are watching for a suitable opening. In time, someone is almost certain to run across something.

Proceeding in this manner, however, assumes the ability to convince a significant number of executives to devote time to these meetings. It also assumes the ability to make a favorable impression; otherwise the requested help will not be granted. Not everyone is able to do this. There are indications that as networking has become more popular, it has also lost some of its effectiveness.

For one thing, corporate executives can spend only so much time meeting with people who ask their aid and advice. Because books which recommend this approach have become common, however, the number of such requests has grown immensely. This is particularly true of the highly visible executives in major corporations, who receive far more requests for these interviews than managers in small and medium sized firms.

In addition to the increased volume of interview requests, there are apparently many "networkers" who lack either social skills or a clear understanding of what they are doing. As a consequence they make a bad impression on potential employers instead of a good one. A survey sent to 500 executives, managers and professionals by an outplacement firm found that 54 percent of the respondents met frequently with persons who were networking. These meetings often did not work out well, however. The managers expressed irritation at having people sent to them by others whom they hardly knew. They reported meeting many networkers who were not clear on what they wanted, and who exhibited a general lack of courtesy and appreciation during the interviews (Eaton, Swain Associates, 1983).

It is certainly wise for those seeking employment to contact friends, relatives and acquaintances. They can describe the type of job they are seeking, and ask for suggestions or leads. Going beyond this to networking through friends of friends and acquaintances of acquaintances, however, requires some social skill and even subtlety. Done properly, such an approach can be effective. It will lead to useful conversations with those who are responsible for hiring. Done badly, however, it not only leads nowhere but gives the whole approach a bad name.

Paying A Reward Uncovers Hidden Openings

A less subtle but intriguing approach to finding job openings was tried by Jones and Azrin (1973). It has never, to the best of our knowledge, been used practically. These researchers realized that although information about most job openings is not widely broadcast, there are nonetheless many persons in the population who know of one or two opportunities. They therefore decided to put an ad in the paper seeking information on job openings.

The newspaper involved served a rural county with high unemployment. The ad offered $100 to anyone who would provide information which led to employment for "one of our job applicants." The ad specifically mentioned a dozen common occupations and requested information about openings in these areas. A total of 14 calls came in as a result of the ad, giving information about 20 job openings. This information was turned over to the local employment service office, which sent 19 applicants to interview for the positions, of whom eight were hired. The results suggest that any widely-broadcast reward for information about job possibilities might well draw out some useful leads.

Practical Implications

If referrals are to be obtained, the person who wants new employment needs to let people know that he or she is looking for work. To whom should this fact be communicated? To everyone in sight! One of us (Wegmann) knows of an inner city job search program which regularly advised its participants to strike up conversations with whomever they met when riding city buses. During this conversation, they were to mention their job search activities. Several got leads that led to employment through these discussions.

The more highly-placed the persons to whom one speaks, the more likely they are to know of job possibilities. Almost everyone, however, runs across information on at least some job openings. People are invited to an office party for a retiring worker; the boss mentions that a new contract has been received; word goes around the office that someone has been fired. In each of these situations, there is a high probability that a job opening has just been created, or soon will be.

Many unemployed individuals withdraw from social contacts. Feeling uncomfortable about their status, they say as little about it as possible to anyone. In addition, they are short of money. They contract their social lives severely, staying home as much as possible.

This, unfortunately, is the worst possible thing they could do. It takes them out of contact with others, and makes it less likely they will run into someone who can tell them about a job possibility. The best advice for the unemployed is, therefore: "Talk to people." It is not essential that these conversations be with executives ("remembrance and referral" interviews). They can be short exchanges with a small business owner, a minister or an insurance agent. So long as they end with a cheerful "give me a ring if you hear of anything," the potential benefit is there. Knowledge of job possibilities is scattered throughout the population. The more people who know what kind of job an individual is seeking, the more likely it is that one of them will run across some useful information. Even people who are barely known will often gladly pass on such information. It costs them nothing, and they enjoy being helpful.

In Conclusion

Information received from personal contacts plays a major if imperfect and often unpredictable role in helping the unemployed find new positions. Jobs obtained through leads and referrals from friends, relatives and acquaintances work out better. They pay more, provide higher job satisfaction, and are kept longer.

There is not, and probably never will be a universal list of all job openings. The reporting of job openings could be mandated by law, but that is highly unlikely. The quality of person hired is too central to the success of a business, and people are too variable in the qualities which they bring to their work, to make hiring anything but a personal process. Computers can match people to positions based on training and experience. Who can work effectively with a particular supervisor in a specific corporate culture, however, will always be a matter for individual judgment — on both sides. Therefore, information received personally from friends and acquaintances will always play a major role in the job search process.

Hiring someone has many similarities to dating and marrying. Both are matchmaking processes, and both seem to work out best when there is as much accurate and trustworthy information on both sides as possible. All the computer capabilities in the world will never motivate either employers or applicants to put their real concerns and problems into a computer, which is why no system of using computers to match people to jobs has ever had much success

Notes✦✦✦

Readers who are interested in a more theoretical discussion of the relationship between a worker's skill and the geographic area in which a job is sought should see Simpson (1980). Simpson raises a concern which we share: low income areas, with their concentrations of poverty and unemployment, often fail to provide enough informal job information. This reinforces and perpetuates a high level of inner city unemployment.

Another useful article for readers of a more theoretical bent discusses majority/minority relationships. This article has a particularly clear and clever discussion of why minority group members are driven back on each other. It also shows mathematically why an "old boy network" is so effective (Rytina and Morgan, 1982).

CHAPTER SEVEN
Another Effective Job Search Method: Approaching Employers Directly

In the last chapter, we reviewed research on obtaining interviews by referral. In this chapter we take a closer look at the second major method by which interviews are obtained: going from employer to employer to see if there are any openings and, if so, to apply for them. This is what people in sales refer to as a "cold call."

It is difficult to say with precision just what proportion of Americans find jobs by approaching employers in this manner. (There is a discussion in the Notes at the end of this chapter on the methodological problems of research on this question.) There is no doubt, however, that it is a commonly used method of finding employment. Given the information in Chapter Four, a reasonable estimate is that one out of every three or four jobs is found using this approach.

There is some evidence that those who find employment most quickly combine following up on referrals with some cold calling. A study of laid off blue collar workers done some years ago found that most heard of their new jobs through friends, relatives and other workers. Reemployment success was greatest, however, when the men also checked with every appropriate company for possible openings, even if they thought it unlikely that the firm was hiring. Although cold calling was far more effective than answering want ads, it did require high motivation. The lower the motivation, the longer it took to find another job (Sheppard and Belitsky, 1968).

Along this same line, other researchers report a relationship between levels of self-esteem and the job search method chosen. Those with higher self-esteem are less likely to use intermediaries such as the want ads or employment services, public or private (Ellis and Taylor, 1983).

Measurements of motivation and self-esteem are always difficult to make. They are, in the nature of things, quasi-measurements at best. Such findings do, however, suggest the value of looking at just what a person must *do* when using different job search methods. Some methods are more stressful than others.

Approaching Employers Works, But Is Hard For Many To Do

Conceptually, the person who goes from one employer to another is using a rational job search method. As we have already seen, there are positions coming open every day. Unfortunately, no one person or institution has a list showing where these openings can be found. Just finding the right places to apply is therefore the first major problem of a person looking for work.

Faced with such a situation, a statistician would suggest taking a sample. If one out of every 20 employers of a certain type has a job opening of a particular kind on any given day, the statistician would take a random sample of 100 of these employers. On average, there should be five job openings of the type sought in each sample of 100.

In theory, this is all straightforward, at least to a statistician. Practically, for the unemployed person, it can involve a lot of very frustrating work. To find those five openings the person looking for work must deal, not only with the five firms where there are openings, but with the 95 where there are not. That may not always be a pleasant experience.

The person who comes to an employer because of a personal referral can open the discussion with a statement such as the following: "My cousin, Tom Smith, who works in accounting, suggested I see you about a secretarial position. He said you were a fine person to work for, and there was a chance you might need someone." Saying this won't guarantee a job, or even an interview. The employer's response is likely to be friendly, however, or at least civil.

If a firm needs another worker, being referred to the employer usually guarantees an interview. Those who answer ads or learn of an opening from the state employment service face much stiffer competition. Usually there will be many applicants. Indeed, the opening may have been filled even before the applicant arrives. But at least the employer has a real need, is expecting people to apply, and is set up to deal with them.

When making a cold call, however, the person looking for work has none of these advantages. He or she runs much more risk of being treated as an unwanted intruder. The employer has not shown any desire to see job applicants. The unemployed person is not expected. If there are no openings, and no likelihood of any, the inquiry is an unproductive interruption in the day's work. Therefore, the treatment received is more likely to be curt or unfriendly. Many people are polite and helpful, of course, but it is difficult to contact all 95 firms where there are no openings of the type sought without meeting at least some brusque treatment.

Emotional reactions being what they are, most people begin to feel, after a few dozen dead ends, that no openings are available. The experience of constant rejection often leads them to slow down or stop well before the hundredth application or phone call.

If human beings were computers, in other words, finding job openings through random sampling would undoubtedly be effective as a job search method. Human beings are not computers, however, and the experience of applying to one employer after another is, as Jackson (1978) suggests, almost inevitably one of meeting obstacles, being turned down, facing disappointments, and bearing with fear and anxiety. It can be a time-consuming, frustrating and sometimes even soul-destroying experience.

Both research and experience therefore suggest a real tension between the benefits of cold calling and the distastefulness of the process. Although direct application to employers is a common and potentially effective job search technique, the number of employers approached by the typical unemployed person is low. Perhaps this is to be expected, given the degree to which applying to employer after employer can be a frustrating experience. Unfortunately, such a low level of activity almost guarantees that it will take months to find employment.

An Average Of Six Contacts A Month Results In Long Unemployment

In reviewing data from the Current Population Survey, Rosenfeld (1977) found an average of six contacts with employers per month by those who were unemployed and looking for work. This includes inquiries made by phone, in person, or by mail. A more recent study confirms this low rate of employer contact. In conducting a random audit of job applications claimed by unemployed persons who were receiving Unemployment Insurance, investigators found that they averaged about 1.8 contacts with employers each week (Louis, Burgess and Kingston, 1986). This is very close to the rate of six per month found in the earlier CPS data.

Stevens (1977) studied 2600 persons receiving Unemployment Insurance payments. They had been out of work for at least seven weeks and none were waiting for recall or union reassignment. He found that a third of the group had approached fewer than 10 employers since leaving their last job, and two-thirds had contacted 20 or fewer. This was too few to generate many job offers. (His figures suggest that it took about 34 contacts with potential employers to generate one offer. This implies that the individuals in his sample had less than a three percent probability of success when approaching any one firm.)

All this may seem very negative. It should be noted that there are some equally positive things to be said for cold calling. Many employers admire applicants who have the initiative (or "gumption," as they often put it) to come in and ask for a job. They are more favorably disposed toward such applicants than they are toward those sent by agencies, whom they view as more passive.

Furthermore, done properly, this method can be quite efficient. With good telephone skills, a person looking for work can easily canvass a hundred small and medium-sized employers a day, determining quickly which ones are worth a personal visit. When dealing with major companies it is sometimes possible to bypass the personnel office and obtain an interview by phone with the appropriate supervisor.

Approaching employers to ask about job possibilities is an ancient and honorable job search method. It is, however, far harder for some people to use this method than it is for others. Personality, the ability to deal comfortably with strangers, telephone skills and the type of job being sought are all important factors. As we shall see in Chapter Ten, a major goal of group job search programs is to provide training in how to make effective cold calls. When this training is supplemented by support and supervision as it is put to use, with help offered as problems develop, the results can be very positive.

Who To Approach — And How

There are many different methods of choosing which employers to approach when trying to find an opening. Some individuals seeking common white collar positions simply pick a large downtown office building. They begin at the top and work down, applying to each firm in turn, floor by floor, until a job is offered. Others take the Yellow Pages and look up firms which employ persons with their occupational backgrounds. They phone one employer after another until they obtain an interview. Lists of employers in certain industries, available in the library or from the local chamber of commerce, can also be used.

Many group job search programs have adopted telephoning from the Yellow Pages as their main search strategy. Phoning can be supervised, and it permits easy access to the hundreds of small employers who are the source of many new jobs. Nichols and Schill (1977) provide a list of Yellow Pages headings for most common occupations. This is a helpful aid in finding groups of employers who hire a given type of worker. The employment service in California also publishes an excellent booklet which lists all the telephone directory headings under which various employers can be found, divided by industry (California Employment Development Research Division, 1983).

In addition to using the phone and making contacts in person, another option is writing to a series of employers to ask about possible employment. This usually involves sending a resume along with a cover letter requesting an interview. Letters are a "thinner" form of communication, however. They are less personal than phone calls or visits. As a result, even mass mailings do not usually produce positive results. More often than not, there is no reply. When responses *are* received, most are negative.

Major firms receive thousands of letters and resumes. One Houston corporation reports receiving 5000 a month. Unless the person applying by mail offers skills which are in high demand, these letters are typically given a 30 second skimming and then set aside. In some firms, they do not even get that. To protect themselves against suits alleging discrimination in hiring, some corporations are being advised to return all unsolicited resumes unread (Rosenblum and Biles, 1982).

Personnel Offices Tend To Damage Self Esteem

Richard Pfeffer, a professor who chose to take a factory job during a sabbatical leave, describes what he experienced as he and others waited in personnel offices to apply for unskilled jobs:

> Mostly, those waiting simply stared vacantly into space. Their eyes rarely met each others'. They did not smile at or respond observably to the few who were active. On their faces were fixed, blank looks. They were there for one purpose, to get a job. That meant they had to wait until they were called for an interview. They had all waited many times before, it seemed, in other personnel offices.

The manner in which job applicants are treated in the personnel offices of large corporations can, even apart from whether they are offered positions (which, necessarily, most are not), make them feel unimportant and even insignificant. Pfeffer describes his experience at a local factory:

> Although the personnel office was empty, no one working there seemed to notice me. My asking for

an application appeared to constitute an unwarranted interruption. Perhaps that was partly because GM had been laying off and was not hiring. But GM outer office personnel employees treated job seekers in a way not very different from what I had experienced elsewhere, making them feel insignificant, beneath notice.

After several weeks of searching, Pfeffer accepted a job driving a forklift. Summing up his experience, he noted that firms had no hesitation about making him wait for hours before telling him that all jobs had been filled. The only time that seemed to be of any importance to those hiring was the company's time. He rarely knew, while waiting, whether a job was available, what it paid, or what it was really like. The fear of another rejection, combined with this lack of information, caused a high level of anxiety and uncertainty.

A strong feeling of powerlessness naturally results when interview after interview makes it obvious there are far more applicants than jobs. The decision-making process seems totally in the hands of the corporation. This experience leaves many job applicants feeling painfully impotent and in need, with their worth and options decided by others (Pfeffer, 1979: 17-28).

Allan Dodd has described the white-collar, managerial equivalent of these experiences in his novel, *The Job Hunter*. They can be equally unpleasant. Shortly after being eased out of his job, the novel's main character finds himself recalling the "There is no opening available in this organization at the moment" notes he has received from the secretaries of former colleagues. "At odd moments throughout the weekend...I would writhe as if someone had jabbed me with a red-hot iron. Those notes, those goddam, contemptuous, snotty notes." (Dodd, 1965:19) Unreturned phone calls, personal letters answered impersonally by secretaries, a series of interviews with an apparently interested firm followed by no actual offer, curt replies to efforts to communicate — all can combine to produce feelings of rage, helplessness, anger and depression.

Being Assertive Gets Interviews

Given the difficulties of cold calling, a willingness to be assertive can make a significant difference when trying to find an opening. Harry Maurer, a journalist, traveled the country interviewing people waiting in line to collect Unemployment Insurance. Many would not talk to him. Those who did told of a sense of violence and invasion when they lost their jobs, followed by feelings of worthlessness, drinking and marital problems, nervousness, and thoughts of suicide. A marked loss of energy and constant edginess were common as the time spent unemployed wore on and their job search efforts led nowhere. What astonished Maurer more than anything else was the degree to which the unemployed blamed themselves for their situations.

One of Maurer's interviews was with Willie Hawkins, a young black man from Alabama who finished high school in 1971 and then spent four years in the air force. He was unemployed for seven months after his discharge. He began to feel desperate, which helped him to come up with something:

> One day me and my brother drove out to this industrial area. We parked the car and walked to every factory. I think it took us something like three hours to run up on a place that would even talk to us. Everyplace we went, they wasn't hiring. They wasn't even accepting applications. Well, we came to this warehouse. The receptionist told us they wasn't hiring. But I had got so aggressive that I told her, "I'm not trying to run your business, but would you make sure? Will you call back there in the plant and ask to speak to the general foreman and ask if he'll accept an application?" She said, "Well, I'll do it, but they're not accepting applications." So she called back there, and he answered the phone and told her that he would accept one. She was all in shock and she told me, "Yeah," and she apologized. (Maurer, 1979: 171)

Willie Hawkins got this job, and worked there a year. Then the place went out of business, and he again faced unemployment for another seven months.

Large And Small Firms Need Different Approaches

The person who decides to apply to employers directly, one after another, has to determine which employers would be most likely to hire for the type of job he or she is seeking. The next decision is whether to concentrate primarily on the small number of large employers in the area, or the much larger number of small employers. This choice involves a clear set of trade-offs.

On the one hand, there are more jobs, and therefore usually more openings, at large corporations. Such firms, however, are also much more visible. Many unemployed persons come to them to apply for work. The competition for available openings is therefore intense.

Furthermore, large corporations are more bureaucratized than small firms. Application forms must first be filled out and screened. Many are rejected at this point; only a fraction of the applicants are usually seen in person by those in the personnel department. Some who are given a first interview are then dropped. Others are sent to supervisors for yet another round of interviews. All these activities require several trips to the firm, followed by intervals spent waiting for a letter or phone call that will move the applicant to the next step. In many cases, after a series of seemingly interminable waits, the applicant is either not given a further interview or is not offered the job.

In almost all large firms the employment application form is the first screening device used to determine which applicants the firm will consider seriously. "The area of greatest concern to the professional is the work history. It is there that the risk indicators are sought: how complete it is; how accurately and precisely the jobs are described; how tight it is chronologically; how rationally periods of non-work or unemployment are explained, including the most recent period; how long people last on jobs, and why they left them. Professionals become very adept at checking time spans, from the period a person left school until the present, or at least in the last five years. Dates are important. Unexplained gaps suggest hidden problems — jail, hospitalization, or living off someone else, a 'red flag' to work-oriented reviewers. School, homemaking, out of the country, self-employment, all are rational explanations. Current extended unemployment is viewed very negatively. In fact, some of the largest private employment agencies are reluctant to grant full interviews to people who have been unemployed for more than two months. Job hopping indicates lack of stability and poor work performance for adults, less so for youth. The knowledgeable professional or employer is usually very aware of inflated job titles: the 'sales/office managers' who managed no one but themselves, the 'chef' who did short-order cooking, the 'mechanic' who can do only tuneups. Hence, the probe for precise job duties." (Johnson, 1982: 97-98)

Although smaller firms may not do such intense screening, they do present other difficulties. These businesses do not usually have the economies of scale that characterize large corporations, and often pay lower wages. Although small firms have many openings collectively, there is a low probability that an opening of the type sought exists at any one. Many small employers must be approached to obtain even a few interviews. Since small firms cannot afford personnel offices, the applicant will ordinarily deal directly with the owner or manager. Although this means much less bureaucratic red tape, it also means that the hiring decision is determined by the needs, perspectives and prejudices of this single individual.

Employers Are Wary Of "Strangers"

Lathrop (1977) complains that the national job market is a chaotic mess, disorganized, unregulated, and lacking a central communications system. He is correct. Our economy is not centrally planned. Each employer is free to hire in whatever way he or she wants. The employer does not have to notify anyone that a job opening exists. Both employers and the unemployed are, as a result, often groping around in the dark as they attempt to find each other. Both want to make a good match, and both are trying to avoid the many problems caused by unwise choices.

Trying to catch the employer's attention under these conditions, some jobseekers are driven to highly unusual approaches. Burdette (1981) tells of one individual who sent an employer a pizza every day for lunch. Another drove a taxi with a sign on the back seat saying, "This taxi is being driven by an unemployed advertising copywriter" (with a supply of resumes). A third sent an employer a letter with a ten dollar bill, betting he would get a reply and an interview. When none was forthcoming he sent a twenty dollar bill, betting again, "double or nothing." (That, at least, did lead to an interview. If nothing else, he showed he was serious!) Most persons, of course, do not have the ingenuity (or the funds) to do this sort of thing.

No matter what method is used (phone calls, going in person, or writing letters), going from employer to employer has all the potential for both pain and profit that salespeople experience when they make any cold call. The applicant comes to the employer unreferred. Both sides to the transaction begin with almost total ignorance. The person seeking work usually knows little about the firm. The person doing the hiring (whether the owner of a small business, or a personnel official in a large corporation) knows equally little about the applicant. Both are understandably wary. In a labor market where there are more applicants than jobs, the employer looks carefully for any negative information and does not hire if there is the slightest doubt. There will always be other applicants to consider.

There are few employers who have not made mistakes when hiring. They know the grief that awaits them if they must deal with new employees whose attendance is intermittent, who steal from them, who show up under the influence of alcohol or drugs, or who easily get into disputes with customers or other employees. Most employers will risk losing a potentially good employee before they will take a chance on hiring someone who may turn out to be a problem. If there are few seeking work, employers may have no choice but to take some risks. There is little reason to take chances, however, when there are a wide variety of qualified applicants from whom to choose.

For all its potential effectiveness, looking for work by going from one employer to another is a challenging task. When job openings are uncovered, the applicant must first deal with the employer's fears. Even when successful, there are still problems. Without an "inside source" the applicant knows little about the working conditions to be expected if a position is accepted.

Without benefit of referral by someone who is known and trusted, the employer must depend on the information provided by the person looking for work. Employers are painfully aware of how both applicants and references regularly exaggerate good qualities and fail to mention glaring problems and deficiencies. Therefore, many are understandably suspicious and mistrustful when they must, in effect, hire strangers. The applicant bears the burden of gaining the employer's trust. Without this trust, statements about skills and past accomplishments will be discounted or ignored by a manager or personnel worker who has been lied to by prior applicants. The person who obtains an interview by going from one employer to another clearly faces a more difficult task than the individual who is referred by a trusted mutual friend or acquaintance.

Tips For Making Effective Cold Calls

Difficult though it may be to use this approach, the potential payoff is too high for most people to ignore it. The best strategy, therefore, is to make cold calls in a manner that has the highest possible likelihood of success.

The first step is to break the list of potential employers into at least two groups: those large enough to have personnel offices and those where the owner or manager hires personally. The first group must usually be approached in person, since an inquiry by phone will typically bring the reply that no interviews are granted until an application has first been screened. Sometimes one can phone a supervisor directly, but most such inquiries will be referred to the personnel office. The most useful issue to raise by phone is whether the corporation has been hiring in the last few months. It is usually a waste of time to go to a firm that has workers on layoff, for example, since they must be called back first before any new employees can be hired.

Many large firms have far more applicants than they can possibly interview. The key is often to go back to them again and again, finally becoming known by name, until an interview is granted. There is a fine line between being persistent and being a pest, but it needs to be walked. Better to be a bit of a pest than invisible and unnoticed.

The smaller firm, on the other hand, is usually best approached by phone. Many cities have directories which give the name of each establishment's manager. A quick personal introduction by phone, including a short summary of skills and experience, and a request for an interview (if not for an opening which exists now, at least for the next one that comes up) will lead to some appointments. Most employers will say no, of course, but persistently dialing the next number will usually lead to something. If the job being sought is a reasonable choice (the unemployed person has the appropriate qualifications and there are positions of that type available in the community), persistent inquiries will eventually turn up some openings.

There are a variety of intermediate strategies which can help in certain cases, depending on the job sought and the mix of available employers. Sometimes a letter can be sent to the supervisor of the appropriate division of a large company, followed by a phone call. Although this may not always lead to an interview, it may make it easier to get useful information before going to personnel. Occasionally a well-written letter arriving at the right time may lead to an immediate interview with the division head.

Writing first can also help with medium-sized employers who are not quite large enough to have personnel offices. This at least allows the caller to tell the manager's secretary that he or she is following up on a recent letter. If this gets the person through, the manager will be expecting the call. He or she may be willing to consider the applicant for an opening (existing or to be created), or at least may suggest some possibility elsewhere.

When phoning small firms, it is usually better to skip those employing only a few people. These are often family enterprises that rarely or never hire. The probability of employment may be so low that it is more psychologically efficient not to phone in the first place. This keeps the total number of rejections at a more tolerable level.

One approach to preparing for these phone calls to employers is outlined and discussed in Farr (1988b). A person can often benefit by practicing what to say on the phone with someone else. It helps to record some practice calls, playing them back to hear how they sound. It is also helpful for the person seeking employment to set a specific quota of places to be visited in person, and of employers to be phoned. The person can then report to a friend or job search group whether the quota was fulfilled, and how things went.

Many people find it helpful to set up a structure so their phoning is not done totally alone. One effective method is for two people to share the same phone, with one calling while the other listens, as they alternate their calls. This gives each a perspective on their own experiences, and doubles the number of interviews each hears granted.

What is needed, in sum, is an approach which combines (1) a strategy which carefully selects the employers to be approached and the message they will be given, so the probability of a favorable reception is as high as possible, and (2) a support system which helps make the inevitable rejections as bearable as possible. If this support system also keeps the unemployed person in touch with as many appropriate employers as possible, interviews will come. Without such support, many will become discouraged and quit before they discover the openings they are seeking.

Being granted an interview is, of course, only the first step. Meeting with an employer to whom one has not been referred by a mutual acquaintance is also a real challenge. How that challenge can best be handled will be discussed at greater length in Chapter Nine. First, though, we need to look at the final method by which interviews are obtained: the use of an intermediary to bring together employers and those looking for work. That will be covered in the next chapter.

Notes✦✦✦

Research on the job search methods which are most effective has been obscured by the failure of most researchers to make a clear distinction between *sources of information* (why did you go to this company to apply for a job instead of some other; where did you hear there might be a job opening at that firm?) and *the search methods used* (answering an ad with a letter or phone call; walking in cold and asking to talk to the supervisor).

The apparently simple question, "How did you get your last job?" combines both of these questions. The question blurs *why* a person applied to a particular firm with *how* he or she went about the application process. A given individual may answer "My brother suggested I apply" or "I called the supervisor and asked for an interview." Both are correct answers, depending on how the question is interpreted.

To give a concrete example of the problems this causes: some studies find personal referrals to be the source of most jobs; others report that more positions are obtained by those who apply directly to employers. Closer examination suggests that the proportion using information received from contacts (and possibly from other sources of information, such as the want ads) is higher than is typically reported. The reason for this is that many respondents, when filling out questionnaires, check "applied directly to the employer" even though the *reason* they made the application was that someone told them of a possible opening, or they learned from an advertisement that a particular employer was hiring. We have, again, a confusion between the source of the information and the method of application.

Granovetter (1974), in his study of the employment process, reports a clear example of this confusion. Those filling out his mail questionnaires reported that 51 percent of their professional, managerial or technical jobs had been obtained through personal contacts. When he interviewed people, however, that figure rose to 66 percent, and the number of positions obtained through direct application declined. During the interviews Granovetter could probe with follow-up questions on just why the respondent chose to apply to the firm which eventually offered a position. A significant number of respondents, as a result of this probing, recalled they made the application because of information received from others.

CHAPTER EIGHT
Other Job Search Methods: Using Labor Market Intermediaries

We have reviewed the two most common ways of finding job openings: hearing of them from friends, relatives or acquaintances; or going from one employer to another until an opening is found. About two-thirds of the jobs in this country are found using one of these two methods.

We now turn to the third major approach which brings together employers and those seeking work: the use of labor market intermediaries. Here a third person or institution intervenes. Some intermediaries broadcast news of an opening widely (through the want ads, for example, or in the job listings of a professional association). Others act as brokers, bringing the employer in contact with appropriate applicants (as is done by a search firm, an employment agency or a college placement office).

Those who use a labor market intermediary are often said to use a "formal" job search method. This is in contrast to the informal methods used by those who simply approach employers on their own, or are referred by friends and acquaintances.

Employers clearly prefer to hire people who are referred to them by those they know and trust. If no one with the appropriate skills is available through referral, employers always have the option of choosing from among the applicants who regularly approach them looking for work.

Given this, why do employers bother to advertise or use employment agencies or other intermediaries? There are many reasons. Some employers are small, or not widely known. They see only a few walk-in applicants. Some have only limited access to personal referrals. In other cases, the job to be filled may be difficult or uncomfortable. If the pay is low, only a small fraction of the potential applicants will accept it. Those who do take such jobs typically leave them quickly (hence the label "high-turnover"). As a result, new workers must be recruited constantly.

Not all use of intermediaries, of course, is for such negative reasons. A new contract or large order can require the rapid hiring of many new employees. A friend at a college placement office may make a concerted effort to send talented graduates to a particular employer. Because of affirmative action requirements, some jobs must be widely advertised and clearly open to all applicants. Or a job may demand uncommon skills; those who are referred or come in on their own initiative will often lack the necessary qualifications.

For a wide variety of reasons, then, employers turn to the want ads, employment agencies, college placement services or similar institutions for help. Those looking for work also regularly turn to these same institutions. This is why it is important to understand how these intermediaries work, the strengths of each, and their inherent limitations.

The Want Ads

By far the most widely used of the labor market intermediaries is the classified ad or want ad, found in both the daily and Sunday editions of almost all American newspapers. About one worker in seven finds employment after answering a want ad, more than through any other labor market intermediary.

Detailed studies have been made of the ads appearing in both the daily and Sunday editions of newspapers in specific cities (Walsh, Johnson and Sugarman, 1975; Johnson, 1978; U.S. Department of Labor, 1978). These studies find the openings listed in the ads to be only a small fraction of the jobs a city has to offer. They are also not a representative sampling of the city's total labor market. A small percentage of employers place most of the ads. Most are large firms in only a few of the city's industries.

TABLE TWELVE

Want Ad Types, Daily and Sunday Editions

Type of Ad	Percent
New ad, local job, placed by local employer	30.5
Repeat of previous ad	33.0
Ad placed by private employment agency	19.2
Ad for job in non-local or unknown location	11.7
Ad for non-job earning opportunity	5.6
Total	100.0
(N = 204,427)	

Source: U.S. Department of Labor, 1978. Adapted from Table 3-4.

In San Francisco, fewer than half of a representative group of employers had used the want ads at any time during the past year. In Salt Lake City, it was less than 60 percent. Firms in finance, insurance and real estate were the least likely to advertise. Employers who did place ads reported they had the most success hiring clerical personnel and salesworkers.

The want ad section requires careful and selective reading. Table Nine shows the kinds of ads found in a large sample of such notices in the newspapers of 12 different metropolitan areas. About a third of these ads were repeats of previously advertised openings. Another fifth were placed by employment agencies; the reader could not tell who the employer was, or where the job was located. Slightly more than one ad in 10 listed an opening in another city. Additional notices in the want ad section were for ways to make money other than taking a job. Only three of every 10 want ads was the type of notice of most interest to the typical unemployed person: a new listing, placed by a local employer, for a local job.

TABLE THIRTEEN

Comparison of Daily and Sunday Want Ads

Type of Ad	Sunday (%)	Daily (%)
Ads placed by employers for local jobs	55.1	71.6
Ads placed by private employment agencies	25.1	13.6
Ads for non-local jobs	14.4	9.2
Ads for non-job earning opportunities	5.4	5.6
Total	100.0	100.0

Source: U.S. Department of Labor, 1978. Adapted from Table 3-5.

The mix of help wanted ads in the daily and Sunday papers are significantly different, as Table Ten shows. The Sunday want ads are much more dominated by employment agencies. Sunday's ads also contain more openings in other cities. The daily paper is more likely to list local openings placed by local employers.

Although want ads notify the public that a job opening exists, many contain little information beyond that. The wage or salary is often not stated, and the industry or nature of the work may not be clear. This is especially true when ads are placed by employment agencies, whose practices we will discuss shortly, but it is often the case for employer-placed ads also. Even the name of the employer may not be given. The so-called "blind ad" requires an applicant to write a box number at the newspaper.

Many applicants are uncertain about what they want. They apply for almost any advertised opening, which makes mismatches highly likely. Breaugh (1981) reports a study of 112 research scientists (none of whom obtained their jobs through personal referral). He found those hired through want ads missing almost twice as many days of work as the scientists recruited from other sources (such as college placement offices, professional journal ads, or self-initiated contacts). It is reasonable to assume that this higher absenteeism indicated less commitment to the work being done and a poorer match between the demands of the job and the characteristics of those hired.

The want ads stimulate such poor matcnes. Often quite short, they usually lack the detailed information an applicant needs to make an informed choice. To make things worse, much of the information which is in the ads can be misleading. "Manager trainee" can mean a clerical or sales job which has a hypothetical potential for promotion to supervisor, for example. Statements of salary potential are often exaggerated. Under these conditions, the probability of a bad match is high.

The years of experience and level of education needed to qualify for advertised jobs are often raised to reduce the number of applicants. Where experience and training are not required, the person looking for work needs to be wary. "No experience needed, we train" usually means a sales position with no salary except the sales commission, and perhaps an hour's training. Those accepting such offers may even be asked to pay for the samples or demonstration materials needed for sales calls. Sometimes these are legitimate products, though they may be overpriced or hard to sell. In other cases, however, more dubious proposals, such as pyramid selling, are involved.

The want ads are, for the unemployed person, somewhat of a mixed blessing. On the one hand, they do announce specific job openings and help those looking for work to find employers who are adding new employees. This eliminates the necessity of dealing with employer after employer who is not hiring. In addition they are cheap, easily obtained, and provide new listings daily. There is no doubt that the want ads play an important and useful role in the American labor market. As has been noted, one worker in seven obtains his or her new job through these ads.

These advantages must be balanced against the disadvantages which have been noted by researchers. The want ads rarely contain detailed information about either the job or the employer; they list a disproportionate number of undesirable jobs; and they announce openings for some occupational groups but rarely for others. Those seeking employment in an occupation in which the ads are strong (secretarial or clerical, for example) can find them a real help. For others they may be much less useful, or even a source of frustration and unnecessary discouragement.

Want Ads Result In Stiff Competition

When applying for an opening listed in the want ads, the person looking for work should expect intense competition. Since the ads broadcast information about only a fraction of the jobs open at any given time, they usually draw large numbers of applicants. Anyone who can read can learn about the advertised jobs; many fewer people know about the others.

This is especially true of jobs advertised nationally. It is not unusual for a Wall Street Journal ad to draw 500 to 1000 resumes, for example. Large responses to local ads are also common. In San Francisco, a sample of 411 employers reported that over 10,000 persons had responded to their advertisements. Only 407 (about one in 24) were ultimately hired. Another study reviewed the want ads in the Sunday edition of a small town newspaper in New York State. It found that only 131 of the 228 ads had been placed by employers rather than employment agencies or others. Some ads listed more than one opening. Of the 142 available jobs, 100 required a specific skill. Despite their specialized requirements, most of these jobs were filled quickly. Employers reported that they were swamped with applicants for the remaining 42 unskilled jobs. As a result, 90 percent were filled within two weeks, and many within a day or two.

Employers advertise frequently either for low paying, high turnover jobs which constantly come open, or for positions requiring specialized skills. The want ads are most lacking in the middle jobs. These positions do not require exceptionally high skill levels, but do provide good pay and opportunity for advancement. They are filled largely through personal referral or direct application. Kaufman (1982) reports that professionals who try to obtain new employment by applying for advertised openings are often given misleading information. As a result, they are more likely to end up underemployed.

The want ads therefore need to be used carefully. It is not necessarily true that an ad means a job exists. Noer (1975) reviews a variety of motives that can lead firms to place ads other than a desire to hire more employees. Blind ads which request that a resume and salary history be sent to a post office box at the newspaper are sometimes used to collect information on local pay. This is useful if a business wants to be sure its salaries are competitive. Or a company may want to interview employees of a competitor to learn more about what the competition is doing. In other cases, an employer who is preparing to bid on a contract will place an ad even though he or she is not yet ready to hire. The response to the ad will provide valuable information on the availability of workers with various skills. This information is used in preparing the bid.

Conclusion: Use Want Ads Knowledgeably

None of the above discussion is meant to suggest that someone looking for work should not read the want ads. They are, after all, readily available and inexpensive. There is no question that they regularly list some good jobs. What is important is that they be used knowledgeably. There are many more jobs open in any community than appear in the want ads, so it is not a good strategy to place one's whole reliance on them. And because some ads contain misleading information, the job openings they list need to be approached with care.

Employment notices are routinely published in the journals and newsletters of professional associations. These notices are important to professionals who seek positions in a national market. Often there are only a limited number of openings for specialized positions in any one city. This makes it difficult to apply in person, as one would for other jobs, or even to get detailed information about potential employers. Notices in professional journals are therefore widely used as a way for institutions and professionals to come together. In addition, affirmative action rules often require such notices. This is one of the few cases where there may be an almost complete listing of particular kinds of openings available throughout the country.

Any list of openings can generate intense competition if the number of positions is significantly below the number of applicants. This is as true for professionals as it is for others. Steinhauser (1985) kept records of his search for a position after completing a PhD in Counselor Education, a very competitive market. Over a 10 month period, he applied for 122 positions, responding to notices in three major professional publications. He was invited to 14 interviews. Four of these occurred at the same national convention. He went to 10; the other four came after he had accepted a position. These 10 interviews generated two job offers; one of these offers was accepted.

Private Employment Agencies

In most industrialized countries, it is a government responsibility to maintain labor exchange offices. These offices serve the unemployed without charge, referring them to available job openings. In the United States, this function is performed by state agencies which operate employment service offices under federal guidelines. These offices will be discussed later in this chapter.

What is unusual about the United States is that, in addition to these government offices, there is also a large and thriving private sector competitor, the private employment agency. These for-profit firms invite the unemployed to apply. They also seek information on job openings from employers, call firms to describe attractive applicants, and generally serve as brokers between employers and those seeking employment. The private employment agency charges either the employer or the person seeking employment each time someone sent by the agency is hired. Although charges vary widely, they are usually substantial (typically at least 10 percent of a year's salary). Individuals who cannot pay the fee in full sometimes have to pay it over time, with interest. This can be a financial burden for lower and middle-income workers.

Private employment agencies come in many sizes, organizational patterns and specialties. There are nationwide chains whose offices can be found throughout the country. Most major cities have at least one or two large local firms with offices scattered throughout the metropolitan area. Small agencies are also common, however, and even one-person firms are not unusual. Some agencies specialize in one occupation (accounting, secretarial and clerical help, or sales people, for example). Others are general service firms which handle a wide variety of positions. Some agencies charge only the employer when a placement is made; they are sometimes called "fee-paid" agencies. Others routinely charge the person seeking employment, though this is becoming less common. Still others will charge either, depending on the situation.

Some employment agencies handle all the needs of particular employers. They act, in effect, as their personnel offices. More commonly, they are told about some openings but not others. The openings sent to the agency are often those the employer has trouble filling, or the ones which come up unexpectedly and must be filled quickly. Sometimes several agencies (including the state employment service) will be told of an opening. An employment agency must then fill the job quickly to earn the commission, before the position is taken by an applicant sent by someone else.

There is another type of intermediary, the executive search firm, which handles only the highest positions. The best of these firms are paid for their efforts "on retainer" — that is, they are paid whether they locate someone who is hired or not. The largest of these recruiters (Korn/Ferry International, Russell Reynolds Associates, SpencerStuart or Heidrick & Struggles, for example) are well known to corporate executives. A call from one of them can mean a chance for a corporate presidency. Executive recruiting firms are popularly known as "headhunters," a term which is also sometimes used for employment agencies which specialize in managerial and professional positions. Agencies, however, are paid only on a contingency basis; that is, only if they find someone whom the corporation hires.

Temporary Help Agencies

One particular kind of employment agency which has experienced rapid growth in recent years is the temporary help agency. These firms serve the employer who needs work done for a limited period. This typically occurs during a seasonal overload, the peak period under a particular contract, or some similar situation. Some years ago most temporary help agencies supplied only secretarial and clerical help. Today they place accountants, computer programmers and operators, lawyers, foreign language translators, and even managers and executives.

Workers, like employers, use temporary help agencies for a variety of reasons. Some individuals want to work odd hours or part time while attending school, looking for a permanent position, or working two jobs. Others simply enjoy working at a variety of worksites. They become "permanent temporary" workers. Although seemingly a logical contradiction, this is a very practical option. The agency sends them from one assignment to another. Some temporary help services, after a probationary period, reward those who stay with them by providing health and pension benefits.

Another common pattern, among both workers and employers, involves using the temporary position as a convenient means to explore a more permanent relationship. Employers, after using a group of temporaries, frequently offer permanent positions to the best and most productive. Similarly, those seeking employment may use a temporary agency to look over the working conditions at several businesses. When they find a suitable employer they apply for a permanent position. This application is more likely to be seriously considered, since now they are known to the employer.

The agencies know that temporary work often leads to permanent positions. They usually include a clause in their contracts providing for a commission if a temporary worker is hired for a permanent position within a certain number of months after an assignment.

How Employment Agencies Screen Applicants And Find Openings

Although the number of temporary help agencies has grown rapidly in recent years, the agencies which list permanent positions are more common. (A few large, full-service agencies provide both services.) The most common use of an employment agency therefore involves an applicant who wants to interview for a full-time, permanent job. Employers, on their part, sometimes list an opening with several agencies, and simultaneously advertise it in the paper.

The private employment agencies in any given city are not difficult to find. They are listed, of course, in the Yellow Pages of the local telephone directory. Their primary method of recruiting applicants, however, is through newspaper advertising. Even a brief look at the daily or Sunday want ad pages will turn up a wide variety of employment agency ads.

At first glance it may seem that the primary purpose of such ads is to find applicants for the jobs they describe. Actually it's not quite that simple. As Gowdey (1978) notes, a significant difference in wording and approach is readily apparent when comparing ads placed by employment agencies with those of individual employers. The employer-placed ads usually describe jobs as demanding a high level of performance, and therefore open only to the totally qualified individual. Inflated levels of education and experience are often demanded. The ad is clearly written to keep away all but the most attractive applicants. One can almost picture the author of the advertisement trying to avoid being deluged with more responses than the firm can handle. (It is because many advertised jobs do not really require the education and skills demanded in an ad that the unemployed are often advised to ignore these requirements if they believe they can do the job.)

Ads placed by employment agencies, in contrast, are written differently. Here the aim is to bring in the largest possible number of qualified applicants. The positions listed in these ads are described in glowing terms, and interested persons are invited to apply. The reason for this is that the purpose of the ad is not primarily to fill the advertised openings. These positions are usually the best the agency has to offer. They could be filled easily with persons who apply to the agency on their own initiative. The primary purpose of the ad is, rather, to draw in a large group of qualified applicants so the most marketable can be selected for serious service. (Some unethical agencies make up attractive but nonexistent jobs and advertise these, in an attempt to generate a large client flow.)

Applicants who respond to the agency's ads are quickly reviewed. Those who do not seem marketable are just as quickly dismissed after a short "courtesy" interview. This can include anyone changing occupations, those without experience, or persons with obvious personal problems such as no permanent address or alcohol on the breath.

The rest are dealt with more carefully. If the applicant is paying the agency's fee, the contract guaranteeing this payment must be signed. Those who match jobs which have been listed with the agency, whether these jobs were advertised or not, are briefed on how to handle the interview and sent to apply. The rest of the marketable group are then described to employer after employer over the phone, in an attempt to find interviews. Mangum (1978) estimates that about 70 percent of the placements of private employment agencies result from this aggressive marketing of applicants by phone. Employment agency placements, in other words, are largely achieved by directly approaching employers. However, it is the agency consultant who first makes the approach rather than the person looking for work.

Even when an employer does list an opening with an agency, the agency often has trouble finding someone to fill it. Mangum quotes one estimate that agencies are able to fill about one job order in five. (Remember that employers often turn to agencies for jobs they find hard to fill by other methods, and also list the opening with more than one agency.)

Employment agencies undoubtedly serve a useful function. There are, however, certain pressures inherent in the way they are structured which can lead them to act against the best interests of the persons who come to them. Most agency consultants are paid on a commission basis. They receive a fraction of the agency's placement fee. Positions as consultants in employment agencies are, in effect, commission sales positions. There is no set income. Turnover in such jobs is high. It is in a consultant's financial self-interest to send an applicant to a job which is open and can be obtained quickly. This is true even if the job is a poor match to the person's education, talent and experience, and is not the best-paying job which he or she could reasonably expect to find. If most of the listings the agency has are for secretaries, the question to an applicant with a master's degree is likely to be, "Can you type?"

Under these conditions, there is a strong temptation to tell applicants that no jobs other than those the agency has listed are realistically available. Noer (1975) describes one agency which sent applicants with high aspirations to interview for jobs which the agency knew would not be offered. Then, returning with egos crushed, they would accept whatever lower level jobs the agency could obtain.

Most agencies, of course, would never engage in such practices. Problems with employment agencies more commonly arise because of subtle pressures than blatant wrong-doing. Still, it is important to know that agencies typically receive a stream of job orders for lower paying clerical positions. There are less frequent requests for assistance in filling jobs requiring higher levels of skill and experience. Since the agency is paid a fee only when an opening is filled, there is always a temptation to move an applicant into whatever position is most easily available.

As a practical matter, then, the person looking for work needs to consider seriously whether an employment agency is likely to help. If so, the next step is to find the agency and consultant likely to do the best job. One obvious thing to look for is how long a consultant has been in the field. An experienced consultant is more likely to have detailed knowledge of the needs and characteristics of local employers than someone new.

Employment Agencies Are More Effective With Certain Types Of People

Agencies work most successfully with experienced persons who have sharply defined skills, continuous rather than intermittent work histories, and consistent employment in the same occupational area. They will usually be less interested in persons seeking blue collar employment (unless this is an area in which they specialize), those just entering the labor market, or people trying to move from one occupation to another. It is not that such persons cannot find employment. Employers, however, have little trouble finding this type of applicant so they see no need to involve an agency. The agency therefore has no financial motivation to provide assistance.

The knowledgeable user of private employment agencies needs to remember that the agency must, above all, keep the good will of employers. The unemployed come and go, but the same employers hire year after year. Unemployed persons are therefore best advised to assume they will have to look after their own best interests themselves. If the person looking for work is clear about what he or she wants, and the agency can help find openings, then the basis exists for a mutually satisfactory relationship. If not, the individual needs to use a different search method.

In understanding how both the want ads and private employment agencies operate, it is important to note that both are of most help when they are needed least. When unemployment is low, employers (having fewer applicants) are most likely to place want ads or seek help from agencies. When unemployment is low, of course, those seeking work are also more able to find openings by asking friends and acquaintances, or by going to employers on their own to apply.

When the economy turns down and unemployment rises, however, the number of want ads drops precipitously. (Want ad linage is therefore used by economists as an index of the state of the labor market.) The openings listed with employment agencies also decline dramatically. All labor market intermediaries, including those run by the government, must operate within the supply-demand relationships of the market. When the unemployed person most needs help from intermediaries, therefore, the intermediaries are least able to provide that help.

The Public Employment Service

Government action to assist people who are looking for work has a long history in the United States. Employment bureaus were first set up by individual cities. New York, San Francisco, Los Angeles and Seattle all established such offices during the 19th century. Then, beginning with Ohio in 1890, the states began to create systems of employment offices. By the early part of the 20th century most of the states had taken this step.

The present state employment service system dates from the Wagner-Peyser Act of 1933. This law mandated employment offices in all the states. They are run by state agencies but financed with federal funds, with minimal standards and operational guidelines set by the federal government. The name of the agency varies from state to state. Employment Development Department, Employment Security Department, Employment Commission, Job Service and other similar titles are used. There are 2500 employment service offices throughout the country, run by 25,000 employees.

Guzda (1983) has reviewed the evolution of these agencies over the last half century. Although theoretically available to any employer to help fill any job, these offices, like their predecessors, primarily handle low-wage positions. More than anyone else, they serve employers seeking unskilled or casual labor.

Employment service offices fill about one job in 20, roughly the same proportion as are filled by private employment agencies. The number of employers listing openings with the employment service is low (5.1%, about one-third the number using the want ads). A small number of large employers provide a high proportion of the openings. The jobs listed are clustered at the low end of the skill-experience-education-pay spectrum.

It is important to note, however, that a local employment service office may have a placement pattern very different from the national average. Offices in small towns often build up an intimate knowledge of the local labor market, and may even negotiate exclusive hiring agreements with many of the area's largest employers. Some offices, usually in larger cities, have divisions concentrating exclusively on clerical or professional jobs. Other local offices, particularly in California, run training sessions which describe the local economy and the most effective ways to find jobs within it. The unemployed can then decide whether they want apply for the jobs listed with the employment service, or use other search strategies.

The state employment service office, like the private employment agency, is dependent on employers for information about job openings. Employers may or may not be interested in supplying this information. In some parts of the country employment service offices are perceived as primarily serving low-income, heavily minority populations. Some employers assume these applicants have poor work records and multiple problems. Hence they not only do not tell the service about their openings, but treat anyone who mentions using the service as an applicant of doubtful promise.

The employment service has traditionally had representatives whose assignment was to contact employers, build good relations with them, and secure their job orders. Many of these positions were eliminated as a result of budget cuts during the early 1980s, however. Employment service offices today are therefore even more dependent than before on the information about job openings voluntarily provided by a small proportion of employers.

Employment service listings, like those found at private employment agencies, vary with the state of the economy. The employment service, despite its desire to provide effective assistance without charge, is (like other intermediaries) of least help when most needed. When a recession hits lines lengthen and personnel must be re-assigned to process unemployment compensation claims. This leaves even fewer personnel to assist the unemployed find new jobs.

A somewhat different perspective on employment service operations is given by Stevens (1978), who argues that the service is more effective than is commonly believed. He notes that most studies of job search methods ask only *whether* a particular search method was used, not *how often* it was used. If data were stated on a placement per contact basis, he argues, use of the employment service would be the most effective of all job search methods.

It is not clear that Stevens' conclusions could be defended today (the data on which they are based are more than a decade old). Nonetheless, the basic issue he raises is worth considering. It is much more efficient to deal only with employers who have openings than it is to go from one employer to another in the hope of finding something. The key question is whether the service knows about many of the available openings. To make an intelligent decision whether and how often to use the employment service, in other words, the unemployed person needs to know whether the service can supply a reasonable number of referrals. The quality of jobs listed would, of course, also have to be considered.

The only practical way a person can determine how well a particular employment service office can serve his or her needs is to use it and see what happens. Hundreds of jobs are listed with local offices every day. Many post openings on bulletin boards. Just reading through the listings can be a good education in what is available. Although many of these jobs will be temporary or have undesirable characteristics, others may be more attractive.

Federal law requires that jobs created by government contracts be listed with the local employment service office. Most of these positions are filled by other methods, since the typical person using the employment service does not meet their requirements. Qualified applicants will find some attractive openings, however.

If it is possible to establish a good working relationship with an employment service counselor, he or she can often be helpful. Experienced counselors are familiar with the local labor market. They will sometimes phone employers they know to recommend a promising candidate. Since their services are provided without charge, it makes sense to use them. Here, as elsewhere, it is persistence and a personal relationship that matters. As one report puts it, "There are hardly any interviewers in the [employment service] who have not responded to individual applicants they have come to know personally or who have not been motivated by the persistent visits or phone calls of individuals. It is often to these individuals that the interviewer's mind turns when an appropriate new job appears, or when there is time for job-development efforts." (Johnson, 1982: 90)

Although the employment service lists fewer jobs than the want ads, their openings cover a wider range of occupations and industries. The want ads are more narrowly focused. Like the want ads, however, employment service lists have clear limitations. Just because no suitable job is found on these lists does not mean that such a job is not open and available somewhere in the community.

The Future Of The Employment Service

The future role of the employment service is a matter of debate. There are those who would like to see it abolished, arguing that labor market operations are best mediated by private sector employment agencies. Others would like to see the service changed to operate more on the European model. This would involve a much more far-reaching role in matching employers and applicants.

Bendick (1983) has described the Swedish approach to job placement, for example, and believes the United States should operate in a similar manner. Swedish law makes private employment agencies illegal. Every employer must list all job openings with the public labor exchange. Each unemployed person works with a case manager until reemployment. This case manager has access to information on all job openings of any given type. Visits to potential employers, and even trial placements, are encouraged in an effort to find a position which is likely to be successful and lasting. Referral to additional training is another option. With computerization, it is hypothetically possible to sit down with an unemployed person and review every opening of a given type anywhere in the country.

Appealing though such a system is in many ways, we doubt it is politically possible in the United States. The freedom of each American employer to recruit and hire in any way he or she chooses is a deeply ingrained tradition. It is not likely to be overturned easily. The most realistic, appropriate, and cost-effective role for the employment service therefore remains an open question. It is likely to be the subject of debate and controversy in the years ahead. Our own vision of how the employment service should operate is spelled out at the end of this book.

The School Placement Office

Almost all colleges and universities, as well as a few high schools, run a placement office to assist graduating students to find employment. (Out-of-work graduates or students seeking part-time jobs to help finance their educations are sometimes also served). Over the years, the process of hiring new college graduates has been institutionalized by the country's major corporations. Dennis and Gustafson (1973) questioned a sample of corporate personnel managers. They reported hiring more college graduates through campus recruiting than by all other methods combined.

More recent information, however, suggests a somewhat different picture. Bowman (1987) reports a survey done by the Maryland State Board of Higher Education. Responses were received from over 2500 of Maryland's 1984 college graduates. Only one graduate in 10 found a job through the placement office. Two-thirds of the group found jobs using informal methods. The small group that did get jobs through the placement office got the best jobs, however. They averaged over $23,000 in starting salary, and three-fourths of the jobs were related to their majors. Those using other means averaged around $17,000, with less than half the jobs related to their majors. These figures indicate how competitive the job market is for college graduates. They are also a good measure of the decline of the major corporation as a source of employment. More and more jobs are with smaller employers who do not send representatives to campus.

Like all intermediaries, therefore, college placement offices offer the student a skewed sample of the jobs for which he or she might apply. Only the larger corporations usually have college recruiters, so a list of those interviewing on campus will typically contain few medium-sized or smaller firms. Even some large employers who do hire a significant number of college graduates (firms in wholesale and retail trade, for example, or the various levels of government) are commonly underrepresented. Smaller colleges, in contrast to large universities, have more trouble attracting corporate recruiters, since they have fewer graduates with any given major. The student, especially at a small school, who relies primarily on the placement office to obtain job interviews will therefore be exposed to only a small and rather unrepresentative sample of available job opportunities.

Not all student placement activities take place in a college's official placement office. Some students obtain introductions or recommendations to employers from professors who do consulting or other work for those same corporations. The professor rather than the placement office serves as an intermediary. This too can be an approach which conceals possibilities as well as opens them. Some major corporations form relationships with academic departments and individual professors out of a conscious desire to identify and recruit the best students. Smaller firms who are less likely to have professors doing consulting work for them, on the other hand, may be less able to develop such relationships.

Other Intermediaries

The want ads, public and private employment agencies, and school placement offices are the major labor market intermediaries. There are others which serve smaller, more specialized populations. Union hiring halls assign union members to jobs in certain occupations. Several trades (building, printing and maritime, for example) have traditionally done this. Many professional associations regularly provide placement services at their annual meetings. There are privately run computerized job banks which attempt to match those seeking professional positions to employer-supplied openings. Various community-based organizations collect information about local job openings to help individuals living within their service areas. Government programs serving the low- income unemployed often hire job developers who go from employer to employer seeking information about job possibilities for program participants.

Recognized leaders in a variety of professional fields often serve as informal employment brokers. When jobs come open, they are routinely asked for recommendations. Some of those seeking employment know this, and therefore make it a point to meet them and ask their help. A somewhat similar function is occasionally performed by priests, ministers and other religious leaders who attempt to help the unemployed in their congregations find work. They are in a convenient position to ask employers in the same congregations if they have any openings.

In contrast to the informal approach of such "switchboard persons," who simply help to put people in touch with each other, federal, state, and local civil service offices act as highly bureaucratized labor market intermediaries. They receive applications at central locations for a wide range of positions with a variety of agencies. Applicants are tested and screened. Those who are selected go for a final interview by the appropriate supervisor. Like the hiring processes typically found in large corporations, such centralized operations put a premium on formal education and prior occupational titles (Grandjean, 1981).

Intermediaries Can Provide A Useful Service

The potential value of the information supplied by labor market intermediaries, formal and informal, is undoubtedly great. Although unemployment was much lower when Stevens did his research (2.4 percent, well below today's levels), he found that males with at least two years of prior work history, seeking full-time nonconstruction employment, had to contact an average of 14 employers before obtaining a job. Today this would be an unusually short and successful job search! What Stevens noted then is therefore even more true now: "The striking result of analyzing job search behavior...is the observed low quality of labor market information available to job seekers. Clearly a substantial amount of fruitless employer contact ensues." (Stevens, 1972: 102).

The value of even basic data when looking for work is shown in an experiment run in the Hayward, California employment service office (Neto and Sugarman, 1974). Those seeking employment in selected occupations were given a package of cards listing possible places to apply. This printed information was attached to a return postcard on which applicants could record whether they were hired, the rate of pay, who did the hiring, and so on. Much of this information was initially collected by phone. Once the program started, those seeking employment kept it up to date by sending back reports on their experiences. Information recorded included the hours during which applications were accepted, any specialized knowledge that was needed, required licenses, the level of education sought, bus lines serving the area, and any minimum age requirement.

What was especially impressive in this study was that more than half of those supplied with this information used it to obtain employment. Indeed, more jobs were found this way than by applying for the specific openings listed with the employment service office where the experiment was done. As the program received more feedback from those looking for work, and the quality of information given to the unemployed improved, the success rate of those seeking work went up.

There can be no doubt about the need for better labor market information, and intermediaries are the logical persons to provide much of it. Employers seek good workers; the unemployed seek steady employment. Both usually approach the hiring interview with far too little information about each other. They therefore can find the interview unsatisfying and full of ambiguity. If intermediaries could fill this void, providing both sides with accurate information, it would make the labor market much more efficient and save both parties much time, trouble and expense.

Problems With Intermediaries

Given the need that both employers and applicants have for information about each other, one would expect labor market intermediaries to flourish, and be widely used. They are indeed widely used, which suggests at least some level of effectiveness. But each also has serious problems. The want ads list only a small proportion of available jobs, and these are concentrated at the two ends of the employment spectrum. The employment service is widely (if not always fairly) viewed as ineffective. It is seen as a place where lower income workers stand in line by the hour for unemployment checks. Often it offers the unemployed only a small number of openings; many of these are for low paying, high turnover jobs. Although the service helps many of the unemployed, it also leaves many others unsatisfied.

Private employment agencies, for their part, fill a useful role in matching employers and experienced workers. The quality of the match, however, varies with the agency. Employers complain that agencies exaggerate the attractive qualities of those they refer, and do not find the kind of workers the employer is really seeking. Applicants, for their part, complain that some employment agencies are guilty of bait and switch advertising, charge excessive fees, and downgrade their skills to obtain quick placements (Mangum, 1978).

In addition to employment agencies which list actual openings, there are also career counseling firms which provide help in finding employment but do not list specific positions. Some of these firms have also been accused of unethical practices. Investigative reporters on programs such as "Sixty Minutes" have featured these complaints. Accusations include charging large fees and claiming high success rates, but providing little real help. Guthrie (1981) reports on one such firm which claimed a success rate of over 90 percent. It was found by the New York Attorney General's office to have helped no more than 38 of 550 clients find a position. Another firm provided counseling but, once the large fee was paid, made it difficult to reach the assigned counselor. In effect, five or six hours of counseling were given at about $400 per hour.

The problems of seeking new employment in today's economy have been widely publicized. As a result, many individuals and groups now offer assistance to those looking for work. A few, such as those just mentioned, are trying to take advantage of the unemployed. Others are well-meaning but inept. Some good counselors know little about the labor market; people with considerable labor market experience may lack the traits and training necessary for effective counseling. Luckily, however, there are an increasing number of people who can provide effective assistance, and who do it at a reasonable price. They understand how the labor market operates, and they provide needed coaching and direction as their clients seek new employment. They are not, strictly speaking, labor market "intermediaries," since they deal only with those seeking employment, but not with employers.

Who Will Pay For The Services Needed?

Although there is a real need for effective labor market intermediaries, then, the evidence suggests this need will remain unmet. The reasons for this seem almost entirely structural. It takes considerable time and money to gather accurate and usable information about the many hundreds of job openings available in a town of any size. This is in addition to what it costs to investigate the persons seeking employment. Who will pay for all this?

Employers are largely inclined to pay only when the job is hard to fill. The unemployed will usually pay only if they are unable to find a position on their own. They are often short of cash even if they are willing to pay. But an operation which is largely set up to match the hardest to fill jobs with the hardest to place applicants will obviously have a difficult time of it.

The government cannot easily afford to provide this service to everyone. Government programs therefore usually serve low income groups, since they have the greatest needs. Employers, for their part, then often become uncooperative if they believe they will be sent only workers from low income backgrounds.

The situation is made even more difficult when various government agencies run a variety of independent, uncoordinated employment programs. Employers (large employers, particularly) find themselves approached regularly by a stream of job developers, all seeking the same job listings (Johnson and Sugarman, 1978).

Even if all these problems could be solved, it would still be impossible to have a central list of all job openings. This is inherent in an economic system based on the independent and uncoordinated entrepreneurial activities of a large number of employers. It is understandable that the greatest desire of adults considering a change in employment is to look at such a list (Arbeiter, Aslanian, Schmerbeck and Brickell, 1978). But a list cannot, in the nature of things, be constructed. One can list the types of jobs in high demand, as the government does regularly, but not specific openings.

Even if such a list were available, it would provide neither side of the employment transaction with the intensive information they both really want and need to bring about a mutually satisfactory match (Granovetter, 1974). What both employer and applicant are primarily seeking is not simply a list of names or openings, but greater knowledge about each other's characteristics.

This being the case, we find ourselves back at the situation which is typical today: people obtain jobs through informal contacts if possible, talking to people they trust and asking for the information they need. Failing that, they go from employer to employer, often rather blindly, or try to find something through an intermediary. In the latter two cases, however, they often have much less information about what they are getting into. The result is often lower pay and less job satisfaction.

Learning To Use Intermediaries Well

Existing labor market intermediaries are clearly useful but also, and equally clearly, imperfect. Since there are two sides to any employment transaction, the question which must be asked of any intermediary is: whose side are you on? If there is a conflict of interest, whom do you serve? Given that every unemployed person has failings, but needs employment anyway, and that every employer also has failings, but needs employees anyway, for whose best interests does the intermediary primarily work? Usually it is the employer who has priority.

What is important, therefore, is that the unemployed person have a clear view of the role intermediaries play in the labor market, so they can be used realistically. Imperfect help is better than no help, but even imperfect help will be of greater benefit if there is a clear understanding of how the system works. Employers control the wording of the want ads they place, and we have already noted complaints about the misleading nature of some ads. (Applicants control the wording of their resumes, which can be equally misleading.) Private employment agencies are in business to make a profit, and that profit comes from the fee collected when a placement is made. This creates the temptation to make any placement possible, however inappropriate, to collect the fee. And, if a choice must be made, it is more attractive for an agency to maintain the good will of the employer, who may hire more agency clients in the future, than to worry about any single applicant. The public employment service has a restricted budget, yet is under government mandate to serve everyone, and especially targeted groups: low-income persons, minorities, veterans and so on. To push too hard to find jobs for some of these persons, however, is to risk the wrath (and future non-cooperation) of employers, especially if some of those who are hired do not work out well. School placement offices face the same problem. They want to serve their students, but there are far more students seeking positions than openings provided by college recruiters. The good will of these recruiters must be maintained to keep them coming back year after year.

None of these structural pressures make unethical or harmful behavior certain. They do, however, create a situation where it is to the applicant's advantage to understand what is going on. Highly effective labor market intermediaries which consistently find work for those who use them are like the proverbial "good five cent cigar." The world may want them, but they are not available and there is little promise they ever will be. Still, for a given person in a particular situation, a specific intermediary, used intelligently, can be helpful.

The key to the effective use of intermediaries may lie not only in an understanding of how they function, but also in a willingness to use them in novel and creative ways. Some persons skim the want ads to see which firms are hiring. Then, instead of answering an ad directly, they try to find someone in the company who can tell them in more detail about the needs of the firm. Sometimes this person can help to arrange an interview with the appropriate supervisor.

Another approach is to wait two weeks or so after an ad has appeared before applying. At that point, if no one from the first group of applicants has been hired, the employer may dread having to readvertise and process another large group of applications. A qualified person who appears at this point will often get a serious and favorable reception.

An approach to employment agencies used by some engineering and computer professionals also shows there is more than one way to use an intermediary. These individuals will build a relationship with a knowledgeable person in an employment agency, keeping in touch with the demand for their specialty. Then, when they are seeking work, they can deal with a person whom they know well and trust. Such knowledgeable use of labor market intermediaries is uncommon, but may be the key to getting the most from them.

The Type Of Job Sought Can Make A Difference

The most important thing to understand about any labor market intermediary is the set of jobs to which that intermediary has access. No intermediary is in touch with all employers, or even (except in a few small towns) with a large proportion of them. Once an unemployed person is clear on the set of jobs a given intermediary is likely to list, the next two decisions follow. First, should the intermediary be used at all; if so, how much use should also be made of other search methods.

A police officer who wants to become a social worker would be wiser not to approach a private employment agency, for example. Agencies almost never handle social work jobs, and they rarely serve people who are changing occupations.

Someone graduating from a college or university, on the other hand, and seeking a job with a major corporation, would be wise to work closely with the college placement office. This is precisely the type of position in which the placement office specializes. Even then, however, the graduating student would be better off also approaching corporations of interest directly. It is not likely that all of them will send representatives to campus, and competition on campus is keen.

An experienced secretary seeking a new position will find a warm reception at almost any employment agency. The want ads, too, will provide many good leads. Even here, however, such an individual will usually benefit from picking a few businesses with particularly attractive locations and stopping by to see if they need someone.

In summary, it is a matter of matching the intermediary to both the person and the position being sought. Surprisingly few people have a clear idea of who is typically helped by each of the many intermediaries operating in the labor market. Approaching inappropriate intermediaries, they often come away discouraged. Some even become convinced there is no job they could possibly obtain.

Their reaction reveals an exaggerated view of what intermediaries can do. No intermediary can get anyone a job. What they do is help some applicants obtain an interview with one of the limited number of employers they serve. The applicant must then meet with the person who hires. If a personnel office is involved, the meeting will be with someone who is able to send the applicant on to the hiring authority. In any case, obtaining the interview is only the first step. The essential second step is the self-presentation made during that interview, since it is this alone which will lead to an actual job offer.

CHAPTER NINE
Effective Interview Strategies

Referrals, cold calls, and the use of intermediaries all have the same goal: a personal meeting with an employer to discuss employment possibilities. Once the interview is scheduled, however, the person looking for work must concentrate on a new goal: turning the employment interview into a job offer.

This offer, of course, may or may not be accepted. A job offer is often only the beginning of a negotiating process. This is particularly true when offers are received from more than one employer. And even an accepted offer does not always mean immediate employment. In some circumstances a new employee may not go to work for several weeks or even months. Clearly, however, the job search process has reached a new and more positive stage once the first job offer has been received.

It is, of course, theoretically possible to be hired without a personal interview. This does occasionally happen, particularly if the applicant is already known or the job being sought is located a great distance away. However, such instances are clearly exceptions. Although there is no hard data, we have no doubt that some kind of employment interview is an essential part of almost all hiring decisions.

What actually happens during these interviews, however, varies widely. At one extreme is an exchange consisting of a few quick questions and a gruff "report to Mike over there." At the other extreme is a process which can include a series of extended meetings with dozens of persons and groups, taking place over several months.

A good sense of this variation in hiring environments was exhibited by a banker working with a program designed to help low-income youth find jobs. "He presents himself to the group in his banker role and conducts mock interviews with the participants. He then leaves the room, changes into jeans and a work shirt, and returns as the foreman of a construction crew, an owner/worker in a restaurant, an owner/worker in a small manufacturing firm or whatever, and roleplays that hiring situation with the youngsters." The banker's behavior provided these young people with a practical sense of the many settings in which interviews can occur. They were able to see what a wide variety of exchanges the word "interview" actually covers (Johnson, 1982: 103).

Because interview situations are so varied, what will help a person obtain a job offer in one situation could be a mistake when dealing with a different employer. Although the discussion in this chapter will concentrate on what is usually true, it should be said explicitly that any generalizations are bound to have exceptions.

It should also be noted that many people who are unemployed, or thinking of changing employment, meet with employers for reasons other than an employment interview. Employers are asked for information by those who are trying to decide what job to seek or where best to seek it. Others come seeking referrals to employers who may be hiring. In some cases the person looking for work takes the initiative, and meets with an employer to propose that a new position be created; this may or may not become an employment interview, depending on the employer's response.

There is, finally, the assessment center approach used by a few major corporations. An account of a Coca-Cola assessment center's operation can be found in Slavenski (1986). Candidates spend one or more days at these centers performing tasks which simulate the work they will do on the job. Their activities are observed and rated, and later discussed with them. Although certainly part of the hiring process, these interviews are based on observation of the applicants' behaviors.

This chapter, however, will concentrate primarily on employment interviews as they are usually understood: the employer has an opening, and is meeting with an applicant who is interested in filling that opening. We will review what research and experience teach about the essential events which are a part of this interview process. We will be particularly concerned with the skills needed for effective self-presentation.

Both The Job Seeker And Interviewer Are Tense

Employment interviews often take place in an atmosphere of great ambiguity. The unemployed person wants the job offer, but is frequently uncertain about many important specifics: pay, working conditions, additional training and potential for advancement, the personality and interpersonal style of the supervisor.

Similar uncertainties are faced by employers and (in large firms) by personnel officials. The personnel interviewer wants to send acceptable candidates on to the supervisor, and fears being criticized if a candidate is found unacceptable, or is hired and then does poorly. The supervisor or owner of a small business wants a good employee, but often lacks enough information to be sure which of several candidates is most likely to do well. Most supervisors and employers have made hiring mistakes in the past, and naturally fear making such errors again.

The employer is therefore in the ambivalent position of wanting to interest the applicant in the job (so it will be accepted if offered) but not wanting to commit to making an offer. Similarly, the applicant wants to convince the employer that he or she would be good for the job, but is often equally hesitant about committing to the position until more information is gained and other offers evaluated.

The lack of important information on both sides is made more difficult by the employer's natural inclination to be optimistic. Positive statements about future opportunities for training and promotion are commonly made. The line between optimism and exaggeration is a thin one, and much of what is discussed may never happen. The applicant often has a parallel inclination to claim experience, skills, and intentions for the future which may be equally exaggerated. And, of course, both sides are inclined to ignore problems or potential difficulties.

The situation is not unlike that of the buyer and seller of a used car. The seller of the car is eager to shine it up, and is not likely to mention every little accident or problem. The buyer, on the other hand, looks carefully under the hood. The buyer may claim there will be no problem paying for the car if favorable terms can be arranged. It would be understandable if the seller were skeptical. Self-interest guides the communication that occurs when buying and selling used cars or hiring and seeking work, and the self-interests of the two parties to each transaction are significantly different. Under these conditions, it is understandable that mistrust and communications problems are common.

Almost Anything Negative Results In Rejection

Springbett (1958) observed both private sector hiring and army personnel decisions. He found that if either the written application form or personal appearance made a poor impression, no job offer would usually made. Unless both were favorable, the odds against final acceptance were ten to one. The job interview itself, he observed, was primarily a search for negative information.

Springbett's findings suggest a pervasive attitude of caution on the part of employers. In fact, such caution is widely observed, and has its own logic. After all, rejecting an applicant who might actually have been a good employee produces no visibly bad results. There is always someone else to consider. Hiring someone who turns out badly, however, can have consequences which are both serious and painfully obvious. The costs of a bad hiring decision therefore seem much higher than the costs of not hiring someone who would have worked out.

Anything which makes an applicant seem unsuitable therefore carries great weight. Many employers spend much of the interview checking out possible problem areas. Several researchers report that interviewers seem to assimilate any negative facts which they do uncover much more accurately than the positive information about an applicant (Clowers and Fraser, 1977).

This pattern may increase with time. Wiener and Schneiderman (1974) report that experienced interviewers in one study rejected more applicants than did inexperienced ones. All the interviewers felt more sure of themselves when turning someone down than when making a favorable decision. (This research involved only written materials, not personal interviews; the individuals participating in the study were business people drawn from local firms.)

A job applicant who realizes how much employers fear making hiring mistakes is more able to handle the interview effectively than one who does not. By consciously aiming to deal with these fears, and to lower them, an applicant can increase his or her chances of coming across as the candidate with the best risk/reward trade-off. The goal is to present oneself as the candidate who offers the most potential to do a good job consistent with the least risk of turning out badly. The applicant who is not aware of the employer's fears may inadvertently increase them, and lose a job offer despite superior ability and experience.

Types Of Interviews

Although employment interviews vary widely in length, nature and context, there are several fundamental distinctions that are helpful in classifying them.

There is, first, the difference between a hiring interview and a meeting with someone in the personnel office. Personnel workers screen applicants, sorting out those who will be seriously considered for employment from those who will not. Occasionally the actual hiring decision is made by the personnel office, but not often. The personnel department will ordinarily send the applicants they believe to be most attractive to the managers who will oversee their work. These supervisors then making the actual hiring decisions.

In a small business the screening interview and the final interview are the same, since there is no personnel office. A few small and medium sized businesses are exceptions. They do most or all of their hiring through employment agencies. In effect, these agencies act as their personnel offices. In this situation the interview at the agency is the screening interview.

In any case, the applicant's goal during a screening interview is to be found acceptable. This usually means that he or she must demonstrate that the required levels of education and experience have been met, with no disqualifying or negative characteristics. In some cases this is enough to be sent on for a final interview. If there are many qualified candidates, however, a favorable enough impression must be made so that he or she is one of the group selected for an interview with the supervisor.

In this final interview, of course, the goal is to be judged as the most desirable of the qualified applicants, and to obtain an offer of employment.

For higher level jobs there may be a variety of people to be met besides the person to whom the new employee will report. It is common to meet with executives a stage or two above the supervisor. These individuals will not usually select the person to be hired, but may have veto power. It is also common to visit with persons in parallel or related jobs with whom the new employee will have to cooperate. They do not usually have formal veto power, but could object if they felt the applicant was someone with whom they could not work well. Also possible are sessions with psychologists or others who administer tests to the applicant. All these meetings are just so many hurdles to be jumped. Doing well in them will not guarantee that the job will be offered. Only the favorable reaction of the decision-maker will do that. Doing poorly, however, will make the job that much harder to obtain.

Another major factor, and one which often sets the tone of the employment interview, is how the interview was obtained. The person who finds a job opportunity during a cold call will often be meeting with an employer who has no information beyond what is on the job application form. In some small firms such a form may not even be used. The applicant may know equally little about the employer. The person referred to an employer by someone who "put in a good word" for him or her, on the other hand, is in a conversation which begins with at least some trustworthy information on both sides. This usually leads to a more relaxed and friendly exchange.

Those sent by intermediaries will often be somewhere between these two extremes. An employment agency will commonly give some favorable information about the applicant to the employer before the interview, and will also brief the applicant about the employer's needs and characteristics. The person answering a want ad, on the other hand, usually has little information beyond the job title and the existence of the opening, perhaps supplemented by some research on the company. How much an employer knows about someone answering an ad usually depends on whether an application was obtained and checked out first.

Another basic distinction which is useful when considering interview behavior is the difference between structured and unstructured interviews. In a structured interview a set of questions has been written out beforehand, and the same questions are asked, in the same order, of all applicants. Research suggests that structured interviews are more reliable. That is, when several interviewers ask the same questions of the same applicants, they are more likely to reach the same decisions than when each conducts the interviews in his or her own way (Mayfield, 1964).

Although this greater reliability might suggest that a structured interview is the superior approach to making a hiring decision, this is not necessarily so. Two different sets of questions may lead the interviewers to agree among themselves on two completely different recommendations.

In other words, reliability is not the same thing as validity (though it is a necessary precondition for it). There is no evidence that *any* approach to interviewing is particularly valid. Neither structured nor unstructured interviews necessarily predict who will succeed once hired. A structured interview leads to consistent results across interviewers, but those results may be consistently right or consistently wrong. From a statistical point of view, Wright's report that over half of a group of insurance managers were willing to make a hiring decision based on a photograph is not as unreasonable as it sounds. There is no solid evidence that doing it this way would be less valid than conducting traditional employment interviews (Wright, 1969).

The Unemployed Have A Psychological Disadvantage

It should now be more clear why many employment interviews go so badly. Both sides want to be friendly and sell the other on what they have to offer, yet both know the painful consequences of a wrong decision. Both sides typically know far less about the other than they need to know to act with confidence. The situation is roughly analogous to having to make or accept a marriage proposal after the first or second date.

The tension heightens when an interviewer, worried about making a hiring error and hence ultra-sensitive to negative information, meets an applicant who is discouraged and defensive after months of looking for work. Irish (1978), who spent some time working in a personnel office, was struck by how incompetent, ineffectual and sullen many job applicants seemed. Under other circumstances, many of them would undoubtedly come across in a much more positive way. The job search process, however, draws out a person's insecurities, thereby creating an impression of negativity and weakness. This is, of course, the worst possible impression to make in an employment interview.

First Impressions Make A Big Difference

The final hiring interview with the supervisor is commonly an unstructured interview, since it is usually trained individuals in the personnel office who use structured interviews. Galassi and Galassi (1978), reviewing 60 years of research on interviewing, stress how important the first few minutes of an unstructured interview can be. First impressions weigh heavily in final hiring decisions.

The candidate's appearance is particularly important, since the employer's first visual perception of the applicant can be a key factor in the impression made during those first few minutes. The employer's first reaction to the applicant's ability to communicate and relate are also of prime importance. If these impressions are favorable, the discussion that follows is more likely to go well.

Kleinke (1975) has summarized the research on first impressions. Certain behaviors or characteristics are particularly likely to generate a positive response when people meet for the first time. These first impressions are strong, and significantly affect later behavior.

Some first impressions can be controlled; others cannot. In either case they can have powerful results. Beautiful women are rarely convicted of crimes. Men over 6' 2" typically receive higher starting salaries. Inmates given cosmetic surgery have lower recidivism rates. Given these and other research findings, there is little doubt that it is unwise to go to a job interview without being sure the employer's first visual impression will be positive. Attractive dress and personal appearance, combined with a friendly and cheerful approach, can give an applicant a head start toward obtaining a job offer.

Molloy (1975) has done research on typical reactions to specific colors and styles of dress and appearance. What is particularly useful in his discussion is the way he relates clothing to the types of people with whom one must deal in a variety of interview situations. Although his work is aimed at those seeking employment at the high end of the pay spectrum, the basic principles he advocates apply to any job. Dress makes a difference, and must fit the situation.

The conservative, dark blue suit and white shirt, Malloy finds, seem to go over best when meeting with middle and upper- middle level executives. A vested pin-stripe suit, in either dark blue or dark gray, is better when meeting the most important or highest level person one will see. A quiet plaid suit would make a better impression on those who are less conservative in their own dress, or who may not react well to conservative business dress.

Molloy takes into consideration the social class background of the person doing the interviewing, variations in dress patterns in different parts of the country, the effect on the interviewer of the perceived cost of clothing, and even the impressions made by certain color combinations. Color, style, and apparent cost all influence perception in those first critical minutes when applicant and employer meet. Although his initial work was with male clothing and its effects, Molloy later did similar research on the effect of women's clothing styles (Molloy, 1978).

If dress makes the first impression, sociability makes the second. Kleinke reports several research findings which are directly relevant to the interview setting. We are more likely to believe people like us if they look at us. Someone who sits about four feet away seems most friendly (closer is threatening and farther is distancing oneself). People are liked more if they lean forward slightly when talking, keep their bodies relaxed, smile, and speak without interruptions (such as stuttering, ah's, you know's, and so on). Most important, we are usually more attracted to people who are similar to us; hence the value of mentioning anything which the applicant has in common with the interviewer. Someone who disagrees mildly, and then agrees after discussion, is liked more than someone who always agrees with everything. If one can somehow find out another's opinions ahead of time, and then express those same opinions *before* he or she has done so, this makes a good impression. Normally, people like to be addressed by name as they are spoken to, although here one must be careful; job applicants who did this in one study were seen as insincere or phony. Finally, Kleinke reports that self-disclosure is attractive as long as a person doesn't go overboard.

Some of these findings may be particularly important to racial and ethnic minorities. Their cultural backgrounds can lead them to behave in ways they believe to be polite, without realizing the bad impression they are making on the interviewer. To look the interviewer in the eye occasionally, for example, is impolite in some cultures. In our culture, not doing so can lead the interviewer to see the applicant as untrustworthy.

Another discussion of first impressions and attractions is presented by Zunin and Zunin (1972). They found that when strangers meet in a social situation (a cocktail party, for example, or a chance meeting), they will almost always chat with each other for about four minutes. After that, however, they must decide whether to continue the conversation or move on, since after about four minutes they may politely leave. The key question is whether some real interest has been generated during those first four minutes. In many ways, this need to connect parallels the early decision-making which often takes place during a job interview (though the interviewer is usually expected to continue beyond four minutes even if a poor first impression is made).

During an employment interview, as during a social meeting, dress, appearance and friendliness make for a good beginning. The next step is for the applicant to project some positive aspect of his or her personality. If this provokes a response, and it usually will, a friendly dialog can develop. A key part of what happens now involves actively listening and responding to what is said by the other person. A relationship is forming; barriers have been broken (Medley, 1978). This is a totally different situation from what occurs in many interviews, during which one or both parties proceed awkwardly, longing for nothing more than a speedy end to the exchange.

The Importance Of Researching
The Organization Or Job

An applicant who shows a sincere interest in a specific firm begins an employment interview on a particularly favorable note. Conversely, ignorance of a corporation's products or industry makes a bad impression. This is not to suggest that a candidate has to announce explicitly that he or she has done a great deal of background research before the interview. Ordinarily an applicant's questions and comments will show clearly enough whether he or she has "done some homework."

Medley (1978) describes his experience, as he was finishing law school, of applying for a job with a division of Litton Industries which manufactured guidance and control systems. Before the interview he went to an engineering major in his fraternity to learn something about the type of work such a division would do. Because of this he was the only candidate who knew any of the language of guidance and control work, and to whom the division counsel did not have to explain inertial navigation. As a result, he got the job.

The applicant who learns as much as possible about the industry of which the firm is a part, the firm itself, and the person with the authority to hire will come across as informed and knowledgeable. With this background information it is much less likely that he or she will say something out of place. Above all, this preparation makes it possible to ask intelligent and thoughtful questions that will interest the interviewer and lead to a good discussion. This ability to draw the interviewer out, involving him or her in a personal exchange, usually makes the difference between a memorable interview and one which is quickly forgotten.

The unprepared applicant, on the other hand, forces the interviewer to ask most of the questions. Often these are standard questions which have been asked many times before of other candidates. The stumbling and shallow answers of an unprepared applicant lead easily to a thoroughly boring interview, which almost guarantees that no job offer will be made.

Understanding Just A Few Interview "Steps" Improves Performance

Greco (1980) argues that it is wise to ask about the demands of a job early in the interview. Marian (1985) has a list of suggested questions to be asked when interviewing for a management position. Questions by the applicant can lead the interviewer to explain in detail what the job demands. As the employer outlines what the position requires, and the applicant responds by discussing these needs, a rapport based on shared agreement about the work to be done can develop. At the appropriate point, the applicant can sum up what has been discussed, demonstrating that he or she really understands what the employer wants. This interviewer/applicant agreement on the job to be done creates a bond between the two without requiring a commitment to hire, although it clearly moves the discussion in this direction.

Now the stage is set for the applicant's self-description. This is the time to describe strengths, skills and experiences, and to relate these to the needs of the employer. If the interviewer accepts this self-description, then he or she has agreed that the applicant *could* do the job. This is the second key step, and puts the applicant only one decision away from the actual job offer.

Although this interview pattern may seem simple and logical, few people can do it spontaneously. Most need considerable preparation and practice. The natural psychology of the interview leads most applicants to sit back, feeling somewhat nervous and defensive. They answer the interviewer's questions and volunteer little beyond that. The interview becomes, in effect, like a tennis match, with the interviewer doing most of the serving. This, unfortunately, gives an impression of passivity and often fails to bring out much that the applicant has to offer. A good interview, in contrast, involves a serious exchange between two people trying to find out whether they can work together to their mutual benefit.

Training And Practice Improve Interview Performance

Downs and Tanner (1982) videotaped two college recruitment interviews, and then showed them to 24 recruiters who evaluated them. The negative effect of lack of preparation and practice was clear. Vague, rambling, incomplete or disorganized answers made a poor impression, as did the inability to articulate either short- term or long-term goals. Hollandsworth (1979) also found that 73 on-campus recruiters who rated 338 interviews were strongly influenced by a candidate's ability to respond to questions concisely, yet fully and to the point. The fluent, thoughtful, articulate applicant was the one who was most likely to be offered the position.

Discussing matters like personal goals and motivations is not easy for many people. Providing positive and appropriate self-descriptions necessarily involves both self-revelation and the ability to speak well of oneself. This often takes considerable practice; the words do not come easily at first. A few people are able to give thoughtful, succinct answers to such questions spontaneously, but not many.

The questions an applicant wants to ask also need to be thought out and practiced ahead of time. Their wording will help determine both the impression an applicant makes, and how much he or she learns about the job. A good question draws out the employer without putting him or her on the spot.

Barbee and Keil (1973) report assisting disadvantaged workers in Denver who were completing skills training. Now they had to find employment using their newly learned skills. Significant improvement resulted when these workers reviewed videotapes of themselves in simulated job interviews, identified areas they needed to improve, practiced new behaviors, and then did another simulated interview. A control group which simply watched such videotapes but did not identify needed changes or practice specific ways to improve did only slightly better on the second simulated interview.

Improved interviewing behavior can be learned, given appropriate training, as Barbee and Keil have shown. Molloy (1982) also describes how this can be done. As in any learning, what is needed is the identification of specific behaviors that need to be changed or acquired, and then enough practice to allow the behavior to become routine and comfortable rather than forced or awkward.

Employers Look For Three Things During An Interview

Half (1985) has summarized his interviewing and hiring experience in a book on how to hire well. Half's book is equally useful reading for those seeking employment. At the heart of learning how to interview well is understanding the major concerns of the employer. This is the essential first step in learning to present oneself in a way that addresses those needs.

Although the specifics will vary with the job in question, in one way or another all employers share at least three major concerns. If a job is to be offered, the employer must leave the interview with these questions resolved.

The first issue, naturally, is whether the applicant can get the job done. The employer needs to know a candidate's skills, training and experience. An employer is also concerned about his or her work habits. Will the applicant show up for work promptly and regularly, and stay with the employer for a reasonable length of time?

The degree of employer concern with performance will vary widely depending on the skills the job demands. About one-third of the country's jobs can be done without further training by workers who have a modicum of manual dexterity, communicate adequately, dress appropriately, relate to others without serious problem, drive an automobile, and do simple arithmetic (Mangum, 1976). When interviewing for these jobs, issues such as dependability and honesty will be of prime importance, since most of the population has the ability to do the work.

The second major area of concern is the kind and quality of relationships that can be expected if the employee is hired. How well will he or she will get along with supervisors, other employees, and customers? Can the applicant be trusted? Is he or she someone who will tell the truth and not steal from the business? Can he or she be counted on to act in the owner's or supervisor's best interests? The fear that applicants cannot be trusted is, as has been mentioned, a major reason that employers suspiciously search for negative information.

Lastly, there is always some uncertainty about what wage or salary offer will be required, and whether the applicant will take the job if it is offered. In some jobs certain conditions of employment (employer-paid benefits, on-the-job training, the potential for advancement) will be more important than salary. The degree of concern about these points will vary widely, of course, as will the character of the negotiations about them, depending on the nature of the job and the applicant.

Each of these three concerns (ability to do the job well, trustworthiness and good interpersonal relationships, and salary) must be addressed in some way during the interview. If any of these issues are left unresolved, the likelihood that the position will be offered to the applicant goes down significantly.

To interview well, then, an applicant must be able to ask questions and intelligently discuss the position involved. Next, his or her skills and personality must be presented in a way that shows how they fit the job's demands. In the process rapport and trust must be developed. The applicant who can successfully relate to an employer in the beginning of the interview can, at the end, express a serious interest in the job with a reasonable likelihood of triggering an offer.

Close The Interview By Asking For The Job

Straightforwardly asking for the job at the end of an interview is difficult for many people. Their discomfort is understandable. The fear of rejection is strong. Yet if there is no clear statement of interest, the employer does not know whether the applicant really wants the job, or would even accept it if it were offered. This uncertainty can make the employer hesitate. An employer wants to hire someone who is enthusiastic about a position.

There may be other reasons for the employer to hesitate. Despite a generally good impression of the applicant, the employer may still feel a bit uncertain about making an offer. The natural thing to do then is to procrastinate. A frank expression of interest, however, may lead an employer to set aside these hesitations and make a favorable decision.

The willingness to ask for the job at the end of an interview is, therefore, a crucial requirement as the job search process reaches its final stages. The applicant's challenge at this point is much the same as that faced by a salesperson who has clearly interested a customer but not yet gotten an order. All the work done up to this point does not pay off unless the customer agrees to buy. How to best handle this last, delicate stage of the sales process is of intense interest to salespeople. *Secrets of Closing Sales* (Roth and Alexander, 1983), which has gone through five editions, has a thorough discussion of the many ways closing can be approached.

There are probably as many effective ways of obtaining a job offer as there are employers and applicants. There are no sure-fire formulas; what counts is judgment and chemistry. The important thing is to turn the discussion from exploration to decision.

Closing the interview, like closing the sales call, requires the ability to judge when a favorable impression has been made and it is time to move on to the final details. A good close is a matter of timing. Traxel (1978) suggests watching for the employer's non-verbal behaviors: taking a deep breath, or sitting back in his or her chair. At this point, he advises, the applicant should stop selling, and begin trying to close. If there is resistance, however, one must again return to a discussion of the job, and one's qualifications for it, and then move back to closing later.

If the interview has gone well, a direct question can lead to an offer: "Everything looks good to me. Is there any problem with my starting Monday?" More subtle approaches involve assuming the job *will* be offered and asking about some other detail: "It sounds good to me; are there any forms I need to fill out?" or "Everything you've outlined is fine with me. When do I start?" or "Do you use a formal contract, or would you like me to simply write a short memorandum pulling together what we've discussed?" A somewhat bolder tactic is suggested by Thompson (1975): if the employer seems favorably impressed, express an interest in the job and offer to shake hands. An outstretched hand is awkward to refuse and yet is universally understood as a symbol of agreement.

Although interest in a position should be expressed at any interview, whether and how hard to try for an immediate offer is always a matter of judgment. The higher the level of the job, and the larger the firm, the more difficult it is to get an immediate decision. Often other applicants already have appointments for interviews. Even if there are no further applicants to be seen, the supervisor in a large corporation may not be able to make a hiring decision independently. Under these circumstances a sincere expression of interest sets the stage for the final decision later on.

Don't Accept Rejection Too Soon

It does happen, of course, that an employer is free to make an offer but decides not to. Faced with a flat no, applicants can accept the decision and leave or they can continue the conversation. There are two good reasons for staying. First, there is a valuable potential for learning in this situation. If a person can learn from the employer why the job was not offered, this information can be a help in future interviews. Second, it is sometimes possible to reverse the decision. A mistaken impression can be corrected or new information presented. Sometimes an alternative proposal can be made.

There is an old sales motto that the sales effort never really begins until the customer says no. Continuing to talk after a refusal must be done with tact, of course, but the issue is never final until the employer stops the discussion.

One approach is to ask the employer, in a direct but friendly way, why the decision was negative, and then probe to see if this is the real reason. Suppose the employer says that the applicant does not have enough experience. One response is, "Just to be sure I understand you, if I were to apply with four years of experience instead of the two I have, would you hire me?" If the answer is no, then one can ask again why the decision was negative. If the answer is yes, one can go on to discuss what was learned in those two years of experience, and whether there is really anything essential that was not encountered.

This is a difficult process. It takes a good deal of self-possession to do in a personable and inoffensive way. It is the only way, however, to surface objections which, once they are out in the open, may turn out to be based on inaccurate assumptions. Once these assumptions are corrected, one can sometimes again ask for the job and get it. Under any conditions this discussion should provide some insight into the employer's motivations, which can be helpful in the next interview.

Salary Negotiation Tips

At some point in most employment interviews, usually toward the end, there will be a discussion of salary. Although there are exceptions, the general rule is to leave the timing of this discussion to the employer. When he or she chooses to raise the topic, it is usually a good sign. The question will not ordinarily be brought up for serious discussion unless a job offer is at least a reasonable possibility.

Some salaries are fixed rather than negotiated. The pay of public school elementary and secondary teachers, for example, is usually determined by a schedule approved by the board of education. For a given degree and a given number of years of experience, there is a set salary. Similarly, workers who begin at entry level factory jobs, particularly where there is a union contract, usually receive a predetermined wage. There is no real possibility of negotiation.

In most situations, however, job applicants have at least some room for discussion and bargaining. Many employers begin interviewing with a salary range rather than a set figure in mind. How much qualified candidates are offered will depend on what they bring to the job, and how well they negotiate. Since it is usually much easier to raise the starting salary than it is to get the same amount as an additional raise later, negotiating well is very much in any applicant's interest.

There are many ways to approach these salary negotiations, and what works for one person or in one situation would be inappropriate in another. In general, the more information about salaries the applicant has before the interview, the easier it will be to handle the situation. A good sense of what is involved in all negotiating also helps; Fisher and Ury (1983) provide an excellent discussion.

The first step in negotiating pay is to locate published salary surveys for the occupation in question. National averages are usually easy to find. Any good library will have several sources. Local salary figures will often take more work to locate. Where nothing is published, some information can usually be obtained from professional associations and other local sources. Enough information should be gathered to estimate a firm's salary hierarchy. With rare exceptions, employees are always paid less than those to whom they report, and more than anyone they supervise. With these figures in hand, it is usually possible to make a good estimate of the salary range the employer is considering.

Without this information, it is easy to mishandle salary negotiations. A salary request which is too high, for example, will seem unreasonable; the applicant can easily appear unrealistic. Naming a figure which is too low, however, can make an equally bad impression. Such a request makes the applicant seem unknowledgeable. Not placing an appropriate value on one's skills and experience suggests poor judgment.

Because of these pitfalls, one approach to the salary question is to ask the employer to be the first to suggest a figure. Chapman and Sanders (1987) make a good case for this approach. "I'm sure a firm like yours would offer a fair and reasonable salary. What did you have in mind?"

Alternatively, an applicant can reply to the salary question with a range rather than a specific number. This makes it clear that the salary is negotiable. In addition, at least part of the range will almost always overlap with what the employer thinks is appropriate

Crystal and Bolles (1974) suggest this range be constructed with the low end in the middle of the employer's probable range, and the high end a bit above it. There is a good chance the employer will offer something toward the middle of an applicant's request. The middle is thus set toward the top of what the employer probably has in mind. For example, if the applicant estimates that the employer is going to offer something around $18,000-22,000, he or she can ask for $20,000-24,000. The low end of this range is clearly realistic. The upper end suggests that the applicant values his or her skills and performance highly. The middle ($22,000), which is a likely offer if the applicant has made a good impression, is the top of the range the employer was thinking of paying.

Whatever approach is taken, the question of salary is both important and difficult. The applicant does not want to lose the job offer. On the other hand, he or she does not want to be underpaid either Because many people are more emotional about pay than they realize, discussions about salary can be more difficult than expected. Salary offers and requests touch a person's sense of self-worth.

Like so much else that is part of the employment interview, then, salary negotiations demand both homework and practice. Chastain (1980) argues that the important thing is to be calm and deliberate, repeating key arguments more than once to be sure they are absorbed. Any salary request must be carefully related to contributions to the organization rather than personal needs or wants. The right words and phrases will usually come more easily if they have been practiced first. Someone else can play the employer and raise objections to the points made. A reversal of roles can also help the applicant see how things look from the employer's perspective.

It is usually wise to complete pay negotiations as quickly as possible. As Marshall (1982) points out, a wise applicant strikes a delicate balance between candor and overconcern, appearing knowledgeable about pay matters but not greedy. The more time that passes, the more difficult this balance may become.

Practice Will Improve Performance

The selection interview is the critical step in obtaining an offer of employment. It can easily be a difficult encounter, with both parties needing to make a decision, often before they are fully ready. There is much to learn and communicate in a short time. Successful interviews are usually the result of careful preparation, so the limited time is used well.

Good interview preparation is difficult to do alone. Although background research can be done on one's own (reading the company's annual report, for example, or going through industry journals) the main concern of the interview is the personal impression which is made. Improving this usually requires helpful comments and observations made by someone else.

Such practice can include playing the role of the employer, and trying to understand how the interview looks from the other perspective. One can then reverse roles and practice addressing the employer's concerns. It is particularly important to answer such typical interview questions as, "Tell me about yourself" in a way that addresses the employer's fears of hiring the wrong person. It is also extremely useful to find something in common with the interviewer. People relax more quickly with someone they see as similar to themselves.

Dress, friendliness, fluent and accurate communication, thoughtful questioning, a smooth discussion of salary, a good close: all come more easily when they have first been practiced with a friend or associate. Sometimes the person playing the employer needs to be a bit gruff or unfriendly. The applicant is much less likely to be rattled by such behavior in a real interview if it has first been experienced in a simulated one. Indeed, the more probing and skeptical the simulated interview, the more friendly and easy the actual interview will seem.

A Final Rule: Don't Stop Looking

If experience offers a final rule to govern the employment interviewing process, it is the necessity of continuing that process without letup. A job search is not over until a definite offer of employment (with a specific wage or salary and a starting date) has been both made and accepted, preferably in writing. And even then one must be careful. It is wise to assume the search is not totally over until the end of one's first day on the new job.

One of the most difficult periods in the job search process comes between a good interview and the receipt of a job offer. A period of weeks or months frequently passes before a definite decision is made. This is a time when much can go wrong. As a result, a job interview which went well, and during which the applicant was almost promised the job, may not lead to an acceptable offer.

There are often several persons whose approval is needed before an offer can be put in writing. One of these individuals may say no or specify unacceptable conditions. The owner's nephew may apply. An unusually talented applicant may show up at the last moment. A contract may be lost, leading to a decision to leave the position unfilled. A general hiring freeze may go into effect. And, of course, it is possible that the employer's reaction was misunderstood. He or she may not have reacted as favorably to the interview as it seemed.

For whatever reason, it regularly happens that individuals looking for work believe a job possibility will shortly turn into something definite. They let up on their job search efforts. The days turn into weeks, and even months, and then they discover that no offer will be made after all. In the meantime job leads have not been pursued, trails have grown cold, and now they must begin all over again, more discouraged than before.

This is a situation whose avoidance is worth some effort. Difficult though it is psychologically, the wise applicant continues his or her job search efforts full steam ahead until a definite offer is made and accepted. This is done no matter how promising a particular situation may seem.

No one would claim this is easy. But then, neither are the other steps in the interview process. Finding a good job is a difficult challenge. A review of the last few chapters on obtaining and doing well in employment interviews strongly suggests that, if the job search process is to be done well, many people could use some help. Although they can be helped one at a time, it is obviously more efficient to provide this assistance in a group setting. This is what is done in programs of job search training, the topic to which we now turn.

PART THREE
Providing Job Search Assistance

Part One of this book reviewed recent changes in the American economy, and discussed the increasingly competitive labor market resulting from these changes. Part Two then reviewed the methods which Americans typically use to find employment, and noted the relationship between the search method used and the employment outcome.

The effectiveness of any given job search method will vary, of course, depending on how many jobs are open, and how many qualified people are applying for the openings. When unemployment is high, even appropriate job search methods will often lead to few job offers; inadequate methods can delay employment by many months.

Part Three discusses the assistance needed by people who are having difficulty locating a suitable job within a reasonable period of time. Many would be helped by more accurate information on how the labor market works. Others need more: interview training, job development, individual counseling, and so on. Government programs offered to low income and other groups with special needs frequently provide this assistance.

There is, in addition, a new approach to helping those seeking employment find jobs more quickly. This is the provision of job search training in a group format. Chapter Ten reviews the origin and structure of these programs. They provide a group of people looking for work with one or more of the following: information about the local labor market and its operations; material support needed during the job search process (photocopying, typing, an answering service); training in the skills used to obtain a job offer (telephone techniques, how to properly make out a job application form, interviewing); and then support and supervision during the job search process itself.

It is this direct involvement in the individual's job search efforts which is new. Government programs have offered instruction and training in job search techniques for many years. At the end of this training, however, individuals were on their own as they approached employers to find work.

Some of the first group job search programs were very successful. A high proportion of their participants found jobs within short periods of time. As this approach has been used more widely, however, significantly lower placement rates have been noted. The major problems encountered by these programs are therefore reviewed in Chapter Ten. The elements which seem critical to successful operation are discussed. The chapter closes with some useful research findings from two job search programs for youth.

Chapter Eleven summarizes the main implications of our findings, both for the individual and for public policy. Knowing how to find a job in our rapidly changing economy is an adult survival skill. Adults today need both an understanding of how the job market works (a mental map, as it were), and the skills needed to find new employment quickly within that labor market. Many unemployed adults lack both this understanding and these skills. It is important that society, as a matter of public policy, provide more opportunities to acquire them.

The most appropriate institution to provide job search training for the general public is the United States Employment Service. Doing this within budgetary limitations will require a refocusing of employment service efforts, and the development of new expertise on the part of employment service personnel.

The service now attempts to locate specific job openings, and then to match the unemployed to these openings. Since most employers do not inform the service about their employment needs, this approach is generally ineffective. The employment service cannot refer people to job openings when it does not know about them. We believe the service should shift its goals and methods, aiming instead to provide detailed, usable information which will help the unemployed find their own jobs more efficiently. Labor exchange efforts should be confined to those areas where there are special needs or disorderly labor markets (that is, where employers and those seeking work are having an unusually difficult time making contact in an efficient and regular manner).

In order to give a concrete illustration of how such an approach would work, an Afterword describes the experiences of six individuals who visit a fictional employment service office which is run as we suggest. This office provides a variety of information and training opportunities, along with lists of job openings in selected sectors of the economy. Each person comes to this office with different needs; each is given services appropriate to his or her situation.

CHAPTER TEN
Job Search Training Programs Get Results

The search for employment can be long and lonely. The unemployed person is on the outside looking in. Around him or her, the world hustles and bustles about its daily business. This very activity can increase the sense of being uninvolved and useless. The person with no job lacks a part in the world's daily affairs.

The job search activities of many people are somewhat intermittent. Reading and replying to want ads, sending resumes, filling out applications for employment, phoning to see if an employer has decided to extend a job offer: these activities are usually done alone; few people devote a full working day to them; and even when done seriously and full-time they may draw only an indifferent response from those busy with "serious" work.

Job search activities are typically unstructured. There is no office or factory to which the unemployed person must report, nor any set schedule of activities to follow. When discouragement becomes overwhelming, and job search efforts slacken, there are neither supervisors nor colleagues to provide counsel or support.

Amundson and Borgen (1982) have described the experience of job loss and job search as an "emotional roller coaster." There is a period of grieving as a person adjusts to losing a job and the way of life that went with it. Then the newly unemployed individual sets an employment goal, and the job search begins. Sometimes it is successful. Often, however, the high hopes and energetic efforts which characterize this search at the beginning are not realistic. Frustration and anger set in as some employers decline to grant interviews and others interview but do not offer jobs. Some people handle this situation well, adjusting their goals and adopting new approaches. Others become apathetic, turn to alcohol or drugs, or seek a scapegoat. Sometimes the individual simply gives up. In a follow-up study, Borgen and Amundson (1987) largely confirmed these findings, though they discovered somewhat different patterns for women who were secondary wage earners, and for youth.

These findings raise several issues. Can the time it takes to find new employment be shortened? How can people be helped to use the most appropriate search methods when their energy is highest? What kind of support is needed when job search activity slacks off? How can the search process be given more structure, so a larger number of employers are contacted more quickly and more effectively?

Origins Of Job Search Training

One of us (Johnson) ran after-hours workshops for low- income, unemployed workers in San Francisco during the 1960s. These sessions provided the unemployed with an opportunity to talk through the discouragement they were experiencing. Many participants gained a greater understanding of labor market structure from these discussions. They also came to a clearer realization of the impression they were making on others.

During the large-scale unemployment experienced by the states of Oregon and Washington during the late 1960s and early 1970s, a group approach to dealing with the unemployed became widespread. Instead of having each unemployed person go about the job search process alone, programs designed to help the unemployed began bringing them together for training in job search techniques. Support and supervision during the job search process were also sometimes provided.

By the middle 1970s, several group job search programs (known by a variety of names: job search assistance, job clubs, job factories, and so on) had been set up. Creative individuals in different parts of the country realized that the unemployed would be greatly helped by training and support during their job search efforts. They designed programs to do this, and refined the programs from experience.

Some of these early efforts were very successful. They clearly shortened the period of unemployment. As a result, the use of group approaches to help the unemployed find new jobs has spread throughout the country. Such programs are commonly employed by corporations for workers displaced by plant closings and large-scale layoffs. There are also a wide variety of government-funded efforts to help unemployed individuals in a group setting.

This chapter will review what has been learned about these programs. The emphasis will be on the factors which contribute to their success or failure. Readers who want a thorough literature review and bibliography should consult Mangum (1982).

Basic Elements Of Job Search Training

Group job search programs vary greatly in length, number of persons served, and curricula. In general, however, they usually provide all or most of the following elements:

1) Information about the job search process generally, and the local labor market specifically. The quantity and quality of information varies greatly from program to program, however. Most group leaders introduce the concept of the "hidden job market," making participants aware that the majority of job openings are not advertised in the want ads or found in other published sources. Sometimes information about the local labor market is methodically gathered and presented. This is more likely to happen if the program is run by a local employment service office. More often, employment patterns are inferred from the experiences of prior participants and informally communicated as the need arises.

2) Training in the key activities which are part of seeking employment. This ordinarily includes what to say on the phone when trying to find openings and obtain interviews, how to fill out a job application form properly, and above all how to handle an employment interview.

Some programs help participants prepare a resume. A script to follow when phoning employers is often provided. Lists of typical interview questions are also frequently used. Usually there is an opportunity for each participant to practice making calls and interviewing. Some programs use teletrainers (closed circuit telephones) to practice telephone techniques. Others type copies of properly completed job application forms for each participant. They can then take these forms to personnel offices and copy from them.

Many programs have videotape machines to record simulated job interviews. Program staff play these taped interviews for participants, and discuss with them how to handle the interview more effectively.

3) Some level of material support. Programs will typically provide services which many in the group would not otherwise have easily available: a phone line reserved for receiving messages from employers, answered by a secretary (in effect, an answering service); typing and photocopying; phone banks; lists of employers obtained from the Chamber of Commerce, Dun and Bradstreet listings, the latest Yellow Pages, or other similar sources; and, for low income groups, lunch money, bus fare, stamps and stationery.

4) Support and supervision during the job search process. It is this, rather than information and training, which is the new element in job search assistance.

Under prior legislation, participants in most federally-funded programs received the minimum wage during their job search activities. Even today, in some programs paid for with state or local funds, receipt of welfare or other benefits is contingent on active participation. Where this is true, many programs require participants to check in at the same hour daily. Job search activities (phoning to request interviews or to follow up on past interviews, writing post-interview thank you notes, checking the want ads, preparing lists of employers to approach) are done under supervision, in a group setting. The actual visits to employers to fill out job application forms or be interviewed are, of course, done alone, but participants typically sign out when leaving for these activities, and report back on their experiences when they return. Those who become discouraged have someone with whom they can talk. Those whose job search activities are diminishing can be spotted. Program counselors can then encourage them, and urge them to renew their efforts.

Federally funded employment and training programs no longer pay stipends. As a result, it is more difficult to convince participants to accept as much structure for their job search efforts. If a program is too demanding, people will not participate. The program will then lose its funding.

Program operators vary greatly in their attitude toward the desirability of providing information about specific job openings. At least some information on job possibilities can be provided by almost all programs. Employers frequently learn about a program and phone to request applicants. Participants often bring back information obtained during their search efforts, including lists of job postings from public and private employers. In some cases job developers are part of a program's staff. They supplement the participants' search activity by visiting employers in search of job orders, which are then shared with the group. The local employment service office may also share its listings. The availability of information about specific job possibilities can be a powerful motivator for continued program participation.

On the other hand, there are group job search programs which consciously avoid giving any information about specific job openings. Usually this is because they are philosophically committed to a totally self-directed job search effort. The next time a participant becomes unemployed, they want him or her to feel confident about using effective search methods to find a new job, whether there are support services available or not.

Job Search Programs Are Becoming More Common

The number of group job search programs has grown rapidly during the past decade. They are now an accepted part of state and federal employment and training efforts. Group approaches are also regularly used by private industry to deal with large layoffs, sometimes with financial help from the government. Some corporations staff these "outplacement" programs with group leaders from their own personnel departments. Others contract for technical assistance from outplacement consultants.

The size of private sector outplacement efforts, which serve both individuals and groups, has grown considerably. In 1982, the Association of Outplacement Consulting Firms was founded. Its president estimates that providing outplacement assistance is now a $350 million industry (Lee, 1987). One of us (Chapman) has also served as president of AOCF, and has played an active part in outplacement's rapid growth into a multi-million dollar industry.

More Job Seekers Could Benefit From Training

Despite this widespread usage, however, it is still true that only a minority of the unemployed have access to group job search programs. This is because these efforts are largely funded by the government under special-purpose legislation, or provided by the private sector only for employees of a particular corporation. As a result, a given program is usually open only to those meeting low-income or other criteria, such as being a veteran or having been displaced by a specific plant closing.

A few programs without government or corporate sponsorship do manage to pay their expenses on a self-help basis. They often use donated space and volunteer staff, and so are free to serve anyone who comes. There are only a small number of these self- help efforts, however. Programs funded by individual states rather than the federal government, though often shorter, are more likely to be open to any citizen who asks for assistance.

There is no doubt that group job search programs can be effective (Wegmann, 1979; Kennedy, 1980). By providing services in a group setting, they reach more of the unemployed than would be practical using one-on-one counseling. When they supervise the job search process, they are able to increase the behaviors which lead to employment. As we have already noted, the search intensity of the average unemployed person is low (6 employer contacts per month). Under supervision, this employer contact rate usually increases dramatically. Some programs set quotas of 100 or more phone calls to employers per day, for example. This increased search intensity can significantly lower the time necessary to find a new position.

Many of the unemployed have only an incomplete understanding of how the labor market works. They are not sure of the best ways to approach employers or how to maximize the probability that an interview will turn into a job offer. Group job search programs fill a real need when they provide instruction and training in these areas. There is now an abundance of printed material which can be used by job search programs. Manuals for program operation are widely available (Azrin and Besalel, 1980; Farr, Gaither and Pickrell, 1987, for example).

Employment service offices, because of their knowledge of the local labor market, have the potential for running highly effective programs. Using funding from the Job Training and Partnership Act (JTPA) and other sources, some offices already have them. One employment service program, aimed at low-income youth, illustrates how detailed information about the labor market can help those who are looking for work:

> "Participants were provided with computer printouts listing all employers in the SMSA [the local metropolitan area], either by zip code, by size of firm, and/or Standard Industrial Classification (SIC) code. Armed with industry/occupational matrixes, the DOT [Dictionary of Occupational Titles], the SIC book, inactive orders [information on jobs formerly listed with the employment service, giving the type of applicant sought, the person who does the hiring, pay, and so on], want ads, and yellow pages, 18-year-olds 'researched' the material and made decisions about whom to phone and where to go, based on the availability of transportation to them, and their preference in regard to size and type of firm. The observer was startled at the ease and pleasure with which these young people grasped and pursued the research task, once the principle and process were made clear." (Johnson, 1982: 73)

In some areas of the country, group programs have become particularly common. Employment service offices in California, for example, regularly run sessions for the general public. Most use a lecture format and lack a supervised search component, however. Because of Michigan's high unemployment, group job search programs have also proliferated there. One article in the Detroit Free Press estimated there were at least 100 programs in southeastern Michigan alone. The largest effort in the country of which we are aware is run in Grand Rapids, Michigan, where participation is required of all welfare recipients.

Problems Running Group Job Search Programs

As the number of group job search programs has grown, observers have become more aware of common difficulties which can lower their effectiveness. However sound the basic concept may be, what determines program effectiveness is how well the concept is understood and put it into practice. Among the most common problems are:

1) Inexperienced and untrained program operators. Few academic institutions provide training in labor market structure and operations. Successful programs therefore often hire or assign operators who have gained a knowledge of labor market workings from prior work experience in personnel offices, the employment service, private employment agencies, outplacement firms or other similar positions which brought them into daily contact with the hiring process.

Many government programs are under-funded, however. To keep within budget, they hire young program operators at low salaries. Although some of those hired may have academic training in counseling or psychology, they often lack any personal experience with personnel procedures and operations. Many have never worked in the private sector. This makes it difficult for them to provide accurate information or speak with authority, particularly if there was little or no time for training before the program began operation. Although sincere and well- intentioned, they have no feel for how private sector employers typically hire.

2) Inadequate operational funding. Some programs attempt to operate without the necessary secretarial help, telephone lines, furniture, space and so on. These programs are often housed in run-down, unattractive locations, using space borrowed from other government agencies. Even before a word is said, the surroundings predispose participants to doubt the program's efficacy.

Under these conditions, how program staff relate to participants becomes particularly important. As a national study of group job search programs reported, "observers came to agree that the setting, the seating arrangement, the organization of space, the areas designated for socializing and coffee drinking, the degree of distance and separation between leaders and participants all had significant impact and imparted hidden messages. Though vital and spirited programs were sometimes conducted in drab and discouraging settings, the leader had a difficult task overcoming the impact of the initial impression." (Johnson, 1982: 36-37)

When program operators structure the setting so its hidden message is consistent with the program's stated goals, on the other hand, positive results can occur. This same national study gave a concrete example:

> "Program A, a resource center, assigns most of the available and quite ample space for the convenience and use of participants. The kitchen or coffee area is shared by staff and participants and becomes a focal point for socializing, both among clients and between clients and staff. People get to know one another, and the formation of the group often occurs more rapidly and more effectively in that setting. Free coffee is provided, and almost from the first day clients are invited to participate in keeping the area clean, washing the dishes, making the coffee, running errands, and generally sharing in the housekeeping and operations of the Center. The Center becomes their own. Independence, equality between staff and client, and active participation in making something happen are not just words. They are enacted at every moment. In the classroom, the leaders had no difficulty maintaining control, and in asserting their rational authority over the curriculum. There was a clear consistency between the implicit message and the overt one, 'You are a valid, independent, adult person who is expected to contribute, just as you are expected to act on your own behalf in getting a job. Our authority here is rationally determined—we're not better than you. We simply have knowledge you don't have which we are happy to share.'" (Johnson, 1982: 37-38)

Program difficulties caused by drab surroundings and inadequate material support become worse when the program is also understaffed. In the extreme case, one program operator must handle everything alone. He or she is responsible for program recruitment and operation, individual counseling, extensive paperwork and the gathering of follow-up statistics. This creates a totally unreasonable workload. When this individual gets sick, quits or goes on vacation the program comes to a complete halt.

3) Problems handling the dynamics of the job search process. Looking for work is difficult. It involves much tedious, time-consuming effort, and some of this effort inevitably leads nowhere. As rejection and failure bruise egos and lower self-confidence, avoidance behavior becomes common. Participants will sometimes go to great lengths to put off contacting another employer.

Program staff, particularly those inclined toward non-directive counseling, often find it difficult to handle such avoidance behavior. They are not comfortable confronting participants, even though they know that participant avoidance behavior is self-defeating. The staff sometimes begins to avoid contact with those who are cutting down on their search activities. Soon the staff are engaged in their own brand of avoidance.

It is not unusual to find both participants and staff spending time during the search period having birthday parties, going to medical appointments, holding meetings to discuss each other and how everyone is relating — *anything* to avoid the horror of having to ask (or supervise someone who has to ask) another employer for an interview or a job. In time, everyone seems to reach an unspoken agreement: the participants will not complain about the program if the staff does not demand more frequent contact with employers.

4) Failure to come to terms with the complexities involved in dealing with the many segments of the local labor market. This is particularly evident in programs which rely on a single job search strategy for every participant, no matter who the participant is or what job is being sought.

One good example of the "single strategy" problem is the use of the telephone as a job search tool. Some designers of early job search programs adopted, from private employment agencies, the technique of finding unadvertised job openings by phoning every employer in town likely to employ workers of a given type. This approach, though tedious, will usually generate at least a few interviews if handled properly.

Not all the early job search programs made extensive use of the telephone. The original Cambridge "Job Factory" model placed little emphasis on the use of phone banks. Program operators believed it was better to approach many employers in person. The Azrin "Job Club" model used the phone, but also placed much stress on asking friends and relatives for leads.

As group job search programs proliferated, however, an almost exclusive reliance on the telephone to find openings became common. Indeed, today many people in the employment and training field think the use of a phone bank is at the heart of the group job search concept.

Although the phone can be a useful job search tool, there are several instances where its use is not only not appropriate, but may even be counterproductive. Participants with foreign accents or nonstandard speech patterns, for example, often do badly over the phone. The young, who are often inarticulate when dealing with strangers over the phone, can also find it more of a hindrance than a help. This is also true of some older persons, particularly those from low income backgrounds, who may be quite shy.

Using the phone can also be an ineffective way to find openings with large employers. Major corporations usually hire entry level workers through a personnel office. These offices will often not deal with an applicant unless he or she first fills out an application form. Phoning for an interview is often a waste of time. Whether openings exist or not, the caller will be told to come in and fill out an application.

Communication by telephone is also not an effective strategy in a small town with few employers, all located within a short distance of each other. In this situation it makes more sense to go in person than it does to phone.

Despite the many differences between one person and another, and between one labor market and another, some group job search programs attempt to make every participant use the telephone and, indeed, to use exactly the same script. As a result, some participants become discouraged and lose all faith in the program.

The telephone is an essential tool for most people who are looking for work. Precisely because it is so useful, it is important to pay close attention to how it is being used. Like a powerful medicine, the telephone is beneficial only when used appropriately; blanket prescriptions are dangerous.

5) Over-reliance on the classroom model. Although group job search programs provide useful information, their primary aim is changing the job search behavior of the participants. This involves training more than teaching. The appropriate format for this discussion/instruction/training activity is not so much a classroom as a workshop. "In its purest form, this is a loose, semi-structured activity in which the curriculum is extremely flexible, and the needs and problems verbalized in the group largely determine agenda emphasis. Discussion, participation, and the surfacing of feelings regarding the job search are encouraged. Though the leader has the responsibility of providing information, the experiences of the group are called forth and used as a base. The leader's role is that of facilitator and consultant to a self-help group, and social support from the group is fostered and encouraged." (Johnson, 1982: 41)

Good Programs Look Simple, But Are Hard To Replicate

The goals and methods of group job search programs are not difficult to understand. The unemployed are gathered together. They receive information about the local labor market and how it works, and are given training in key job search activities like filling out job application forms and interviewing. Program staff then provide support and supervision during the job search process. As a result, participants in these programs are both more active and more effective than they would be on their own. They engage in more job search activities, and they do them better. The process of finding new employment is therefore speeded up, so that the time spent unemployed is reduced.

Though conceptually simple, such programs are not easy to run well. The first challenge is locating and training program operators. It takes some effort to find people who understand labor market operations. Effective program staff must also know how to train adults. They have to do more than simply communicate ideas; behaviors have to be changed. It is not difficult to hire staff with teaching backgrounds. Those with skill and experience at training in a workshop context are much harder to find.

Even leaders who have appropriate skills and backgrounds will often need help in mastering certain areas peculiar to group job search programs. A good example is the challenge of leading a discussion based on simulated job interviews. Playing videotapes of these interviews and then discussing them can help participants to communicate more effectively when meeting with employers. Too much criticism, however, can be counterproductive and even devastating. Handling this activity well is not easy. Most new leaders of job search groups need training in this area.

Observers at one program noted the positive results with a good trainer:

> "We all go into a separate room to watch the video replays. The only instruction we are given in what is usually a 'critique' session is to make only positive remarks about ourselves and others. 'We're all trained to be critical. This time, look for the things you like instead.' First the person on the tape makes comments about him/herself, then others make comments. A dramatic change now takes place in the group. It welds together. People come through this session feeling good about themselves since something good was pointed out in every case. There's a purpose — at its base it builds self- confidence." (Johnson, 1982: 43)

We have observed job search programs where the effects of videotaping were not as positive. Interviews were taped perfunctorily. Sometimes other participants played the role of the employer. Often they were not able to do this realistically because they had never hired anyone, and had no experience at interviewing.

As participants watch the tapes, it is easy to let their comments become overwhelmingly critical. This negative emphasis can lead to discouragement. The discussion can also be too general, failing to identify specific behavioral changes which would allow each unemployed person to make a better impression. If it is important to see how not to handle an interview, it is even more important to provide role models of good interview behavior.

Once improved approaches are identified and understood, participants need to practice these new ways of behaving during a follow-up interview. This is often not done. Frequently program operators schedule time to tape only one interview per participant. As a result, there is no opportunity to observe change and improvement.

Program participants regularly report that having a simulated job interview videotaped is a memorable experience. This does not necessarily mean it leads to any significant changes in behavior during actual job interviews, however. In too many programs a videotape machine is purchased and handed to an untrained, inexperienced program operator to do with as he or she wishes. There is no opportunity to observe how others use this tool effectively or to practice its proper use under careful supervision.

Other serious problems occur when providing support and assistance during the search process. Ideally, a high level of group morale has been generated, so that participants regularly provide each other with help and understanding. This can make it easier for everyone to deal with the inevitable difficulties and discouragements encountered while looking for work. However, it's not easy to take a group of strangers and, in a week or so, mold them into an effective support group.

There is an underlying current of fear in most job search groups: fear of never finding work and being permanently shut out of the economic system; fear of being treated curtly when inquiring about job possibilities; fear of rejection in the employer's place of business, either before, during or after the interview; fear of accepting a job which turns out to be unpleasant or undesirable; even fear of being the only one in the group who doesn't get a job. Most of these fears, although exaggerated, are not without some rational basis, and they are always part of the group's dynamic.

Providing job search training in a group setting can make that training more effective, since the group itself is potentially a great resource. The opportunity to discuss job search problems, vent feelings and exchange information with other group members can be invaluable. In well-run groups, even youth groups, the participants will regularly come up with job leads for each other. The opportunity to receive praise and constructive criticism from other group members can be a powerful force for behavioral change. Positive group dynamics can speed up improvement in both the quality and quantity of job search activities. The members can also help with much of the work (running the videotape machine, rehearsing telephone approaches, cleaning up, running errands, and so on).

What is clear when observing job search groups, however, is that although they *may* do all the things mentioned above, they often do not. It takes skilled leadership to draw a group together and produce such results; it does not happen automatically.

Working effectively with a group of unemployed individuals is much more difficult than it might seem. Asking someone to intensify his or her job search activity, for example, is like asking a soldier to stand up and charge under fire instead of crawling forward slowly or huddling in a foxhole. It is not easy to take greater risks and experience more pain, nor is it easy to ask others to do this.

Reports from welfare recipients who were part of one group job search program are typical (N.A., 1982). These Work Incentive Program participants unanimously reported that their job search activities had been frustrating and difficult. Among their most discouraging experiences were nasty responses and rejection by employers, and the awkwardness and discomfort they felt phoning employer after employer trying to find a job opening. Johnson (1982) also reports that many job search program participants find phoning for interviews difficult and tedious. This technique is particularly frightening for the non-verbal and timid.

Program staff do not like to supervise those who are phoning employers. Despite claims to the contrary, there was little actual supervision observed in most of the phone rooms visited during Johnson's study. This was a real lack, because some participants clearly needed help in tailoring their telephone approach to the kind and size of company they were calling. Most quickly abandoned the scripts with which they had been provided. No one was available to determine whether they were using the phones effectively.

The "Job Club" Model

These operational difficulties, which are commonly observed in group job search programs around the country, must be kept in mind when interpreting the favorable results achieved by particular programs. Talented, experienced group leaders can produce placement rates which newer programs will find difficult to duplicate.

Nathan Azrin, a behavioral psychologist, has done several important studies of group job search assistance. His approach stresses positive reinforcement of the behaviors most likely to lead to employment. Although his program provides participants with only rudimentary information on local labor market structure and operations, it has (when properly implemented) achieved consistently high placement rates.

What Azrin emphasizes is that the constant negative experiences which are part of looking for work must, if intensive search activity is to continue, be counterbalanced by positive reinforcements or success experiences. The "job club," as he calls his approach, is therefore a place where counselors provide that reinforcement. They also urge participants to seek work full time, to ask all friends and relatives for referrals and suggestions, and to do anything they can to help each other.

Job club participants keep careful records of the number of phone calls made, applications filled out, interviews obtained, and so on. These are posted for all to see. Program staff urge participants to emphasize their positive personal characteristics as well as their job skills when talking to employers.

Job club counselors go from one participant to another, spending only a short time with each. They constantly praise whatever participants have done properly. Every check on a chart, every completed exercise, every improvement in interviewing behavior is praised as a success in itself, and an action which brings a job that much closer. The unemployed person, however discouraged he or she may have been previously, should now finish each day saying, "At last I'm doing things right."

Azrin's work was first reported in Azrin, Flores and Kaplan (1975). Working in Carbondale, Illinois, Azrin and his colleagues invited individuals who were unemployed and not receiving unemployment compensation to join their newly formed job club. Applicants were matched, and a coin toss determined who participated. Those not participating served as a control group. The job club met for three hours at first, and then for an hour or two each day. All the clients who attended regularly found jobs. It took 14 days for half of the job club members to find employment, compared to 53 days for half of the control group.

At the request of the Work Incentive (WIN) Program, Azrin then supervised the training of counselors to run similar job clubs for welfare recipients in five cities (Harlem, New Brunswick, Tacoma, Wichita and Milwaukee). These groups began operation during 1976 and 1977. The study ended in March, 1978. Researchers randomly assigned some clients to job clubs, and others to control groups.

When the project concluded, 62 percent of those assigned to the job clubs had found work, compared to 33 percent of the control group. Not counting those who dropped out of the WIN program, the figures are 80 percent and 46 percent, respectively. A six month followup of those in the Harlem and Tacoma clubs (which were the first two groups to begin, and therefore ran the longest) found 62 percent of the job club group and 28 percent of the control group still employed.

The success of this pilot program led to the widespread adoption of the job club approach by WIN programs around the country. As local officials launched these programs, however, the training and supervision given program operators apparently became more and more diluted. As a result, not all program operators had a clear understanding of the basic principles Azrin had used to make his approach successful.

An assessment of WIN job clubs in Texas (Jordan-DeLaurenti, 1981), for example, found entered employment rates at 13 sites ranging from 19 to 69 percent. The second week sessions (the actual search process) were "weak in almost all projects. The counselors appeared less directive and more insecure about the methodology." Although they had the title "job clubs," what staff and participants were doing differed significantly from Azrin's prescriptions. Despite the problems, however, these groups were still 15 percent more efficient than using employment service personnel to place clients in the traditional one at a time manner.

Job Search Programs For Youth

In response to high youth unemployment rates, the Department of Labor funded studies of two group job search programs for young people to determine whether this approach might help them find employment more quickly. One program investigated was the Job Factory, run in Massachusetts by the Cambridge Office of Manpower Affairs. This program, created by Joseph Fischer and Albert Cullen, began serving an adult population in 1976. The Job Factory for Youth (JFFY) began in June, 1979.

Shapiro (1978) studied the original Job Factory program for her doctoral dissertation. She found a 69 percent placement rate at the end of the four week program, compared to 33 percent in a control group. Those in the program significantly increased the number of job interviews they were able to obtain. Job Factory clients averaged 18 interviews during the period studied, compared to five for the control group. There was also a notable increase in the level of self-esteem, an effect found even in participants who did not find employment.

The JFFY project was designed to see if similar results could be obtained with a younger population. The findings were positive; participation did shorten the time it took these youth to find work.

Five groups took part in the JFFY program, 203 youth in all. Another 165 were assigned to control groups and received no JFFY services. Those who took part in the program received the minimum wage while they participated. Program operators emphasized that looking for a job was a job. Participants earned their pay by working at their job search activities. Program cost was $989 per youth served.

The value of stressing full-time job search efforts is confirmed by data from the National Longitudinal Survey (Holzer, 1987). Young men aged 16 to 23 who were not in school and had sought work in the previous month were studied. Some were employed but seeking other positions. It was the unemployed, however, who were able to spend more time on their job search efforts. They also used more search methods, and as a result received and accepted more job offers.

Ten weeks after enrollment, 64 percent of the JFFY group (compared to 48 percent of the control group) had found employment. Follow-up studies found that the employment gap between JFFY participants and the control group declined over time. After 45 weeks the employment rate for the two groups was essentially the same. JFFY participants earned slightly higher wages, worked more hours, had slightly better jobs, and were a bit less likely to leave the jobs they obtained. The major effect of the program, however, was in speeding up the employment process or (saying the same thing backwards) decreasing the time it took these youth to find work (Hahn and Friedman, 1981).

The California Employment Service was responsible for the second youth program, which was run in San Francisco with technical assistance from one of the authors (Johnson, 1982). Called Job Track, this program did not pay stipends to those attending. It was also considerably shorter. The program was equally successful, however, in speeding up the employment process. During the first five weeks after the two and a half day training program, 44 percent of the participants found jobs. This compares with 21 percent of a matched comparison group. At the last follow-up, 12 weeks after program participation, these figures had risen to 66 and 49 percent, respectively.

Although Job Track was open to any San Francisco youth who wanted to participate, 81 percent of the 145 youth who chose to do so met government low-income standards. The group was 72 percent male and 90 percent minority. The curriculum emphasized labor market information and the construction of job search strategies. Each participant had an opportunity to videotape practice job interviews.

One unexpected finding was the regularity with which this low-income youth population returned to school. The follow-up survey found 36 percent of the group back in school (10 percent full time and 26 percent part time), and 40 percent of those not in school seriously considering it.

Interestingly, those who had been through Job Track did not increase their job search intensity, although what they did was ahead of the comparison group, where activity decreased. The major effect of Job Track training, however, appears to show up in the quality of participant activity. Contacts with employers more often led to job offers. The program evaluation estimated that 49 percent of the group would have found jobs within 12 weeks without the program; with help from the program, 66 percent did. These results were obtained at a cost of $336 per participant, which was significantly lower than the $989 per youth cost of the JFFY program.

Without a stipend to draw them back, many participants in Job Track did not return regularly after the initial training period. They made little use of the job search facilities which the program offered. This obviously made it difficult to provide much support or supervision during the job search period. The program also had a recruitment problem, which led to smaller groups than the staff wanted.

During 1981-1982, therefore, Job Track began to offer a $5 per day cash expense allowance to participants to cover their lunch and travel costs. This allowance was payable for a maximum of 10 days. More extensive advertising helped the program become better known. As a result, both group size and use of the job search facilities went up substantially. Although this advertising drew in some youth who had college experience, 76 percent of the participants still met government low-income criteria.

Program staff discovered, as have other programs, that delivering support and supervision during the job search process is far more difficult than delivering instruction and training. The results, however, were positive. With more extensive staff involvement during the search process, the placement rate at six weeks rose to 57 percent, an increase of 11 percentage points over the previous results. Black youth and those on welfare now did as well as the other participants, which had not been true previously. The larger groups made more efficient use of staff time. Cost per youth served fell to $117, despite the greater use which each participant made of program facilities and staff time.

Follow-up studies discovered that both the quantity and quality of job search efforts now increased. Each dimension had an independent and positive effect on the speed with which employment was found. More selective, better informed, better targeted approaches to employers, combined with more effective self-presentations during interviews, led to more job offers. Some participants found employment, not because they were seeking more interviews than before, but because they were now looking for them in the right places, and presenting themselves more effectively when they got there. Doing more also helped, however; both factors, quality and quantity, contributed to a successful outcome.

These findings of an independent and positive effect for both the quality and quantity of job search efforts by youth are consistent with the results reported by Dyer (1973). He surveyed unemployed middle-aged managers who were members of the Forty Plus Club of Southern California. Dyer found that those managers who started their job search activities without delay and used an aggressive and wide-ranging approach experienced a shorter period of unemployment. He also found that those who contacted more employers per week experienced fewer weeks between jobs.

More Group Job Search Programs Are Justified

Several years ago, the widespread use of group job search activities was a new phenomenon. Because of the high placement rates obtained by several early programs, there was great hope for this approach. Time, however, has made it clear that group job search programs are not automatically successful (Wegmann, 1982). They will fail if not run properly.

Group efforts help people find job openings more quickly; they do not create them. A program will not work in situations where there simply aren't enough jobs to be had (small towns where the main employer has just shut down, for example).

Although less expensive than counseling and job development done for one person at a time, group job search programs do require adequate budgets. There must be enough money to make possible careful selection and training of group leaders, clerical and other support, and experienced management.

The leaders of job search groups need to be knowledgeable about the local labor market and its operations. They must be able to handle the difficult dynamics of group support and supervision. They have to be directive without being authoritarian. This isn't easy. As two individuals with extensive group outplacement experience put it, "The leader's attempt to focus attention, build trust, teach a complex process and enhance self-awareness must take place among people who may be scared, angry, impatient, cynical, depressed — or any mixture of such feelings, scarcely an ideal situation for excellent group dynamics" (Broussard and DeLargey, 1979: 855).

Despite these problems, useful and cost-effective job search training is clearly possible. These programs require preparation, training and support, but operated properly they can significantly shorten the period of unemployment. A small financial reward for continuing participation (even $5 a day in cash will do), provides a useful incentive to keep participants at their job search efforts. Experience suggests that this incentive is particularly helpful when working with young or low- income groups.

Operating these groups is clearly hard and demanding work. It requires a high level of energy and initiative and a deeply optimistic spirit. Dealing with a multitude of daily problems (and an occasional crisis) is particularly challenging because the leaders of such groups so rarely have supervisors who have themselves done this kind of work. This obviously makes it difficult for them to provide helpful advice and assistance, and throws program operators back on their own resources.

Despite these difficulties, however, group job search assistance still seems like Churchill's description of democracy: it may be an imperfect process, but it works better than any of the alternatives (Burtless 1984).

Practical Implications

It would help everyone if more detailed information on labor market operations and demands were routinely communicated by high schools and colleges. It is becoming more and more obvious that a "one life, one occupational choice" approach to career counseling is unrealistic. Post-secondary education is becoming more oriented toward multiple occupations (and multiple periods of schooling) throughout the lifespan. The sooner more extensive information on the labor market and its workings can be integrated into school curricula, the more students will be prepared to handle occupational and employer changes efficiently. Kimeldorf (1985) has prepared some excellent materials for use with high school students.

Even if the schools do all they can, however, there will still be a need for job search training. This does not mean that every unemployed person needs to be part of a group job search program. Many people know where their skills are needed, and will find new employment on their own without difficulty. Providing a full program of job search training for every unemployed person would also be very costly. There is no obvious source of funding for such efforts.

What is realistic, however, is the provision of assistance to the unemployed on what might be called a "sliding scale." Most people can handle employment transitions on their own or with only short and inexpensive assistance. Those with greater needs, however, require more intensive assistance.

Mathews and Fawcett (1985) were struck by how poorly unemployed adults scored on simulated job search behaviors compared to employed adults. Training raised these scores and also led to employment offers. Even highly skilled adults can remain unemployed if their job search skills are poor.

To be successful, any proposed program must deliver the needed instruction in a practical and cost-effective way. The most obvious institution to do this is the federal/state employment service, with its existing offices in every town of any size throughout the country. These offices could provide the public with basic information on how the labor market operates, as well as regularly updated reports on local employment needs. This information could be delivered in several inexpensive forms (printed booklets or audiovisual presentations, for example).

Where needed, specific training in interviewing skills, telephone techniques, the proper way to handle job application forms, and so on, could also be provided. The service could use either regularly scheduled group workshops or computer-assisted instruction. Support groups could serve those whose main need is assistance during the job search period. A full program of job search training would then be reserved for those with special needs and problems (examples would include displaced homemakers, the handicapped, low-income youth, or workers who are part of mass layoffs). Properly conceived, these services need cost no more than the total amount now being spent on the employment service and JTPA's job search programs.

The guiding principle is the need to provide a high quality of useful and accurate information and job search training in the most cost-effective way possible. To make our suggestions concrete, an Afterword to this volume describes the experience of six people who approach a Midwestern employment service office seeking help in their efforts to find new employment. The needs of each are different, and so what is offered to each is different. Yet each person receives significant help in shortening the time which he or she must spend looking for work.

Notes♦♦♦

Outplacement consulting firms, like government-funded efforts, must design programs and produce results with only minimal guidance from research findings. Leana and Ivancevich (1987) make a strong case for more research funding to study employment transitions and their effects.

The early history of job search training is not entirely clear. We are not sure which effort is most appropriately described as the first group job search program. Group instruction in interviewing behavior, filling out job application forms properly, and other job search tasks has been provided by government programs for many years. A variety of group job search efforts such as that run by the Self Directed Placement Corporation of San Diego were in operation by the 1970s. Many of these programs had their roots in earlier efforts. It would not surprise us if there were some early programs of which we are not aware. What is certain is that widespread awareness of these programs, at least in the employment and training community, dates to the middle and late 1970s.

CHAPTER ELEVEN
Conclusions And Recommendations

In Part One we reviewed the changes which have, over the last decade, transformed the American labor market. The effect of these changes has been to increase the competition for all employment possibilities, and particularly for well-paid positions. In Part Two we took a closer look at what unemployed individuals do when looking for work. The process of finding employment is challenging under any circumstances. It is particularly difficult given today's competitive conditions. As a result, many people need help finding work in a reasonable period of time. In Part Three, therefore, we have been reviewing both the promise of group job search programs and the difficulties they often experience.

We believe the facts reviewed in this book support the following conclusions:

First, knowing how to find an appropriate job in a reasonable period of time is a neccesary adult survival skill. The set of available job openings changes daily as new technology is applied and America reacts to the demands of a dynamic world economy. Our labor market is marked by much change and movement, and a high level of competition. Many adults suddenly discover they must find new employment, often on short notice. There is nothing in the available research that suggests any way to make these employment transitions particularly pleasant experiences. Like any other difficult or stressful situations, however, they will be handled best by people who know how to get through them as quickly and efficiently as possible.

Second, adults facing a move from one job to another will be greatly helped if they understand what is happening and why. This understanding will help them decide what they need to do, and how to do it in an intelligent and effective manner. They need, in other words, a good mental map, an adequate conceptual understanding of how the labor market works. They also need a clear idea of the different means which can be used to penetrate that market, and some sense of which approaches are most effective under particular circumstances.

Third, we are convinced that the art of finding new employment can be broken down into a series of learnable tasks. There are a finite number of things a person needs to do when searching for a new position: inventorying the skills he or she has to offer; researching the local labor market; identifying the firms likely to need his or her accumulated skill and experience; approaching friends, relatives and acquaintances (new and old) to learn about these firms and to get help finding openings; handling written materials (application forms, resumes, letters) competently; preparing the self-presentation which is at the heart of a job interview; knowing how to negotiate the details of a job offer and then begin well on the new job. Every one of these activities can be described and discussed, modeled and practiced.

Fourth, it would significantly help many people if the opportunity to brush up on these job search skills were routinely available, preferably in a group setting, before they began seeking new employment. Looking for work is often a stressful and lonely activity. Help from someone who knows the local labor market and its operations can make the job search process both shorter and more bearable than doing everything alone.

A Need To Understand The Labor Market

The "local labor market," although a useful concept, can also be a confusing abstraction. What we are really talking about is the net effect of actions and decisions made by thousands of uncoordinated, independent employers. The American hiring process is a strikingly decentralized operation. Unlike a centralized market (the New York Stock Exchange, for example, or a commodities market), there is no uniform reporting of job openings, no composite list of what is available at any given time, and no one, central place where employers and prospective employees meet. It is, to mix metaphors, a market in which many ships pass in the night.

As a consequence, the unemployed person must ordinarily deal with many people before finding a new position. There are job openings available, but no one person knows where they all are. A job search quickly becomes a search for information. Much effort can be required to find that information. Then the marketing effort begins.

A Need To Learn Job Seeking Skills

In addition to an understanding of how the labor market works, a person seeking employment also needs the appropriate job search skills. Here the focus is on the ability to do, and do well, those things that can turn a job possibility into a job offer. These are learnable skills which many unemployed individuals lack. Despite the need, none of the institutions in our rapidly changing society has accepted responsibility for routinely providing this training to those who need it.

Much of the evidence for the potential payoff from such training has already been cited. Some of this evidence has been around for a long time. Over 30 years ago, an experimental, non-credit course in Job Finding and Job Orientation was offered to high school seniors in Geneva, New York (Cuony and Hoppock, 1954). The curriculum included information on the local job market, practice job interviews with local employers, and so on. A follow-up one year later found that, compared with a control group from the same school, those who took this course reported more job satisfaction, higher earnings and more weeks of employment.

This project, like many others already cited, was small in scale. Results from small studies are usually reported only in little-known journals with limited circulations. They have little effect on public policy. Finding a job, for most people, is still something they are supposed to figure out on their own. If there are problems all they can do is ask around, do the best they can and muddle through.

This approach was always inefficient. It is dangerously so under today's competitive conditions. Unplanned, random learning is not likely to bring people the information they need to understand the increasingly complex American labor market. Furthermore, most people seek work only at intervals of several years. It is inefficient to ask each person to research what is needed, pay little attention to such issues after they have found employment, and then do it all over again some years later. In this area of life, as in many others, specialists are needed. The unanswered question is who will provide these specialists.

Recent studies have shown how high the personal and social costs of prolonged unemployment really are. It is not a question of avoiding costs. The only issue is whether to spend money now on preventing prolonged unemployment, or to spend it later meeting the needs generated by unemployment's negative effects on physical and mental health.

Prolonged Unemployment Causes Health Problems

The economic effects of long-term unemployment are obvious. Savings drain away, poverty sets in, welfare must be requested. The effects of unemployment on mental and physical health are not always as obvious. Only in recent years have we had data on how major these health costs are.

We have already mentioned the research of M. Harvey Brenner, a sociologist at Johns Hopkins University. His work has related unemployment to morbidity and mortality rates (Brenner, 1977). More recent research (Brenner, 1984) has confirmed these findings. In addition, additional factors (decline in labor force participation, decline in average weekly hours worked, an increasing rate of business failure) have been found which, like unemployment, correlate with increased death rates.

It is not just the unemployed person whose health suffers. Cobb and Kasl (1972) studied married men aged 40 to 59, with at least five years seniority, who worked in factories which were about to close. They found increases in uric acid levels (a potential cause of gout), blood pressure and cholesterol levels. The nurses who took the measurements reported that the men seemed depressed. There were two suicides. Both the workers and their wives were potential ulcer victims. Three wives were hospitalized for peptic ulcers in the first four months after their husbands lost their jobs. There was a noticeable increase in arthritis symptoms. These health problems were particularly stressful because the men now had no health insurance. The researchers concluded that serious secondary health effects from unemployment could be expected if reemployment did not take place within six weeks.

A more recent study followed 40 blue-collar and 40 white-collar families after the father's involuntary loss of employment. The physical and mental health of these families was compared with control families where no family member was unemployed. The unemployed husbands were found to exhibit more psychiatric symptoms. One husband who was part of the pilot interviews committed suicide. Children exhibited moodiness at home, new problems in school, and strained relationships with their peers. Wives became significantly more depressed, anxious, phobic and sensitive about interpersonal relationships. As time went by and husbands were not able to find new employment, wives became less supportive. There was three times as much marital separation among the unemployed families as in the control group (Liem and Rayman, 1982).

Leventman (1981) reported similar patterns in her study of unemployed professionals. In addition to mental breakdowns, physical illnesses, high blood pressure and heart attacks, she found a pattern of divorce occurring after reemployment. The marital bond of trust and mutual faith, broken during the period of unemployment, could not be restored.

Harry Maurer, a journalist, traveled around the country visiting offices where unemployment compensation checks were being distributed. He asked those waiting in line if he could interview them. Many said no. Those who did speak to him, however, gave vivid accounts of their experiences (Maurer, 1979). These unemployed individuals spoke of drinking problems, marital conflicts, being hounded by creditors, compulsive eating and weight gain, constant touchiness, explosive bursts of anger directed at spouses and children, thoughts of suicide, feelings of guilt and anxiety, periods of crying, and a general loss of energy. The term which came up over and over when the unemployed described how they felt about themselves was "worthless."

The Unemployed Benefit From Social Support

A period of unemployment does not have to be devastating. Gore (1978) found significantly fewer unemployment-related health problems among those displaced by a plant closing in a close-knit rural community, compared to workers who were part of a similar closing in a large urban area. This was true even though the rural workers were unemployed for longer periods of time. (All were blue-collar workers, with a mean age of 49 and mean seniority of 20 years.)

Social support occurred naturally in the rural setting. We believe that consciously designed support groups can serve many of the same functions during periods of unemployment in urban settings. Group job search training has a dual potential: stress reduction through social and emotional support, and faster reemployment through better job search methods.

Producing these results, however, requires that programs be properly designed and well run.

Designing Group Job Search Programs

There are number of fundamental issues which must be addressed when a job search training program is being planned. Program philosophy, structure, and staffing will vary depending on how these issues are resolved.

First, program administrators need to reflect on the major problems faced by the group of unemployed individuals who will participate in the program. Why have they not yet found new employment? Is it lack of knowledge of the local labor market and how it works? Few marketable skills? Poor job search skills? Unwise job search strategies? The inability to keep at their search activities because of feelings of rejection and embarrassment? The collapse of a major industry? Lack of transportation? Program design must take these problems into account.

Second, how much can be spent on the program? The most immediate effects of budget size will be on such decisions as the amount and quality of space to be rented, the number and experience of staff who can be hired or assigned, program length, the size of each job search group, and the quantity and quality of audio-visual and printed material that can be purchased.

Whether support and supervision will be available during the job search period is a particularly important budgetary consideration. Participants can be trained in job search methods in a short time, but the search period will extend for several weeks, and sometimes for months. Failure to stay in touch with the unemployed during the job search period means having no control over whether the newly learned job search skills are put into practice.

Third, program designers must decide how much they want to venture into related problems often experienced during unemployment. These include difficulties making an occupational choice, financial problems generated by lack of income, the provision of day care for children, and so on.

Fourth, what will be the relationship between program goals, operating procedures and evaluation standards? It is important to avoid inconsistencies.

Suppose, for example, that a program's primary objective is helping participants obtain the best possible positions they can. This means information about the local labor market will have to be emphasized. Logically, program evaluation should stress the quality of jobs obtained. Better jobs often take longer to find; the evaluation process should therefore not stress job search length.

Any inconsistency between a program's goals, design, and evaluation standards can have a detrimental effect on staff morale. Staff are understandably sensitive to evaluation standards and results. Inconsistencies can lead them to ignore the stated program goals and produce whatever results are necessary to guarantee a positive evaluation.

A Program Design Check List

Let us assume that an identified population needs job search assistance. A program must be designed to provide information and training before beginning the job search, and then support and supervision as employment is sought. The goal is to help participants reach both a higher quality and a higher rate of job search activity. We will further assume that enough funding is available to cover reasonable costs, and that the program has decided to focus only on the job search process. Occupational counseling, transportation, child care problems and other difficulties will be handled by others.

Given these assumptions, the issues which program planners need to address are:

A. Where and how will the program be housed? Pleasant surroundings, an informal atmosphere and a lack of barriers between staff and participants all contribute to program morale.

B. What will be the program's organizational structure? How many meetings per week will be involved? How long will each session last? For how many weeks can someone participate? How many staff will be present at each group session? The answers to these questions will vary depending on the population being served, the labor market sector in which they are seeking employment, and the size of the budget.

C. Should time for venting of anger and frustration be provided at the beginning of the program? This is often necessary in plant closing or mass layoff situations, particularly when there has been little advance notice. Failure to work through these emotions can reduce program effectiveness. An angry, emotionally upset participant will not hear what others are saying. Negative feelings are almost certain to come through during an employment interview, making a poor impression on the interviewer.

D. Should instruction take place in a workshop setting, or should a classroom model be used? The answer will depend, to some extent, on group size. A group of 25 can be instructed using a classroom model; it is difficult to run a workshop in a group of this size.

E. How much time will the staff spend building group cohesion? Mutual respect and concern can be generated as a byproduct of many training activities. A program which provides support and supervision during the job search process will want to make a particular effort to build group cohesion. If only a few days of training are provided, on the other hand, these efforts are less defensible; they use up the limited training time.

F. How much effort will go into training staff in role-playing and discussing videotaped employment interviews, handling the dynamics of workshop behavior, and using the program's printed and audio-visual materials? How much time is available to gather labor market information, find the best available employer lists, and recruit employers to help at appropriate points in the program?

These are important issues. Many programs get off to a weak start because they must begin on short notice. As a result, they are in operation before either facilities or staff are properly prepared. Furniture has not arrived, the printed materials are not ready, the phones are not yet installed, and yet the program is supposed to start operations. This is upsetting for the staff and confusing for the participants.

G. How large a part will employers play in the program? In an hour or two a week, employers can make a significant contribution. They can explain hiring procedures, help role-play realistic job interviews, discuss what they look for when hiring, and so on.

H. How will the local employment service office be involved? A cooperative relationship can involve sharing information, job listings, counselors, and so on.

I. Should information about job openings be given to program participants? We think so. This need not be a major focus of the program. However, any list of job openings that can be obtained by staff, participants, or anyone else will contribute to the goal of helping everyone in the program find a job. Having the listings available also keeps participants coming back during the job search period, when the temptation to drop out is strongest.

J. How much secretarial help will be available? For most programs, at least one full time secretary is essential. Help will be needed with program paperwork as well as resume and other typing required by participants. The secretary can also answer a designated phone line which serves as an answering service. This allows participants to go about their job search activities without fear of missing an employer's call. Equally important, providing this service keeps people coming back to check for messages.

K. How much can participants help out? The more they do the better. It is important, however, not to ask them to do anything for which they do not have the background (such as playing the role of the employer in interviews if they have no experience hiring). It is also important not to let them get wrapped up in "helping out" as a way of reducing their job search efforts. There is nothing more characteristic of the job search period than avoidance behavior. Almost any available excuse for putting off contacts with employers can and will be used.

L. Which of the available job search techniques should be emphasized (asking for referrals from friends and contacts; visiting employers in person; phoning one firm after another; mailing resumes or letters with requests for interviews; using the want ads; using the local employment service office or private employment agencies, and so on)? The important thing is to work with each person to develop a job search strategy which simultaneously makes sense for the person involved and is appropriate for the type of job being sought.

M. Within available funds, how will priorities be set? Funds will be needed for help with problems that arise during program operation. If administrators are inexperienced, the program will need funds to pay outside consultants.

N. Are funds available to rent or purchase needed equipment (a photocopying machine, films, typewriters or word processors, videotaping equipment) and printed materials (reference books, handouts, workbooks)?

O. How will the program balance the importance of finding *some* employment and the desire to find a *good* job (however the definition of "good" may vary with the participants and the setting)? The program evaluation should include measures of both the proportion of participants employed within some reasonable time frame (usually one to three months), and the quality of job obtained (usually measured by the level of wage or salary). If only the placement rate is measured there is an inherent pressure to push participants toward jobs which can be obtained quickly. Because of their low wages and other undesirable characteristics, these jobs are often abandoned almost as quickly as they are found.

P. Should participants of varying educational and social levels be mixed? We think so. Each race, age level, educational level and so on is tempted to believe that only *they* are having a hard time finding employment. When they are together in the same group they are much more likely to realize that the fundamental problem is the difficult job market, and not their personal characteristics.

Ordinarily, the only limits on program eligibility should be the exclusion of those whose personal problems are so great that they could not realistically keep a job if one were offered to them. Examples would be severe drug or alcohol dependency, illiteracy, serious psychological difficulties or the inability to speak English. Job search training is not designed to solve these problems. An individual for whom job search activities are hopeless or meaningless can easily become bored and resentful. Sometimes the entire group is disrupted as a result.

The Need For Shared Program Information

There is great value in keeping careful records, and being willing to share what is learned with the administrators and staff of other programs. Although group job search programs have become more common, staff turnover is high and there are still only a limited number of people in any one city who have extensive experience running them. The opportunity to learn from others conducting similar programs is invaluable. In addition, federal research funds were cut severely just as group job search programs were widely adopted. As a result, there is a need for more detailed information on how these programs can be run most effectively.

The state of the art in this area is still somewhat primitive, with many wheels being reinvented and many mistakes repeated. It is difficult, in the midst of the thousand practical demands of program operation, to keep the detailed records and do the methodical experimenting that would advance our knowledge of what works best. Any programs which make the effort to do this will be making an important contribution.

Other Approaches

Group programs are, of course, not the only possible way to provide help for the unemployed. They are attractive because of their low per-person cost and their potential as a way to provide mutual support. A study done a few years ago in

Nevada suggests, however, that almost any consistent assistance will reduce unemployment time for the general population.

The employment service in Nevada formed four teams of two job service employees each. One member of each team was a specialist in Unemployment Insurance regulations; the other was a placement specialist. A sample of unemployed individuals receiving UI was then drawn, along with a second sample used as a control group. The team interviewed those selected for the program. They gave them help with their resumes, offered job leads and suggested job search strategies. Counselors offered to help them speed up or improve their job search activities in any way possible. Interviews took about a half hour; coming was a condition of receiving the weekly UI check. The unemployed then reported back each week on their job search efforts, and received any additional suggestions or help that seemed appropriate.

As a result of these efforts, those in the treatment group found 3.2 times as many jobs as those in the control group. Only nine percent of the treatment group (compared to 35 percent of the control group) stayed unemployed long enough to exhaust their UI benefits. UI funds were saved because of the reduction in the time it took to find new employment, and also because more individuals were disqualified during the careful review of their UI eligibility which was part of the program. These efforts saved $6.50 in UI funds for every dollar expended to pay the program's costs. Unemployed persons who were counseled remained unemployed and on UI for an average of 8.5 weeks; the control group was on UI for an average of 12.4 weeks (Steinman, 1978).

More recently, Washington State has also begun an extensive program to help those receiving UI return to work more quickly. Participants put together a job search plan; workshops teach job search skills; employers are contacted for unadvertised openings; referrals are made to listed openings. Initial results show these efforts reducing the average period of unemployment by 2.3 weeks. The cost of providing UI has been reduced by about $6 for each dollar spent on the program (Employment Security Department, 1987).

These results, along with other findings already reviewed, argue strongly for taking the process of finding new employment more seriously than has been the case in the past.

Unemployment — Cyclical, Structural And Frictional

Economists have traditionally divided unemployment, for analytical purposes, into three categories. Their intent is to distinguish between the diverse sources of unemployment, since different causes demand different remedies.

Some persons are unemployed because there is a downturn in the business cycle. During a recession there are simply too few jobs. This is called cyclical or demand deficiency unemployment.

Other persons are unemployed because of a mismatch in the economy. The jobs exist in one city but the unemployed workers are in another. Or there are job openings available in a given city, but the unemployed workers there do not have the skills these jobs require. This is called structural unemployment.

The final category of unemployment, frictional unemployment, has been of less interest to economists. It is often dismissed (or even defined) as an inevitable phenomena not much affected by government policy. Frictional unemployment exists because there are always people who are "between jobs." A person is looking for work, jobs of the appropriate kind exist and are open, but the worker and one of these opening have not yet come together.

Some frictional unemployment is clearly inevitable. There will always be people who have just left one job but not yet found another, even when job openings are plentiful. Decentralized markets are inherently inefficient.

Although some frictional unemployment is inevitable, this does not mean it should not be taken seriously. Many people remain unemployed for far longer than is necessary. The issue of how long it takes to find new employment is no small matter. As we have argued throughout this book, some individuals search far more efficiently than others because they have a better understanding of how the labor market operates. They know how to find what they want as quickly as possible. They are also committed to doing what is necessary.

Others lack this understanding or commitment. They are much more likely to flounder and fail and become "discouraged workers," to use the Labor Department's term for those who want work but do not believe they can find anything, and so do not actively search.

If more effective search methods reduced the average time during which jobs sit unfilled, or even spread unemployment more evenly among those seeking work, it would have significant and positive social benefits. We therefore argue that frictional unemployment requires both serious study, and active government efforts toward its reduction.

Information Needed In The Information Age

It is ironic that adjustment to the information age is creating so many problems for the unemployed, who lack detailed information on what is happening. The irony, however, does not make the situation any less painful.

For now, both unemployed individuals and those running job search training programs need to use the information already available. A major purpose of this book has been to gather what is known about the job search process into one place, in order to make this easier. Specific information on any particular labor market will still have to be gathered locally, of course, in as much detail as is practical.

What the country most needs is to have more labor market information routinely provided to everyone who needs it. The logical place to provide general instruction is in high schools and colleges. The employment service would then be responsible for providing specifics to meet the particular needs of individuals. How the service could do this is illustrated more concretely in the Afterword which follows this chapter.

A Final Word

We have done our best, in these pages, to synthesize the limited and incomplete data now available on the process of seeking employment. If this information, incomplete though it is, is of value to those planning and delivering job search training, then it will have been well worth the efforts that went into producing this book. We realize how difficult it is to run such programs effectively. We can think of no better way to close than to express our deep respect for those who are working on this difficult but important task.

CHAPTER TWELVE
Afterword: How The Employment Service Might Operate A Job Search Program

This Afterword illustrates one way the United States Employment Service could provide more effective assistance to the unemployed. We attempted to be as realistic as possible when writing this fictional description of one day at a reorganized Job Service office. We assumed a budget no higher than what is now available. Every aspect of the operation is computerized. The number of staff needed to run the operation has been kept as low as possible.

All the computer hardware described here is available off the shelf at reasonable cost. Lists of employers are also already available. They are regularly produced by firms such as Dun and Bradstreet (in the process of collecting information for credit ratings), and by businesses which provide mailing lists to bulk mailers. These lists are available in computer-compatible form. A Job Service office could purchase them at reasonable cost and then reorganize the information for use as we describe.

In fact, many employment service offices around the country are already using a variety of new approaches, including computer-based systems. The Job Training and Partnership Act of 1982 amended the Wagner-Peyser Act (the legislation which originally created the U. S. Employment Service) for the first time in half a century. These changes, along with administrative decisions made by the Department of Labor, have allowed experimentation that was not possible in the past.

Local employment service budgets are no longer tied to the number of persons placed in jobs listed with the service by employers. The reporting system used by the service now recognizes that training the unemployed in job search techniques may lead to employment in positions not listed with the service, but obtained by the unemployed through their own (but now more effective) efforts.

This Afterword, then, describes the experiences of six citizens who come to a reorganized Job Service office for assistance in finding employment. The office works no miracles. Each person, however, leaves with a clearer view of his or her options, and a realization that practical help is available.

The primary responsibility for finding work rests, inevitably and properly, with the person seeking a new position. What the Job Service can do is guide these efforts so they are not futile, but instead have a high probability of success.

One Day At The Cedar Falls Job Service Office

The chilly September breeze whirling around the Cedar Falls Job Service office had a sharp edge to it. Later the sun would begin to take that edge off, but at 6:30 in the morning, applicants shivered as they began lining up, waiting for first crack at the day labor jobs that would be available when the doors opened at 7:00 a.m. Inside the office Tim Farrington, who had come on duty at 6:00, was taking job orders by phone. He typed them directly into the microcomputer which both stored the data and printed the job tickets.

Most of the callers were familiar. The same construction, waste disposal and day labor firms used the service on a regular basis. There was also a scattering of retail stores and service firms calling for someone to fill in for a vacationing worker, or to help with a temporary overload. As the information was typed in, a printer automatically created a half dozen job notices for each opening. This allowed for applicants who would take a card but not show up, and others who would apply but not be hired.

At 6:30 a.m., Diane Sheehy came in and began posting the notices. Each card listed the employer's name and address, the number of persons needed, the nature of the work, the pay, and the hours of employment. Most of the work was unskilled and paid the minimum wage or a bit above it, but there were exceptions. Where specific skills or experience were needed this was listed. The cards were posted in sectors and divisions, grouped by both the nature of the work and the location of the workplace. Bus routes that passed near the worksite were noted on the card

Mike Deutscher

Mike had been through the routine many times before. He knew which bus to take so he would arrive at almost exactly 6:45 a.m. Arriving earlier wouldn't get him much closer to the head of the line. Arriving after 7:00 could mean waiting for at least an extra half hour, since only 20 people at a time were allowed in to scan the day labor postings.

He got in line quickly and waited silently. The door opened promptly at 7:00, and the first 20 people entered the day labor area. One or two were new and had to fill out the basic application form first, but most had already taken care of this chore and were able to go immediately to the postings. The regulars knew what they were looking for: what working conditions they could tolerate, who was least likely to reject applicants, which worksites could be reached quickly by convenient bus routes, who would be likely to pay the best or offer a job that would last for more than a day or two. New applicants, on the other hand, took longer to scan the cards and weigh their options.

As each person left the room with one, two or three job cards (three being the maximum allowed) another person entered and the line shortened. Mike made it in by 7:10. He much preferred something in his part of town, so he went immediately to these listings. Spotting an employer for whom he had worked before, he took that card and then another for a "fall- back" job not too far away, and left quickly to catch the next bus.

Mike is 58. He had worked at a series of factories when he was younger. The last plant closed three years ago and he had been unable to find another steady job. His last factory job, however, had lasted for 11 years, long enough to be eligible for severance pay. He had had the option of either a lump sum settlement or a small monthly payment that would continue until his social security checks began. The latter option paid part of his health insurance premium until he was eligible for Medicare and kept him in a group plan. After some agonizing he had chosen it. Now he was glad he had, since his search for another factory job had been fruitless. Automated equipment was now so common that very few factories hired semi-skilled workers.

Mike lived alone in a small apartment in a working class section of town. What he earned doing day labor plus his monthly severance check managed to pay his bills and keep him off welfare.

Mike's experience at the Job Service office was unusual. He had gone there to find information about a specific job opening (or about two of them, to be exact). About a year ago, local Job Service offices had formally abandoned their efforts to list openings for all types of jobs. They now concentrated instead on providing labor market information. Job listings for specific openings were handled only when there was a pool of applicants likely to use them, and a set of employers willing to provide the listings.

The Cedar Falls office, after reviewing the local labor market, had set up two job listing services. One was for day laborers, the other for secretarial and clerical workers. Private employment agencies had protested the latter, seeing this as their "turf," but the Job Service had held firm. Employers were eager to list these openings, and some of those seeking employment were not being well served by the private agencies. As a practical matter, agencies now handle openings primarily for the more skilled and experienced executive secretarial positions. The Job Service places a large proportion of lower paid clerical and secretarial workers.

In Mike's case, the day labor exchange was a real godsend. Once he gained some experience with the system he began to pick up the better jobs, since he was a steady and dependable worker. Some employers who got to know him would even call him directly when they needed help. Mike wished he were earning more, as he had in the old days, but he did appreciate the freedom to take a few days off without any hassle if he was not feeling well, or had something else he wanted to do. It was an imperfect situation, but the centralized listings at the Job Service office both increased his options and decreased the time and expense he would otherwise incur looking for work.

Kathy Jones

Unlike Mike, Kathy Jones did not arrive early. In fact, it was almost 10:00 a.m. when she walked into the Job Service office. It was her first visit, and she was nervous. Kathy, 17, had quit school the previous April. With a little over a month to go in her junior year, she became convinced she would not pass most of her subjects. She walked out without taking the final exams. After looking for restaurant or clerical work without success until June, she got a "clerical trainee" position through the Cedar Falls Summer Youth Program. That, however, had ended in August and now it was September. Kathy had no interest in being an over-age high school junior, but she didn't look forward to resuming her futile job search activities either. The counselor at the summer youth program had referred her to the Job Service. After a week or two of putting it off, she finally decided to stop by.

Entering the office, she saw a large sign which read INFORMATION — BEGIN HERE, and got in line. There were four people ahead of her, each waiting to talk to the woman working at the counter position under the information sign.

In 10 minutes or so, Kathy made it to the head of the line. "Have you ever used this Job Service office?" she was asked. She had not. "Have you used any other office in another part of the city, or anyplace else in the state?" The answer again was no, so there would be no data on Kathy stored anywhere in the system's computers. She was given a form and directed to some school-type desk-chairs in one corner of the lobby.

This form was not unlike those she had already met when applying for jobs at several large firms. It asked for her name, address, phone number, educational level, type of job desired, prior work experience, wages sought, social security number, and so on. Kathy filled in the blanks slowly. She never felt comfortable with these forms, knew she was misspelling several words, and felt inadequate listing so little education or experience. It was past 10:30 when she finished and again got in line under a large sign which read APPLICANT REGISTRATION.

This time it was a 15 minute wait before she made it to the head of the line. Dan Rogers took the form after a perfunctory "good morning" and began entering it into the computer. As he did so he corrected an occasional spelling error. He also asked her about some entries that weren't clear. A few minutes later Kathy was handed a small, computer produced registration card. This card would admit her to the office's other services. Since she had expressed an interest in clerical employment, she was directed to an office on the second floor.

Entering the second floor office, Kathy saw two lines. Several people were waiting near a sign reading NEW APPLICANTS NEEDING TESTING. A second and longer line had formed in front of an alcove. Here job notices hung on pegboards. They were classified by required typing speed and clerical abilities scores, and grouped by location.

Kathy soon found herself talking to the person in charge of the testing room. She showed her registration card and said it was her first visit.

Most employers who listed secretarial and clerical openings specified the typing speeds and skill levels they needed. As a rule, the pay offered increased with the skills demanded. Hence every applicant was tested before being allowed to review the job postings. The higher the test scores, the more openings a person could consider. No test result was final; anyone was free to come back another day and repeat any of the tests. There were, of course, multiple versions of each examination. The computer was programmed to print out the highest score obtained if a test was taken more than once.

Kathy was assigned to a computer terminal. Her registration card was passed through a card reader, identifying her to the computer. On an upright stand next to the terminal she found a full sheet of paper with three paragraphs of text. The computer instructed her to type what was on the sheet, and Kathy began to do so. Her typing was slow, so it took her some time to finish. When she had typed the last word, the computer screen changed to a series of clerical tasks. There were lists to be alphabetized, a spelling test, and some multiple choice questions. Again, Kathy worked slowly. She did not know what some of the words being alphabetized meant, and was unsure of her spelling. It was an hour before she finished.

Standing up, she left the computer terminal and went back to the person in charge of the testing room. The computer at his desk produced a card with her typing speed (18 words a minute ignoring errors, and less than zero with errors counting off). The card also had the results of her other tests.

She was asked to see a counselor who was sitting toward the back of the room. This time there was no wait in line. The counselor was on the phone, but the call ended a minute or two after Kathy walked over. Mrs. Nettles smiled and asked her to sit down. She took Kathy's registration card, waved it through the card reader, and looked at the computer terminal in front of her. Both Kathy's registration data and test scores appeared.

Mrs. Nettles asked a few questions about Kathy's summer position, and then looked at her with a kind but blunt expression. "Kathy," she said, "there is no realistic way you can expect to be hired as a secretary or clerical worker. Your skills are simply too low. You can barely type, have trouble reading, and don't alphabetize or spell well. You'll either have to get some more training in the clerical area, or you'll have to consider something else. Let's talk about some possibilities."

As Kathy answered Mrs. Nettles' questions, it quickly became clear she had very few options. Kathy had tried working as a waitress the summer before last but had not done well. She had looked unsuccessfully for a similar job this past summer. It wasn't really what she wanted to do, but it was all she could think of.

Mrs. Nettles asked a few more questions. She learned that Kathy came from a low-income family and would probably be eligible for government assistance. This led to a discussion of the Pre-Employment Preparation (PEP) program run by the Cedar Falls Employment and Training Administration. Kathy said she wanted to learn more about this program, so Mrs. Nettles typed PEP into the referral blank on the computer screen. The printer quickly produced a program description. It included the name of the person Kathy should see and even had a small map showing the program's location.

Kathy took the printout, thanked Mrs. Nettles, and headed home. It was past her usual lunch time and she was hungry. In addition, she had had enough of lines and forms for one day. Perhaps tomorrow she would go down and take a look at the PEP program.

Tom Bender

Tom Bender, 22, arrived at the Job Service office a little after lunch. He felt somewhat out of place. He knew the Job Service could be used by any citizen, but the people in line looked rather less affluent than most of his friends and neighbors.

Two months ago, Tom never dreamed he would be waiting his turn in front of the INFORMATION — BEGIN HERE sign. He had been immersed in finishing his degree at the University of Minnesota. Tom had moved through his degree program more slowly than most of his friends. Because he was working almost full time as a waiter, it was hard to carry a full load of classes. He had taken out student loans in order to cover part of his tuition and living expenses. His parents would have helped if they could, but their medical bills had been heavy because of his father's heart condition, and Tom didn't want to ask them for money. As soon as he graduated, he told himself, his marketing degree would help him get a good job, pay off his debts and help his parents until his dad got better. He intended to visit the university placement office early in his last semester but hadn't gotten around to it.

When an automobile accident killed both his parents he was as unprepared emotionally as he was financially. There was the funeral to arrange, the will to attend to, the debts to be paid off. Somehow he managed to finish his last two exams and graduate but he never did get to the placement office. Graduation day found him exhausted and almost penniless. His uncle, who lived in Cedar Falls, invited Tom to come for an extended visit until he got established. The invitation was gratefully accepted.

So here he was, in a strange town, degree in hand, trying to find his first post-college job. None of the ads he had answered seemed promising, so he decided to stop by the Job Service office and see what they could do for him.

His first two steps were the same as Kathy's: information and then registration. Dan Rogers at the registration desk gave him his card, smiled, and said the Job Service no longer listed specific openings for most jobs. However, they could provide overall information on the local economy and then some suggestions on how to find a marketing job. They could also supply the names of specific employers who might be worth approaching.

Dan directed Tom to a large room at the opposite end of the first floor from the day labor area. His card was waved through the Information Center reader and he was asked if he wanted to begin with an overview of the Cedar Falls labor market. He said fine, and was directed to a booth with a 13" TV screen and a set of earphones. Tom put on the earphones and pushed the start button. A videotaped presentation appeared on the screen. The narrator reviewed the major industries in Cedar Falls and then went on to discuss the mix of large and small employers. She pointed to several tables of statistics on the town's occupational mix and described the shortages and surpluses of workers in different occupations. Locations where jobs were concentrated were shown on a town map.

When the program was over a menu appeared on the screen. The following choices were offered:

> What Goes Into a Sound Occupational Choice?
> Doing Informational Interviewing
> Job Search Methods: Word of Mouth
> Job Search Methods: Direct Application
> Job Search Methods: Lists and Intermediaries
> Looking Good on Job Application Forms
> Using the Phone Wisely While Looking for Work
> Using the Library to Help With Your Job Search
> Constructing a List of Potential Employers
> Putting A Resume Together
> Doing Well in the Job Interview
> Finished For Today

Looking over the list, Tom realized he had not yet done a resume. He selected that choice. The operator of the Information Center, reacting to a light that flashed on his console, walked over and handed Tom several printed sheets with sample resumes. They would be discussed during the taped presentation and could also be taken home so he could review them again as he made out his own.

Tom took notes as he watched the instructions on how to prepare a resume. When the menu appeared again at the end of the presentation, he chose "Making A List of Potential

Employers." This tape was also preceded by the delivery of some printed sheets. One was an order form for the Job Service Employer Listing Printout (JSELP).

After this presentation Tom chose the "Finished for Today" option. He took off his earphones and filled out the JSELP form as the presentation had directed. It was getting late and he felt tired. He wanted to get home, work on a resume and get some rest. Tomorrow he would get out to see a few employers.

Tom viewed this presentation with intense interest. It explained how Job Service Employer Listings were cross-indexed by location, type of employment, size of employer and industry. The presentation explained each category, gave examples, and showed how to code the JSELP form. The Job Service had no way of knowing whether there were any specific openings at any of these firms, of course, but the listings at least showed where to look.

He made a mental note to return to the Job Service office at least once next week. Now that he was registered, he could come directly to the Information Center to view more of the instructional materials. He felt confident about handling himself once he got to an employer's office. What he had seen so far had been useful, however. He decided it was worth his time to watch the rest of the videotaped presentations.

Tom then went over to the JSELP desk at the back of the Information Center. Tim Carter, who ran the JSELP computer, greeted him and asked if he had used the service before. Since he had not, Tim checked to be sure the videotaped instructions had been followed properly. They had. On the completed JSELP form, Tom requested the names of medium to large employers located downtown who employed marketing personnel. He did not specify any particular industry.

Tim sat down at the computer console. He first put Tom's registration card through the card reader and then ran Tom's JSELP form through an optical scanner. After a moment or two the computer responded. There were 87 employers meeting the requirements which had been entered. Tim asked how many places Tom thought he could contact in the next week or so. The office policy was to give no more than 20 names at a time. Tom would always be free to return again for another 20 later. Tim also mentioned the job searcher support groups that the office ran each evening from 7:00 p.m. to 9:00p.m. If Tom ran into problems during his job search, he could join a group of others who were in the same situation. With the help of an experienced leader, he could try to improve his approach.

Tom said a list of 20 employers was fine, and he would consider the group if he ran into problems. Tim produced the printout. The computer would record which 20 names Tom had been given. There would be no duplication the next time he came in.

The high-speed printer typed out 20 listings that began with:

Employer:	Allied Chemical Service Company
Address:	537 Main Street
	Cedar Falls 55666
Phone:	678-9012
Employees:	150-200
Location:	Downtown
Industry:	Business Services
Category:	Private Sector, Traded (AMEX)
Marketing Staff:	20-25
Office Manager:	Nathan Cross, Division VP
Dept. Manager:	Nancy Edwards, Marketing DTR
Personnel:	June Doyle, Personnel DTR
Education Req.:	BA; Marketing Major preferred

Tom had requested downtown listings because he intended to spend two or three days downtown, going from firm to firm. At each firm he would ask to see the person in charge of marketing. The printouts would help him find the firms most likely to need him, and now he could ask for the marketing director by name. If that person was not available, Tom would ask for an appointment later. These visits should either produce a job offer or at least a good sense of what his chances were.

When Tom left it was late afternoon. The experience had been more useful than he expected. He now had several things he needed: help with his resume, a clearer understanding of the town's economy and a list of specific people to see about the kind of job he wanted.

He didn't know where there were any openings, of course, but he was pretty sure at least some of these people would see him. If they didn't have anything now, they might at least give him a shot at the next opportunity that came along. In addition, they might know of an opening at another firm.

Tom decided he would do his best on the first 20. If he did not found anything by the time he finished visiting these firms, he would come back to the Job Service office to watch more of the instructional tapes and pick up another list of employers. He would also drop in on one of the evening job searcher meetings to see if they could help. There was a lot of work to do, but at least he now had a plan of attack.

Peter Hook

Like Tom Bender, Peter Hook arrived shortly after noon. Peter, however, was not coming for the first time. Bypassing information and registration, he went immediately to the JSELP office, filled out the form and requested an additional 20 employer names. After a short wait in line, he handed his request form, along with his registration card, to Tim Carter.

Tim waived the card through the card reader and Peter's records came up on the computer screen. Because it had been over 90 days since Peter first visited the office to register for unemployment insurance, a flag appeared.

Tim reviewed the computerized record. Peter's job as a warehouse bookkeeper disappeared when that operation was computerized. He had come to the employment service every three or four weeks since then, each time picking up another list of 20 employers. Tim asked how many of the last group of employers he had spoken to, and whether he had gotten any interviews. Peter had little success to report. At first he had visited many of the employers on his list in person. More recently he had been writing them. Only one or two had been willing to talk to him, however, and no one had offered him a job.

Tim took a closer look at Peter. He was obviously depressed. Unsmiling and not very well dressed, Peter said as little as possible. Trying to draw him out a bit, Tim asked if he had any alternative job search plans. Peter, however, had little to say.

Not wanting to delay the others who were waiting in line, Tim explained that state regulations required job search training for anyone receiving unemployment compensation payments for over 90 days. These training sessions were held every afternoon from 1:00 to 4:00. A new group would begin next Monday and continue until Thursday; the members would then be assigned to an evening job searcher support group. The evening groups met every night, Monday through Friday. Those receiving unemployment compensation were required to attend at least one session a week.

Peter nodded his head in assent and Tim registered him for next week's workshop. While being registered, Peter glanced at the short brochure which described the four training sessions. A few minutes later Tim handed him a list of 20 new employers to contact and wished him well.

Once outside the building, Peter sat down on a bench by the bus stop and read through the job search training brochure. The first day, he learned, was devoted to a discussion of job search strategies. Group members described how they tried to get job interviews and discussed their experiences. The group leader then related their experiences to research findings on what usually works best. A discussion of the methods used by newly employed participants in recent support groups helped illustrate successful job search methods. The purpose of this discussion was to help each participant develop a job search strategy appropriate to the job he or she was seeking. The group leader's job was to be sure the participants' approaches were likely to be successful.

The second session dealt with resumes, job application forms, and letters. Each participant brought any written materials which he or she had been using. Each also filled out a typical job application form. Particular emphasis was placed on describing for the employer what the applicant did particularly well in prior jobs. Employers want to know what prospective employees are good at. They want more than a list of job titles and responsibilities. Finally, there was a discussion of how written materials can be used as tools to help make personal contacts. While written documents are important, it is personal contact which is most likely to lead to a job offer.

The third and fourth sessions are totally devoted, the brochure explained, to interview preparation. Practice interviews are videotaped. Ways to improve each person's interview approach are identified and practiced. Each participant is taped at least twice. Two or three additional taping sessions are provided for those who need the extra practice. The emphasis is on keeping the interview positive, volunteering information about past accomplishments, coming across as friendly and congenial, and asking for the job.

When these four days of intense work are over, each participant (1) is better able to handle the paperwork which is part of any job search; (2) has a sound strategy for obtaining interviews; and (3) is better prepared to handle the employment interview and therefore more likely to generate a job offer. The evening support group sessions then provide assistance as the participants put what they learned into action. A high proportion of past groups, most unemployed for at least three months, have obtained employment within four to six weeks.

Peter was skeptical. A shy person, he had been profoundly shocked at losing his job. Despite considerable effort he had only obtained a few interviews. He was deeply pained by some of his experiences during the job search process. He didn't feel most employers took him seriously. Peter had recently been trying to limit the pain by making his initial approaches to employers by mail, but this wasn't working.

He wasn't sure these training sessions would change things much but he reluctantly concluded they were worth a try. His unemployment insurance payments would not last forever, and he had already spent most of his savings. Each day of unemployment increased his anxiety. So, next Monday afternoon at 1:00 he would be back. At this point, anything was worth a try.

John Hill

John Hill arrived at the Job Service office in mid-afternoon. Like Peter Hook, he came reluctantly. A short, energetic man of 47, John had worked for almost 17 years at the Johnson Mill Works on the south side of Cedar Falls. The works had been closed for a month now. Like the death of an elderly relative, the plant's closing was both expected and still a shock.

Most of the younger workers had been laid off as plant operations wound down. When the final closing came, there was no one on the payroll with less than a dozen years seniority.

Despite months of advance warning, John felt disoriented and depressed.

Johnson Mill Works, in cooperation with the union local and the Job Service office, had offered job search workshops in the weeks before and after the plant closed. John hadn't responded to the invitation to take the training. He had a generous severance package so he didn't feel any immediate financial need. In addition, he really didn't anticipate much trouble finding another job. So he took a few weeks to do some work on his house, with a couple of long weekends to go fishing. Then, several weeks ago, John began going from plant to plant applying for semi-skilled openings.

It had been a much more discouraging experience than he had expected. Most of the plants were not hiring. Everyone else from Johnson had also been coming by. Some of the plants wouldn't even give him an application form. They said they had their own people on layoff and, if any openings came up, would be calling them back first. John heard of two new, small plants some distance from town that might be hiring but the commute was too long and, from what he heard, the wages were lower than he was used to. John now began to get worried. He decided to drop by the Job Service office and see what they had to offer.

John went first to the information desk and then to registration. At registration "Johnson Mill Works" was typed in as his last place of employment. The computer responded with a flag showing John as eligible for displaced worker assistance. Along with his registration card, he was given a second card with the title of a videotaped presentation on the challenge faced by displaced workers and the name of the person (Carol Pepper) who specialized in assisting them.

John went to the Information Center as directed and soon found himself watching a tape on factory closings. He was surprised to find how accurately the presentation described what he had experienced: the younger workers leaving first, his feelings when the plant closed, his initial disinterest in the group job search program and then the unexpected problems finding a new job. As he watched the tape and listened to its explanation of the changing set of jobs available in Cedar Falls, he became even more convinced that he could use some help after all. So, when the tape was over, he put the earphones aside and asked directions to Carol Pepper's desk.

Carol Pepper had been hired a year ago when the staff was reorganized. Her salary came from funds earmarked for assistance to displaced workers. Carol was an older woman who had gone back to school after her children were grown. Her husband, a factory worker, lost his job when a Cedar Falls factory closed several years ago. This experience helped Carol get her present job. She convinced the office manager that she understood what displaced workers were experiencing. She and her husband had been through it themselves.

John was a bit uncomfortable with Carol at first, but as they talked he began to relax. She knew a few of his friends and acquaintances, which helped. He sensed she knew what she was doing and, equally important, was not going to talk down to him. Unlike the other people in the office, she was not dealing with a long line of persons waiting to see her. She took the time to draw John out, letting him describe what he had been doing over the last month and how he was feeling.

John's reactions at this point were mixed. The videotape had convinced him the Job Service people understood what he was going through, a belief that was reinforced as he talked to Carol. This was only partially reassuring, however. The videotape had been quite blunt about the small number of openings available in local factories, the lower pay that many new factories were offering and the probability of further manufacturing layoffs due to automation and foreign competition. What could he do? He had done factory work all his life and had not seriously considered anything else.

Sensing how he was feeling, Carol began to move the conversation away from the past and into the future. John had, she said, essentially five options. None of them were perfect solutions to the situation in which he found himself. He would have to decide which was the least imperfect.

First, he could do day labor if he needed to bring in some immediate income, either immediately or when his UI payments ran out. The pay wouldn't be much, but with his solid work record he would have no trouble getting the better jobs.

Second, he could get a computer printout of every factory in town and go from one to the other, applying at each. The printout would include some of the smaller and less well-known firms he might have missed. The odds that he would get a job this way were not good. There were far more applicants for these jobs than openings. But, if he was lucky, he might find something.

Third, he could be trained in a new skill and then look for a different type of job. Because he qualified as a displaced worker, he was eligible for tuition-free retraining. It made sense to sign up now, while he still had UI and his severance pay to live on. Carol gave him a brochure which discussed the training programs available at Cedar Falls Community College. These programs were designed by a board which included local employers and a Job Service labor market analyst. Training was concentrated in the areas of greatest demand in Cedar Falls. Admittedly, the pay for some of these jobs would be below what John had earned in the factory, but it would be above the day labor rate and would increase with experience. Carol offered to arrange for aptitude testing if John wanted to apply for one of these programs.

John's fourth option was to join a group job search program. Program staff would help him identify jobs which he could do without any further training. He could then use the employer lists to begin applying. He could try for some factory jobs but the emphasis would be on positions where there were more openings. There would be heavy competition for these jobs, of course, but the interviewing training would help John present himself in the best possible light.

Finally, he was free to continue on his own. But, as Carol pointed out, the labor market had changed a great deal in the 17 years since John last sought work. While he might run across something, looking for a factory job today was usually a very prolonged, discouraging and unproductive experience.

John accepted the brochure on the training programs and another describing the group job search option. He didn't want to decide today. Carol said that was fine and suggested an appointment in two or three days. John thanked her but said no; he wanted to sort out his own feelings first.

Carol had been very helpful, but the whole situation bothered him. None of the options she mentioned gave him what he really wanted, which was his old job back or something just like it. The pay at Johnson had been good, he knew the people and he had his place. Now all of this was gone. He walked out quickly, feeling upset, not really seeing the others standing in line. Mrs. Pepper was trying to help, he knew, but somehow he wanted to be alone for awhile.

Jane Gilbert

It was 4:20 p.m. when Jane Gilbert hurried into the Job Service office. She had to work until 4:00 p.m. at her present job; this was as early as she could arrive. She had taken her tests several weeks ago, so she went directly to the secretarial and clerical placement center. Giving her registration card to the worker at the gate, she watched while he waived it through the card reader and verified the jobs for which she was eligible.

Jane, 24, had worked as a secretary for two years now. Before that she had been a waitress for four years, a job she took immediately after graduating from high school at 18. She liked being a waitress at first, particularly when the tips were good, but after awhile she began to feel a need for something "better." This led her to an early morning secretarial course at a community college. She would go to class and then leave for work around 11:30 a.m. She worked through lunch and dinner, leaving at 8:00 p.m. It was a long day.

When her training was finished, the college placement office helped get her a secretarial job with a local wholesaler. At first her income went down some but she stayed with it and now, after three raises, was doing well. The somewhat rundown, hurried environment of the wholesale office wasn't really what she wanted, however. A month ago she decided it was time to look for something downtown.

Her test scores and two years of full-time work experience qualified her for jobs at levels one to three, but not level four. (All jobs were classified by levels, depending on the skills and experience the employer demanded and how much the job paid.) Jane immediately went to the level three job postings and began scanning those in the downtown section. She found only two that paid what she was now earning.

She had been surprised to learn that, for her level of experience, she was well paid. At least some decrease in pay might be the price of better working conditions. She considered this idea and rejected it. Better to continue her search until she found a position where both the working conditions and pay were an improvement. If it took quite a while to find what she wanted, so be it. She worked to increase her typing speed and improve her secretarial skills. That way, if nothing else turned up on her weekly visits, she could qualify for a level four job in another year.

Taking the two postings, she hurried to the check-out lane and let the clerk waive her registration card and the two job openings through the card reader. She went out to the bus stop, hoping to beat the worst of rush hour traffic. She had not told her employer she was looking for something else. It would be a challenge finding a time tomorrow when she could get in a quiet phone call requesting late afternoon interviews for these two openings. If necessary, she could use the pay phone in a restaurant down the block from where she worked. It was noisy there, though, unless she left for a very early lunch, in which case she got terribly hungry around the end of the day.

But that's the way it is, looking for work. It's often an awkward and uncomfortable business.

REFERENCES

Citations identified with an asterick (*) are available directly from JIST Works, Inc., 720 N. Park Avenue, Indianapolis, Indiana 46202, 317/637/6643 or 800/648/5478.

Abraham, Katherine. "Structural/Frictional vs. Deficient Demand Unemployment: Some New Evidence." American Economic Review, 73 (September 1983): 708-724.

Aho, C. Michael and James Orr. "Trade-Sensitive Employment: Who are the Affected Workers?" Monthly Labor Review, 104 (February 1981): 29-35.

Alexander, Charles. "That Threatening Trade Gap." Time (July 9, 1984): 62-64.

Amundson, Norman and William Borgen. "The Dynamics of Unemployment: Job Loss and Job Search." The Personnel and Guidance Journal, 60 (May 1982): 562-564.

Anderson, Harry. "Jobs: Putting America Back to Work." Newsweek (October 18, 1982): 78-84.

Andreassen, Arthur, Norman Saunders and Betty Su. "Economic Outlook for the 1990's: Three Scenarios for Economic Growth." Monthly Labor Review, 106 (November 1983): 11-23.

Arbeiter, Solomon, Carol Aslanian, Frances Schmerbeck and Henry Brickell. 40 Million Americans in Career Transition. New York: College Entrance Examination Board, 1978.

Armington, Catherine and Marjorie Odle. "Sources of Job Growth: A New Look at the Small Business Role." Economic Development Commentary, 6 (Fall 1982): 3-7.

Azevedo, Ross. "Scientists, Engineers and the Job Search Process." California Management Review, 17 (Winter 1974): 40-49.

Azrin, Nathan. "The Job-Finding Club as a Method for Obtaining Employment for Welfare-Eligible Clients: Demonstration, Evaluation and Counselor Training." Anna, Illinois: Anna Mental Health and Development Center, 1978.

Azrin, Nathan and Victoria Besalel. Job Club Counselor's Manual. Baltimore: University Park Press, 1980.

Azrin, N. H., T. Flores and S. J. Kaplan. "Job-Finding Club: A Group-Assisted Program for Obtaining Employment." Behavior Research and Therapy, 13 (1975): 17-27.

Barbee, Joel and Ellsworth Keil. "Experimental Techniques of Job Interview Training for the Disadvantaged." Journal of Applied Psychology, 58 (October 1973): 209-213.

Bass, Gwenell. The U. S. Steel Industry: Recent Economic Developments. Congressional Research Service Issue Brief IB83048. Washington, DC: 1983.

Beck, Melinda, Gloria Broger and Diane Weathers. "Women's Work — And Wages." Newsweek (July 9, 1984): 22-23.

Becker, Eugene. "Self-Employed Workers: An Update to 1983." Monthly Labor Review, 107 (July 1984): 14-18.

Becker, Eugene and Norman Bowles. "Employment and Unemployment Improvements Widespread in 1983." Monthly Labor Review, 107 (February 1984): 3-14.

Beckwith, David. "Solo Americans." Time (December 2, 1985): 41.

Bednarzik, Robert. "Layoffs and Permanent Job Losses: Workers' Traits and Cyclical Patterns." Monthly Labor Review, 106 (September 1983): 3-12.

Bell, Daniel. The Coming of Post-Industrial Society. New York: Basic Books, 1973.

Bellante, Don and Mark Jackson. Labor Economics (2nd edition). New York: McGraw-Hill, 1983.

Belous, Richard and Andrew Wyckoff. "Trade Has Job Winners Too." Across the Board, 24 (September 1987): 53-55.

Bendick, Jr., Marc. The Swedish "Active Labor Market" Approach to Reemploying Workers Dislocated by Economic Change Washington, DC: The Urban Institute, 1983.

Berlin, Gordon and Andrew Sum. Toward A More Perfect Union: Basic Skills, Poor Families and Our Economic Future. New York, NY: Ford Foundation, 1988.

Bielby, William and James Baron. "Men and Women at Work: Sex Segregation and Statistical Discrimination." American Journal of Sociology, 91 (January 1986): 759-799.

Birch, David. "Who Creates Jobs?" The Public Interest, 65 (Fall 1981): 3-14.

Birch, David. Job Creation in America. New York, NY: Free Press, 1987.

Blau, Francine. Equal Pay in the Office. Lexington, MA: Lexington Books, 1977.

*Bolles, Richard. The Three Boxes of Life. Berkeley, CA: Ten Speed Press, 1978.

*Bolles, Richard. What Color Is Your Parachute? Berkeley, CA: Ten Speed Press, Annual Editions.

Borgen, William and Norman Amundson. "The Dynamics of Unemployment." Journal of Counseling and Development, 66 (December 1987): 180-184.

Bostwick, Burdette. 111 Techniques and Strategies for Getting the Job Interview. New York: John Wiley, 1981.

Bowers, Norman. "Probing the Issues of Unemployment Duration." Monthly Labor Review, 103 (July 1980): 23-32.

Bowers, Norman. "Employment on the Rise in the First Half of 1983." Monthly Labor Review, 106 (August 1983): 8-14.

Bowes, Lee. No One Need Apply. Boston, MA: Harvard Business School Press, 1987.

Bowman, William. "How College Graduates Find Good Jobs." Journal of Career Planning and Employment, 48 (Winter 1987): 32-36.

Boyer, Edward. "Restarting Europe's Job Engine." Fortune (August 20, 1984): 183-184, 186, 189-190.

Bregger, John. "The Current Population Survey: A Historical Perspective and BLS' Role." Monthly Labor Review, 107 June 1984): 8-14.

Brand, Horst and John Duke. "Productivity in Commercial Banking: Computers Spur the Advance." Monthly Labor Review, 105 (December 1982): 19-27.

Breaugh, James. "Relationships between Recruiting Sources and Employee Performance, Absenteeism, and Work Attitudes." Academy of Management Journal, 24 (March 1981): 142-147.

Bregger, John. "The Current Population Survey: A Historical Perspective and BLS' Role." Monthly Labor Review, 107 (June 1984): 8-14.

Brenner, M. Harvey. "Health Costs and Benefits of Economic Policy." International Journal of Health Services, 7 (#4 1977): 581-623.

Brenner, M. Harvey. Estimating the Effects of Economic Change on National Health and Social Well-Being. Joint Economic Committee, Congress of the United States. Washington, DC: U.S. Government Printing Office, 1984.

Bridges, William and Richard Berk. "Sex, Earnings, and the Nature of Work: A Job-Level Analysis of Male-Female Income Differences." Social Science Quarterly, 58 (March 1978): 553-565.

Bridges, William and Wayne Villemer. "On the Institutionalization of Job Security: Internal Labor Markets and Their Corporate Environments." Unpublished Paper, University of Illinois at Chicago, 1982.

Bridges, William and Wayne Villemez. "Informal Hiring and Income in the Labor Market." American Sociological Review, 51 (August 1986): 574-582.

Broussard, William and Robert DeLargey. "The Dynamics of the Group Outplacement Workshop." Personnel Journal, 58 (December 1979): 855-857, 873.

Bucalo, Jr., John. "Administering a Salaried Reduction-in-force....Effectively." Personnel Administrator, 27 (April 1982): 79-89.

Bunzel, John. "To Each According to Her Worth?" The Public Interest, 67 (Spring 1982): 77-93.

Bureau of the Census. Current Population Reports, Series P-60, No. 140. "Money Income and Poverty Status of Families and Persons in the United States: 1982 (Advance Data from the March 1983 Current Population Survey)." Washington, DC: U. S. Government Printing Office, 1983.

Bureau of Labor Statistics. Analyzing 1981 Earnings Data from the Current Population Survey. Bulletin 2149. Washington, DC: U. S. Department of Labor, 1982.

Bureau of Labor Statistics. News (October 22, 1987). Washington, DC: U. S. Department of Labor.

Burkhauser, Richard and John Turner. "Labor-Market Experience of the Almost Old and the Implications for Income Support." American Economic Review, 72 (May 1982): 304-308.

Burtless, Gary. "Manpower Policies for the Disadvantaged: What Works?" The Brookings Review, 3 (Fall 1984): 3-11.

Bylinsky, Gene. "The Race to the Automatic Factory." Fortune 107 (February 21, 1983): 52-64.

California Employment Development Research Division. Cross Reference Index: An Aid for More Effective Use of the Yellow Pages for Job Development and Job Search. Sacramento, CA: California Employment Development Department, 1983.

Carey, Max and Alan Eck. "How Workers Get Their Training." Occupational Outlook Quarterly, 28 (Winter 1984): 2-21.

Cashell, Brian. Median Family Incomes and Budgets. Congressional Research Service Mini Brief MB81251. Washington, DC: Library of Congress, 1983.

*Chapman, Jack with Steve Sanders. How to Make $1000 a Minute Negotiating Your Salaries and Raises. Berkeley, CA: Ten Speed Press, 1987.

Chastain, Clark. "Bridling Corporate-Takeover Warfare." SAM Advanced Management Journal, 50 (Autumn 1985): 4-11.

Chastain, Sherry. Winning the Salary Game. New York: John Wiley, 1980.

Chesney, Margaret, Gunnar Sevelius, George Black, Marcia Ward, Gary Swan and Ray Rosenman. "Work Environment, Type A Behavior, and Coronary Heart Disease Risk Factors." Journal of Occupational Medicine, 23 (August 1981): 551-555.

Clark, Rosanne. "Robots at the Front: The New Industrial Revolution." Houston, 54 (May 1983): 17-20, 49-50.

Clowers, Michael and Robert Fraser. "Employment Interview Literature: A Perspective for the Counselor." Vocational Guidance Quarterly, 26 (September 1977): 13-26.

Cobb, Sidney and Stanislav Kasl. "Some Medical Aspects of Unemployment." In Gloria Shatto, ed., Employment of the Middle-Aged. Springfield, IL: Charles C. Thomas, 1972: 87-96.

Congressional Budget Office. Dislocated Workers: Issues and Federal Options. Washington, DC: U.S. Government Printing Office, 1982.

Congressional Budget Office. Strategies for Assisting the Unemployed. Paper prepared by the staff of the Human Resources and Community Development Division. Washington, DC: Congressional Budget Office, 1982.

Congressional Budget Office. Reducing Poverty Among Children. Washington, DC: Congressional Budget Office, 1985.

Congressional Budget Office. Trends in Family Income: 1970-1986. Washington, DC: Congressional Budget Office, 1988.

Cooper, Jr., C. Joseph. "White-Collar Salaries Vary Widely in the Service Industries." Monthly Labor Review, 110 (November 1987): 21-23.

Corcoran, Mary, Linda Datcher, and Greg Duncan. "Most Workers Find Jobs Through Word of Mouth." Monthly Labor Review, 103 (August 1980): 33-35.

*Crystal, John and Richard Bolles. Where Do I Go From Here With My Life? New York: Seabury Press, 1974.

Cuony, Edward and Robert Hoppock. "Job Course Pays Off." Personnel and Guidance Journal, 32 (March 1954): 389- 391.

Davidson, Kenneth. "Do Megamergers Make Sense?" Journal of Business Strategy, 7 (Winter 1987): 40-48.

DeBoer, Larry and Michael Seeborg. "The Female-Male Unemployment Differential: Effects of Changes in Industry Employment." Monthly Labor Review, 107 (November 1984): 8-15.

Decker, Phillip and Edwin Cornelius III. "A Note on Recruiting Sources and Job Survival Rates." Journal of Applied Psychology, 64 (August 1979): 463-464.

Dennis, Terry and David Gustafson. "College Campuses vs. Employment Agencies as Sources of Manpower." Personnel Journal, 52 (August 1973): 720-724.

Devens, Jr., Richard. "Displaced Workers: One Year Later." Monthly Labor Review, 109 (July 1986): 40-43.

Devens, Jr., Richard. "A Movable Beast: Changing Patterns of Regional Unemployment." Monthly Labor Review, 111 (April 1988): 60-62.

DiPrete, Thomas. "Unemployment over the Life Cycle: Racial Differences and the Effect of Changing Economic Conditions." American Journal of Sociology, 87 (September 1981): 286-307.

*Djeddah, Eli. Moving Up. Berkeley, CA: Ten Speed, 1978.

Dodd, Allen Jr. The Job Hunter. New York: McGraw-Hill, 1965.

Downs, Cal and Jeanette Tanner. "Decision-Making in the Selection Interview." Journal of College Placement, 42 (Summer 1982): 59-61.

Driscoll, David. Services Trade in the U.S. Current Account. Congressional Research Service Report 80-170 E. Washington, DC: Library of Congress, 1980.

Drobnick, Richard. Debt Problems, Trade Offensives, and Protectionism. Washington, DC: American Council of Life Insurance Trend Analysis Program, 1985.

Drucker, Peter. "The Changed World Economy." Foreign Affairs, 64 (Spring 1986): 768-791.

Duncan, Greg and Saul Hoffman. "The Incidence and Wage Effects of Overeducation." Economics of Education Review, 1 (Winter 1981): 75-86.

Dyer, Lee. "Managerial Jobseeking: Methods and Techniques." Monthly Labor Review, 95 (December 1972): 29-30.

Dyer, Lee. "Job Search Success of Middle-Aged Managers and Engineers." Industrial and Labor Relations Review, 26 (April 1973): 969-979.

Eaton, Swain Associates. Job Search Networking: Is It Working? Unpublished paper. New York: Eaton, Swain Associates, 1983.

Ellis, Rebecca and M. Susan Taylor. "Role of Self- Esteem Within the Job Search Process." Journal of Applied Psychology, 68 (November 1983): 632-640.

Employment Security Department. Special Employment Assistance. Olympia, WA: Employment Security Department, 1987.

Executive Office of the President. Twenty-Sixth Annual Report of the President of the United States on the Trade Agreements Program 1981-1982. Washington, DC: U.S. Government Printing Office, 1982.

Farr, J. Michael. Getting the Job You Really Want. Indianapolis, IN: JIST Works, 1988a

Farr, J. Michael. Job Finding Fast. Mission Hills, CA: Glencoe Publishing, 1988b.

Farr, J. Michael, Richard Gaither, R. Michael Pickrell. The Work Book. Mission Hills, CA: Glencoe Publishing, 1987.

Farrell, Dan and James Petersen. "Withdrawal of New Employees: An EDA Approach." Unpublished paper, Departments of Management and Sociology, Western Michigan University.

Farrell, Michael and Stanley Rosenberg. Men at Midlife. Boston, MA: Auburn House Publishing Company, 1981.

Faux, Marian. The Executive Interview. New York, NY: St. Martin's Press, 1985.

Felmlee, Diane. "Women's Job Mobility Processes Within and Between Employers." American Sociological Review, 47 (February 1982): 142-151.

Ferber, Robert and Neil Ford. "The Collection of Job Vacancy Data Within A Labor Turnover Framework." In Arthur Ross, ed., Employment Policy and The Labor Market. Berkeley, CA: University of California Press, 1965: 162-190.

Fine, Sidney and Wretha Wiley. An Introduction to Functional Job Analysis. Kalamazoo, MI: Upjohn, 1971.

Fisher, Roger and William Ury. Getting to Yes. New York, NY: Penguin, 1983.

Flaim, Paul and Ellen Sehgal. "Displaced Workers of 1979-83: How Well Have They Fared?" Monthly Labor Review, 108 (June 1985): 3-16.

Flax, Steven. "Pay Cuts Before the Job Even Starts." Fortune (January 9, 1984): 75-77.

Fogel, Walter. "Illegal Aliens: Economics Aspects and Public Policy Alternatives." San Diego Law Review, 15 (1977): 63-78.

Foulkes, Fred and Jeffrey Hirsch. "People Make Robots Work." Harvard Business Review, 84 (January/February 1984): 94-102.

Freeman, Richard. Unionism and the Dispersion of Wages. Working Paper 248. Cambridge, MA: National Bureau of Economic Research, 1978.

Freeman, Richard. "The Effect of Demographic Factors on Age-Earnings Profiles." Journal of Human Resources, 14 (Summer 1979): 289-318.

Freeman, Richard. The Evolution of the American Labor Market 1948-1980. Paper prepared for the NBER Key Biscayne Conference on Postwar Changes in the American Economy. Cambridge, MA: National Bureau of Economic Research, 1980.

Freeman, Richard. "Troubled Workers in the Labor Market." In National Commission for Employment Policy, Seventh Annual Report: The Federal Interest in Employment and Training. Washington, DC: National Commission for Employment Policy, 1981: 103-173.

Fuchs, Victor. How We Live. Cambridge, MA: Harvard University Press, 1983.

Fullerton, Jr., Howard and John Tschetter. "The 1995 Labor Force: A Second Look." Monthly Labor Review, 106 (November 1983): 3-10.

Fullerton, Jr., Howard. "Labor Force Projections: 1986 to 2000." Monthly Labor Review, 110 (September 1987): 19-29.

Galassi, John and Merna Galassi. "Preparing Individuals for Job Interviews: Suggestions from more than 60 Years of Research." American Personnel and Guidance Journal, 57 (December 1978): 188-192.

Gall, Norman. "Will the US become a Pauper Nation?" Forbes, 131 (February 28, 1983): 80-83, 86.

Gannon, Martin. "Sources of Referral and Employee Turnover." Journal of Applied Psychology, 55 (June 1971): 226-228.

Garfinkle, Stuart. "The Outcome of a Spell of Unemployment." Monthly Labor Review, 100 (January 1977): 54- 57.

General Accounting Office. Advances in Automation Prompt Concern Over Increased US Employment. Washington, DC: General Accounting Office, 1982.

Germann, Richard and Peter Arnold. Bernard Haldane Associates' Job and Career Building. New York: Harper & Row, 1980.

Ginzberg, Eli and George Vojta. "The Service Sector of the U.S. Economy." Scientific American, 244 (March 1981): 48-55.

Giuliano, Vincent. "The Mechanization of Office Work." Scientific American, 247 (September 1982): 149-164.

Glueck, William. "Decision Marking: Organization Choice." Personnel Psychology, 27 (Spring 1974): 77-93.

Goldstein, Harold and Bryna Fraser. "Computer Training and the Workplace: A Little Goes a Long Way." Occupational Outlook Quarterly, 29 (Winter 1985): 25-29.

Gordus, Jeanne, Paul Jarley and Louis Ferman. Plant Closings and Economic Dislocation. Kalamazoo, Michigan: Upjohn, 1981.

Gore, Susan. "The Effect of Social Support in Moderating the Health Consequences of Unemployment." Journal of Health and Social Behavior, 19 (June 1978): 157-165.

Gould, Roger. Transformations. New York: Simon and Schuster, 1978.

Grandjean, Burke. "History and Career in a Bureaucratic Labor Market." American Journal of Sociology, 86 (March 1981): 1057-1092.

Granovetter, Mark. Getting A Job. Cambridge, MA: Harvard University Press, 1974.

Granovetter, Mark. "The Strength of Weak Ties." American Journal of Sociology, 78 (May 1973): 1360-1380.

Grant Commission. The Forgotten Half: Non-College Youth in America. Washington, DC: The William T. Grant Foundation Commission on Work, Family and Citizenship, 1988.

Greco, Ben. How To Get The Job That's Right For You (Revised Edition). Homewood, IL: Dow Jones-Irwin, 1980.

Greene, Richard. "Tracking Job Growth in Private Industry." Monthly Labor Review, 105 (September 1982): 3-9.

Griffin, Larry, Arne Kalleberg and Karl Alexander. "Determinants of Early Labor Market Entry and Attainment: A Study of Labor Market Segmentation." Sociology of Education, 54 (July 1981): 206-221.

Grossman, Allyson. "More than Half of all Children Have Working Mothers." Monthly Labor Review, 105 (February 1981): 41-43.

Guthrie, Lee. "Career Counselors: Will They Lead You Down the Primrose Path?" Savvy (December 1981): 60-73.

Guzda, Henry. "The U.S. Employment Service at 50: It Too Had to Wait Its Turn." Monthly Labor Review, 106 (June 1983): 12-19.

Guzzardi, Jr., Walter. "How To Foil Protectionism." Fortune (March 21, 1983): 76-86.

Guzzardi, Walter. "Big Can Still Be Beautiful." Fortune (April 25, 1988): 50-64.

Gwodey, Eve. Job Hunting With Employment Agencies. Woodbury, NY: Barron's Educational Series, 1978.

Hahn, Andrew and Barry Friedman. The Effectiveness of Two Job Search Assistance Programs for Disadvantaged Youth. Waltham, MA: Brandeis University, 1981.

Haldane, Bernard. How to Make a Habit of Success. Washington, DC: Acropolis, 1975.

Haldane, Bernard, Jean Haldane and Lowell Martin. Job Power. Washington, DC: Acropolis, 1980.

*Half, Robert. Robert Half on Hiring. New York, NY: Crown, 1985.

Hardiman, Philip and Marged Sugarman. Employment Service Potential: The Dimensions of Labor Turnover. Sacramento, CA: Employment Development Department, 1979.

Haugen, Steven. "The Employment Expansion in Retail Trade, 1973-1985." Monthly Labor Review, 109 (August 1986): 9-16.

Hayghe, Howard. "Working Mothers Reach Record Number in 1984." Monthly Labor Review, 107 (December 1984): 31-34.

Hayghe, Howard and Steven Haugen. "A Profile of Husbands in Today's Labor Market." Monthly Labor Review, 110 (October 1987): 12-17.

Hedin, Diane, Howard Wolfe, Jerry Fruetel, and Sharon Bush. Youth's Views on Work: Minnesota Youth Poll. Minneapolis, MN: University of Minnesota, 1977.

Herzberg, Frederick. "One More Time: How Do You Motivate Employees?" Harvard Business Review, 41 (January/February 1968): 53-62.

Hodson, Randy and Robert Kaufman. "Economic Dualism: A Critical Review." American Sociological Review, 47 (December 1982): 727-739.

Hoffman, Saul. "On-the-Job Training: Differences by Race and Sex." Monthly Labor Review, 104 (July 1981): 34-36.

Hollandsworth, Jr., James, Richard Kazelskis, Joanne Stevens and Mary Dressel. "Relative Contributions of Verbal, Articulative, and Nonverbal Communication to Employment Decisions in the Job Interview Setting." Personnel Psychology, 32 (Summer 1979): 359-367.

Holzer, Harry. "Job Search by Employed and Unemployed Youth." Industrial and Labor Relations Review, 40 (July 1987): 601-611.

Horvath, Francis. "Job Tenure of Workers in January 1981." Monthly Labor Review, 105 (September 1982): 34-36.

Horvath, Francis. "The Pulse of Economic Change: Displaced Workers of 1981-1985." Monthly Labor Review, 110 (June 1987): 3-12.

House, James. "The Effects of Occupational Stress on Physical Health." In James O'Toole, ed., Work and the Quality of Life. Cambridge, Massachusetts: MIT Press, 1974: 145-170.

Howe, Louise. Pink Collar Workers. New York: Avon Books, 1977.

Howe, Wayne. "The Business Services Industry Sets Pace in Employment Growth." Monthly Labor Review, 109 (April 1986): 29-36.

Howe, Wayne. "Education and Demographics: How Do They Affect Unemployment Rates?" Monthly Labor Review, 111 (January 1988): 3-9.

Howell, Frank and William Reese. "Sex and Mobility in the Dual Economy." Work and Occupations, 13 (February 1986): 77-96.

Hudson Institute. Workforce 2000: Work and Workers for the Twenty-First Century. Indianapolis, IN: Hudson Institute, 1987.

Hunt, H. Allan and Timothy Hunt. "Executive Summary from Human Resource Implications of Robotics." Paper distributed at Congressional Research Service seminar on robotics and the implications of automation for employment, 1983.

Hunter, William. "Yes, More U. S. Households are Becoming Affluent." Gracescope (July/August 1984): 1-3.

Hymowitz, Carol. "Layoffs Force Blue-Collar Women Back into Low-Paying-Job Ghetto." Wall Street Journal (March 6, 1985): 33.

*Irish, Richard. Go Hire Yourself an Employer (Revised Edition). Garden City, NY: Doubleday Anchor, 1978.

*Jackson, Tom. Guerrilla Tactics in the Job Market. New York: Bantam, 1978.

Jacobs, Jerry. "Industrial Sector and Career Mobility Reconsidered." American Sociological Review, 48 (June 1983): 415-421.

Jencks, Christopher. "The Hidden Prosperity of the 1970s." The Public Interest, 77 (Fall 1984): 37-61.

Johnson, Mark. "Import Prices Decline, Export Indexes Mixed in the First 6 Months of 1983." Monthly Labor Review, 106 (November 1983): 59-70.

Johnson, Miriam and Marged Sugarman. Job Development and Placement: CETA Program Models. Washington, DC: U.S. Government Printing Office, 1978.

Johnson, Miriam. "The Role of Help Wanted Ads." In Labor Market Intermediaries. Washington, DC: National Commission for Manpower Policy, 1978: 169-193.

*Johnson, Miriam. The State of the Art in Job Search Training. Salt Lake City, UT: Olympus Research Centers, 1982.

*Johnson, Miriam. Getting Youth on the Job Track. Salt Lake City, UT: Olympus Research Centers, 1982.

Jones, R. J. and N. H. Azrin. "An Experimental Application of a Social Reinforcement Approach to the Problem of Job-Finding." Journal of Applied Behavior Analysis, 6 (1973): 345-353.

Jordan-DeLaurenti and Associates. "An Assessment of WIN Job Club Programs Within the State of Texas and Selected Projects within Region VI." Final Report, 1981.

Joslin, Leeman. "Strictly Speaking, Vocationally." Vocational Guidance Quarterly, 32 (June 1984): 260-262.

Kahn, Lawrence and Stuart Low. "The Relative Effects of Employed and Unemployed Job Search." Review of Economics and Statistics, 64 (May 1982): 234-241.

Kandel, Denise and Kazuo Yamaguchi. "Job Mobility and Drug Use: An Event History Analysis." American Journal of Sociology, 92 (January 1987): 836-878.

Kanter, Rosabeth and Barry Stein, eds. Life in Organizations. New York: Basic Books, 1979.

Katchadourian, Herant. Fifty: Midlife in Perspective. New York, NY: W. H. Freeman, 1987.

Kaufman, H. G. Professionals In Search of Work. New York: Wiley, 1982.

Kaufman, Robert and Seymour Spilerman. "The Age Structures of Occupations and Jobs." American Journal of Sociology, 87 (January 1982): 827-851.

Keith, Robert, James Engelkes and Bob Winborn. "Employment-Seeking Preparation and Activity: An Experimental Job-Placement Training Model for Rehabilitation Clients." Rehabilitation Counseling Bulletin, 21 (December 1977): 159-165.

Kellner, Irwin. "The Tail Wags the Dog." The Manufacturers Hanover Report (December 1984): 1-3.

*Kennedy, Bart. Self-Directed Job Search: An Introduction. Washington, DC: U.S. Department of Labor, 1980.

Killingsworth, Mark. "Comparable Worth in the Job Market: Estimating Its Effects." Monthly Labor Review, 108 (July 1985): 39-41.

*Kimeldorf, Martin. Job Search Education. New York, NY: Educational Design, 1985.

Kirkland, Jr., Richard. "The Bright Future of Service Exports." Fortune (June 8, 1987): 32-38.

Klein, Deborah. "Labor Force Data: The Impact of the 1980 Census." Monthly Labor Review, 105 (July 1982): 39-43.

Kleinke, Chris. First Impressions. Englewood Cliffs, NJ: Prentice-Hall, 1975.

Koziara, Karen. "Comparable Worth: Organizational Dilemmas." Monthly Labor Review, 108 (December 1985): 13-16.

Kutscher, Ronald. "An Overview of the Year 2000." Occupational Outlook Quarterly, 32 (Summer, 1988): 2-9.

Kutscher, Ronald. "Overview and Implications of the Projections to 2000." Monthly Labor Review, 110 (September 1987): 3-9.

Kutscher, Ronald and Jerome Mark. "The Service-Producing Sector: Some Common Perceptions Reviewed." Monthly Labor Review, 106 (April 1983): 21-24.

Kuttner, Bob. "The Declining Middle." Atlantic Monthly, 252 (July 1983): 60-64, 66-67, 69-72.

Lacombe II, John and James Conley. "Major Agreements in 1984 Provide Record Low Wage Increases." Monthly Labor Review, 108 (April 1985): 39-45.

Lacombe, John and Joan Borum. "Major Labor Contracts in 1986 Provided Record Low Wage Adjustments." Monthly Labor Review, 110 (May 1987): 10-16.

Lamar, Jake. "A Worthy But Knotty Question." Time (February 6, 1984): 30.

Langerman, Philip, Richard Byerly and Kenneth Root. Plant Closings and Layoffs: Problems Facing Urban and Rural Communities. Des Moines, IA: Drake University, 1982.

Latack, Janina and Janelle Dozier. "After the Ax Falls: Job Loss as a Career Transition." Academy of Management Review, 11 (April 1986): 375-392.

*Lathrop, Richard. Who's Hiring Who. Berkeley, CA: Ten Speed Press, 1977.

*Lathrop, Richard. The Job Market. Washington, DC: National Center for Job-Market Studies, 1978.

Leana, Carrie and John Ivancevich. "Involuntary Job Loss: Institutional Interventions and a Research Agenda." Academy of Management Review, 12 (April 1987): 301-312.

Lee, Chris. "Outplacement: Throwing Them Life Preservers." Training, 24 (July 1987): 39-47.

LeGrande, Linda. Employment Status of the Nation: Data and Trends. Congressional Research Service Issue Brief IB82097. Washington, DC: Library of Congress, 1983.

LeGrande, Linda. Unemployment During the Great Depression and the Current Recession. Congressional Research Service Mini Brief MB83215. Washington, DC: Library of Congress, 1983.

Leon, Carol. "Occupational Winners and Losers: Who They Were During 1972-1980." Monthly Labor Review, 105 (June 1982): 18-28.

Leontief, Wassily. "The Distribution of Work and Income." Scientific American, 247 (September 1982): 188-204.

Leventman, Paula. Professionals Out of Work. New York: Free Press, 1981.

Levin, Henry. "Youth Unemployment and Its Educational Consequences." Educational Evaluation and Policy Analysis, 5 (Summer 1983): 231-247.

Levinson, Daniel. The Seasons of a Man's Life. New York: Knopf, 1978.

Levitan, Sar and Clifford Johnson. Second Thoughts on Work. Kalamazoo, MI: Upjohn, 1982.

Liem, Ramsay and Paula Rayman. "Health and Social Costs of Unemployment." American Psychologist, 37 (October 1982): 1116-1123.

Lin, Nan, Walter Ensel and John Vaughn. "Social Resources and Strength of Ties: Structural Factors in Occupational Status Attainment." American Sociological Review, 46 (August 1981): 393-405.

Linden, Fabian. "Myth of the Disappearing Middle Class." Wall Street Journal (January 23, 1984): 20.

Louis, Robert, Paul Burgess and Jerry Kingston. "Reported Vs. Actual Job Search by Unemployment Insurance Claimants." Journal of Human Resources, 21 (Winter 1986): 92-117.

Mangum, Garth. "The Private Employment Agency As a Labor Market Intermediary." In Labor Market Intermediaries. Washington, DC: National Commission for Manpower Policy, 1978: 283-307.

*Mangum, Garth. All You Ever Wanted to Know About Youth Labor Markets and Didn't Know Who To Ask: A Handbook for Practitioners. Unpublished Paper; 1976.

*Mangum, Stephen. Job Search: A Review of the Literature. San Francisco: Olympus Research Centers, 1982.

Mangum, Stephen. "Recruitment and Job Search: The Recruitment Tactics of Employers." Personnel Administrator, 27 (June 1982): 96, 99-102, 104.

Manning, Richard and John McCormick. "The Blue-Collar Blues." Newsweek (June 4, 1984): 52-53, 55.

Mark, Jerome. "Technological Change and Employment: Some Results from BLS Research." Monthly Labor Review, 110 (April 1987): 26-29.

Marshall, Ann. "The Salary Subject: When Students Should Speak Up." Journal of College Placement, 42 (Summer 1982): 19-20.

Marshall, Ray. "High Tech and the Job Crunch." Texas Observer, 76 (April 6, 1984): 7-11.

Mathews, R. Mark and Stephen Fawcett. "Assisting in the Job Search: A Behavioral Assessment and Training Strategy." Journal of Rehabilitation, 51 (Spring 1985): 31- 35.

Maurer, Harry. Not Working. New York: Holt, Rinehart and Winston, 1979.

Mayfield, Eugene. "The Selection Interview—A Re- Evaluation of Published Research." Personnel Psychology, 17 (Autumn, 1964): 239-260.

McKee, William and Richard Froeschle. Where the Jobs Are. Kalamazoo, MI: Upjohn, 1985.

McMahon, Patrick and John Tschetter. "The Declining Middle Class: A Further Analysis." Monthly Labor Review, 109 (September 1986): 22-27.

McPherson, J. Miller and Lynn Smith-Lovin. "Women and Weak Ties: Differences by Sex in the Size of Voluntary Organizations." American Journal of Sociology, 87 (January 1982): 883-904.

McPherson, J. Miller and Lynn Smith-Lovin. "Sex Segregation in Voluntary Associations." American Sociological Review, 51 (Februry 1986): 61-79.

*Medley, H. Anthony. Sweaty Palms. Belmont, CA: Lifetime Learning Publications, 1978.

Mellor, Earl and George Stamas. "Usual Weekly Earnings: Another Look at Intergroup Differences and Basic Trends." Monthly Labor Review, 105 (April 1982): 15-24.

Meyer, Herbert. "Jobs and Want Ads: A Look Behind the Words." Fortune, 98 (November 20, 1978): 88-90, 94, 96.

Miller, Arthur and Ralph Mattson. The Truth About You. Old Tappan, NJ: Fleming H. Revell, 1977.

Mirvis, Philip and Edward Hackett. "Work and Work Force Characteristics in the Nonprofit Sector." Monthly Labor Review, 106 (April 1983): 3-12.

*Molloy, John. Dress for Success. New York: Warner, 1975.

*Molloy, John. The Woman's Dress for Success Book. New York: Warner, 1978.

Molloy, John. Molloy's Live for Success. New York, NY: Bantam, 1982.

Moore, Charles. The Career Game. New York: Ballantine Books, 1976.

Morse, John. "Person-Job Congruence and Individual Adjustment and Development." Human Relations, 28 (December 1975): 841-861.

Morton, John. "BLS White-Collar Pay Survey Now Covers Small Firms." Monthly Labor Review, 109 (October 1986): 26- 27.

Muller, Thomas. The Fourth Wave: California's Newest Immigrants. Washington, DC: The Urban Institute Press, 1984.

Nasar, Sylvia. "To the U.S. from the IMF: Shape Up!" Fortune (May 23, 1988): 77-79.

Nelson, Richard. "State Labor Legislation Enacted in 1983." Monthly Labor Review, 107 (January 1984): 59-75.

Neto, James and Marged Sugarman. A Systematized Approach to Using Jobseeker Information As A Means of Maintaining A Localized Job Search Information System. San Francisco, CA: State of California Employment Development Department, 1974.

Nichols, Harold and William Schill. Yellow Pages of Careers. Danville, IL: The Interstate Printers and Publishers, 1977.

Nilsen, Sigurd. "Recessionary Impacts on the Unemployment of Men and Women." Monthly Labor Review, 107 (May 1984): 21-25.

Noer, David. How To Beat the Employment Game. Radnor, PA: Chilton, 1975.

Norton, Janet. "Perspectives on Comparable Worth: An Introduction to the Numbers." Monthly Labor Review, 108 (December 1985): 3-4.

Norwood, Janet. "Labor Market Contrasts: United States and Europe." Monthly Labor Review, 106 (August 1983): 3-7.

Norwood, Janet. Jobs and Prices in a Recovering Economy. Bureau of Labor Statistics Report 704. Washington, DC: U.S. Department of Labor, 1984.

Nowak, Thomas and Kay Snyder. "Women's Struggle to Survive a Plant Shutdown." The Journal of Intergroup Relations, 11 (Winter 1983): 25-44.

Nulty, Peter. "Will the Big Guys Hire Again?" Fortune (April 30, 1984): 253-256.

Office of Technology Assessment. Technology and the American Economic Transition. Washington, DC: Office of Technology Assessment, 1988.

Passel, Jeffrey. "Estimating the Number of Undocumented Aliens." Monthly Labor Review, 109 (September 1986): 33.

Pechman, Joseph and Mark Mazur. "The Rich, the Poor, and the Taxes They Pay: An Update." The Public Interest, 77 (Fall 1984): 28-36.

Personick, Martin and Carl Barsky. "White-collar Pay Levels Linked to Corporate Work Force Size." Monthly Labor Review, 105 (May 1982): 23-28.

Personick, Valerie. "The Job Outlook through 1995: Industry Output and Employment Projections." Monthly Labor Review, 106 (November 1983): 24-36.

Personick, Valerie. "Industry Output and Employment through the End of the Century." Monthly Labor Review, 110 (September 1987): 30-45.

Pfeffer, Richard. Working for Capitalism. New York: Columbia University Press, 1979.

Plewes, Thomas. "Better Measures of Service Employment Goal of Bureau Survey Redesign." Monthly Labor Review, 105 (November 1982): 7-16.

Podgursky, Michael. "Sources of Secular Increases in the Unemployment Rate, 1969-82." Monthly Labor Review, 107 (July 1984): 19-25.

Quester, Aline and Janice Olson. "Sex, Schooling and Hours of Work." Social Science Quarterly, 58 (March 1978): 566-582.

Rees, Albert. "Labor Economics: Effects of More Knowledge." American Economic Review, 56 (May 1966): 559-566.

Regan, Mary, and Helen Roland. "University Students: A Change in Expectations and Aspirations over the Decade." Sociology of Education, 55 (October 1982): 223-228.

Reich, Robert. "An Industrial Policy of the Right." The Public Interest, 73 (Fall 1983): 3-17.

Reskin, Barbara and Heidi Hartmann, eds. Women's Work, Men's Work. Washington, DC: National Academy Press, 1986.

Riche, Richard, Daniel Hecker and John Burgan. "High Technology Today and Tomorrow: A Small Slice of the Employment Pie." Monthly Labor Review, 106 (November 1983): 50-58.

Roberts, David. Evaluation of Job Track: A Youth Job Search Demonstration. San Francisco, CA: Olympus Research Center, 1982.

Rones, Philip. "The Labor Market Problems of Older Workers." Monthly Labor Review, 106 (May 1983): 3-12.

Rones, Philip. "Recent Recessions Swell Ranks of the Long-term Unemployed." Monthly Labor Review, 107 (February 1984): 25-29.

Rosen, Benson and Thomas Jerdee. "Too Old or Not Too Old." Harvard Business Review, 55 (November/December 1977): 97-106.

Rosenblum, Marc and George Biles. "The Aging of Age- Discrimination—Evolving ADEA Interpretations and Employee Relations Policies." Employee Relations Law Journal, 8 (Summer 1982): 22-36.

Rosenfeld, Carl. "Job Search of the Unemployed, May 1976." Monthly Labor Review, 100 (November 1977): 39-43.

Rosenthal, Neal. "The Shrinking Middle Class: Myth or Reality?" Monthly Labor Review, 108 (March 1985): 3-10.

Roth, Charles and Roy Alexander. Secrets of Closing Sales, 5th ed. Englewood Cliffs, NJ: Prentice-Hall, 1983.

Rozen, Marvin. "Job Quality, Labor Market Disequilibrium, and Some Macroeconomic Implications." Journal of Economic Issues, 16 (September 1982): 731-755.

Rubin, Lillian. Women of a Certain Age. New York: Harper Colophon, 1981.

Rytina, Nancy. "Earnings of Men and Women: A Look at Specific Occupations." Monthly Labor Review, 105 (April 1982): 25-31.

Rytina, Nancy. "Occupational Changes and Tenure, 1981." Monthly Labor Review, 105 (September 1982): 29-33.

Rytina, Nancy. "Comparing Annual and Weekly Earnings from the Current Population Survey." Monthly Labor Review, 106 (April 1983): 32-36.

Rytina, Nancy and Suzanne Bianchi. "Occupational Reclassification and Changes in Distribution by Gender." Monthly Labor Review, 107 (March 1984): 11-17.

Rytina, Steve and David Morgan. "The Arithmetic of Social Relations: The Interplay of Category and Network." American Journal of Sociology, 88 (July 1982): 88-113.

Sandell, Steven. "Job Search by Unemployed Women: Determinants of the Asking Wage." Industrial and Labor Relations Review, 33 (April 1980): 368-378.

Sargent, Jon. "The Job Outlook for College Graduates During the 1980's." Occupational Outlook Quarterly, 26 (Summer 1982): 3-7.

Sargent, Jon. "An Improving Job Market for College Graduates: The 1986 Update of Projections to 1995." Occupational Outlook Quarterly, 30 (Summer 1986): 3-7.

Saunders, Norman. "Economic Projections to the Year 2000." Monthly Labor Review, 110 (September 1987): 10-18.

Schiller, Bradley. "'Corporate Kidnap' of the Small- Business Employee." The Public Interest, 72 (Summer 1983): 72-87.

Schoepfle, Gregory. "Imports and Domestic Employment: Identifying Affected Industries." Monthly Labor Review, 105 (August 1982): 13-26.

Schrank, Robert. Ten Thousand Working Days. Cambridge, MA: MIT Press, 1979.

Secretary of Labor's Task Force on Economic Adjustment and Worker Dislocation. Economic Adjustment and Worker Dislocation in a Competitive Society. Washington, DC: U.S. Department of Labor, 1986.

Sehgal, Ellen. "Occupational Mobility and Job Tenure in 1983." Monthly Labor Review, 107 (October 1984): 18-23.

Sehgal, Ellen. "Work Experience in 1983 Reflects the Effects of the Recovery." Monthly Labor Review, 107 (December 1984): 18-24.

Sewell, William and Robert Hauser. "Sex, Schooling, and Occupational Status." American Journal of Sociology, 86 (November 1980): 551-583.

Shank, Susan. "Women and the Labor Market: the Link Grows Stronger." Monthly Labor Review, 111 (March 1988): 3-8.

Shapiro, Barbara. Employment and Self Esteem: An Evaluation of the Cambridge Job Factory, a Manpower Program under the Comprehensive Employment and Training Act (CETA). Unpublished PhD Dissertation, Tufts University, 1978.

Shaw, Lois and David Shapiro. "Women's Work Plans: Contrasting Expectations and Actual Work Experience." Monthly Labor Review, 110 (November 1987): 7-13.

Sheppard, Harold and A. Harvey Belitsky. Promoting Jobfinding Success for the Unemployed. Kalamazoo, MI: The W. E. Upjohn Institute for Employment Research, 1968.

Siebert, Glenn. Employment Service Potential: Indicators of Labor Market Activity. Sacramento, CA: Employment Development Department, 1977.

Siegelman, Ellen. Personal Risk. New York, NY: Harper & Row, 1983.

Silvestri, George, John Lukasiewicz and Marcus Einstein. "Occupational Employment Projections through 1995." Monthly Labor Review, 106 (November 1983): 37-49.

Silvestri, George and John Lukasiewicz. "A Look at Occupational Employment Trends to the Year 2000." Monthly Labor Review, 110 (September 1987): 46-63.

Simic, Tomislava, ed. Mergerstat Review 1985. Chicago, IL: W. T. Grimm, 1986.

Simpson, Wayne. "A Simultaneous Model of Workplace and Residential Location Incorporating Job Search." Journal of Urban Economics, 8 (November 1980): 330-349.

Slavenski, Lynn. "Matching People to the Job." Training and Development Journal, 40 (August 1986): 54-57.

Smith, D. Alton and Jane Kulik. The Downriver Community Conference Economic Readjustment Activity Program: Impact Findings from the First Phase of Operations. Cambridge, MA: Apt Associates, 1983.

Smith, Shirley. "New Worklife Estimates Reflect Changing Profile of Labor Force." Monthly Labor Review, 105 (March 1982): 15-20.

Snipp, C. Matthew. "Occupational Mobility and Social Class: Insights from Men's Career Mobility." American Sociological Review, 50 (August 1985): 475-493.

Sommers, Dixie and Alan Eck. "Occupational Mobility in the American Labor Force." Monthly Labor Review, 100 (January 1977): 3-19.

Spenner, Kenneth. "The Upgrading and Downgrading of Occupations: Issues, Evidence and Implications for Education." Review of Educational Research, 55 (Summer 1985): 125-154.

Spilerman, Seymour. "Careers, Labor Market Structure, and Socioeconomic Achievement." American Journal of Sociology, 83 (November 1977): 551-593.

Springbett, B. M. "Factors Affecting the Final Decision in the Employment Interview." Canadian Journal of Psychology, 12 (#1 1958): 13-22.

Stanback, Jr., Thomas, Peter Bearse, Thierry Noyelle and Robert Karasek. Services: The New Economy. Totowa, NJ: Allanheld, Osmun, 1981.

Steinberg, Bruce. "The Mass Market is Splitting Apart." Fortune (November 28, 1983): 76-82.

Steinhauser, Larry. "A New PhD's Search for Work: A Case Study." Journal of Counseling and Development, 63 (January 1985): 300-303.

Steinman, John. The Nevada Claimant Placement Project. Carson City, NV: Nevada Employment Security Department, 1978.

Sternlieb, George and James Hughes. "Running Faster to Stay in Place." American Demographics, 4 (June 1982): 10-19, 42.

Stevens, David W. "Job Search Techniques: A New Index of Effectiveness." Quarterly Review of Economics and Business, 12 (Summer 1972): 99-103.

Stevens, David. Unemployment Insurance Beneficiary Job Search Behavior: What is Known and What Should be Known for Administrative Planning Purposes. Washington, DC: U.S. Department of Labor, 1977.

Stevens, David. "A Reexamination of What is Known About Jobseeking Behavior in the United States." In Labor Market Intermediaries. Washington, DC: National Commission for Manpower Policy, 1978: 55-104.

Stewman, Shelby and Suresh Konda. "Careers and Organizational Labor Markets: Demographic Models of Organizational Behavior." American Journal of Sociology, 88 (January 1983): 637-685.

Stolzenberg, Ross. "Bringing the Boss Back In: Employer Size, Employee Schooling, and Socioeconomic Achievement." American Sociological Review, 43 (December 1978): 813-828.

Sugarman, Marged. "Employer Dualism in Personnel Policies and Practices: Its Labor Turnover Implications." In Malcolm Cohen and Arthur Schwartz, eds., Proceedings of the Employment Service Potential Conference. Ann Arbor, MI: Institute of Labor and Industrial Relations, 1978: 117-148.

Taylor III, Alex. "Lee Iacocca's Production Whiz." Fortune (June 22, 1987): 36-44.

Terkel, Studs. Working. New York: Avon, 1972.

Terry, Sylvia. "Work Experience, Earnings and Family Income in 1981." Monthly Labor Review, 106 (April 1983): 13- 20.

Thompson, Melvin. Why Should I Hire You? New York: Jove/Harcourt Brace Jovanovich, 1975.

Toffler, Alvin. The Third Wave. New York: Bantam, 1981.

Traxel, Robert. Manager's Guide to Successful Job Hunting. New York: McGraw-Hill, 1978.

Ullman, Joseph. "Employee Referrals: Prime Tool for Recruiting Workers." Personnel, 43 (May/June 1966): 30-35.

Ullman, Joseph and Thomas Gutteridge. "Job Search in the Labor Market for College Graduates: A Case Study of MBA's." Academy of Management Journal, 17 (June 1974): 381- 386.

U. S. Department of Labor. Jobseeking Methods Used by American Workers (Bureau of Labor Statistics Bulletin 1886). Washington, DC: U.S. Government Printing Office, 1975.

U. S. Department of Labor. Recruitment, Job Search, and the United States Employment Service (R&D Monograph 43). Washington, DC: U.S. Government Printing Office, 1976.

U. S. Department of Labor. The Public Employment Service and Help Wanted Ads (R&D Monograph 59). Washington, DC: U.S. Government Printing Office, 1978.

Urquhart, Michael. "The Employment Shift to Services: Where Did It Come From?" Monthly Labor Review, 107 (April 1984): 15-22.

Urquhart, Michael and Marillyn Hewson. "Unemployment Continued to Rise in 1982 as Recession Deepened." Monthly Labor Review, 106 (February 1983): 3-12.

Waldman, Elizabeth. "Labor Force Statistics from a Family Perspective." Monthly Labor Review, 106 (December 1983): 16-20.

*Walsh, John, Miriam Johnson and Marged Sugarman. Help Wanted: Case Studies of Classified Ads. Salt Lake City: Olympus, 1975.

Wanous, John. "Realistic Job Previews: Can A Procedure to Reduce Turnover Also Influence the Relationship Between Abilities and Performance?" Personnel Psychology, 31 (Summer 1978): 249-259.

*Wegmann, Robert. "Job-Search Assistance: A Review." Journal of Employment Counseling, 16 (December 1979): 197-226.

Wegmann, Robert. "Group Job Search at the Crossroads." County Employment Reporter, 11 (April 1982): 7- 9.

*Wegmann, Robert and Robert Chapman. The Right Place at the Right Time. Berkeley, CA: Ten Speed Press, 1987.

Westcott, Diane. "Employment and Commuting Patterns: A Residential Analysis." Monthly Labor Review, 102 (July 1979): 3-9.

White, Martha. "The 1988-89 Job Outlook in Brief." Occupational Outlook Quarterly, 32 (Summer, 1988): 10-45.

Wiener, Yoash and Mark Schneiderman. "Use of Job Information as a Criterion in Employment Decisions of Interviewers." Journal of Applied Psychology, 59 (December 1974): 699-704.

Wilensky, Harold. "Orderly Careers and Social Participation: The Impact of Work History on Social Integration in the Middle Mass." American Sociological Review, 26 (August 1961): 521-539.

Wilson, John. "America's High-Tech Crisis." Business Week (March 11, 1985): 56-67.

*Wright, John. The American Almanac of Jobs and Salaries. New York: Avon, 1984.

Wright, Orman, Jr. "Summary of Research on the Selection Interview Since 1964." Personnel Psychology, 22 (Winter 1969): 391-413.

Yochelson, John and Gordon Cloney, eds. Services and U.S. Trade Policy. Washington, DC: The Center for Strategic and International Studies, 1982.

Young, Anne. Educational Attainment of Workers, March 1979 (Special Labor Force Report 240). Washington, DC: Bureau of Labor Statistics, 1981.

Young, Anne. "Recent Trends in Higher Education and Labor Force Activity." Monthly Labor Review, 106 (February 1983): 39-41.

Young, Anne. "Youth Labor Force Marked Turning Point in 1982." Monthly Labor Review, 106 (August 1983): 29-32.

Young, Anne. "One-Fourth of the Adult Labor Force are College Graduates." Monthly Labor Review, 108 (February 1985): 43-46.

Young, Anne and Howard Hayghe. "More U.S. Workers Are College Graduates." Monthly Labor Review, 107 (March 1984): 46-48.

Zunin, Leonard and Natalie Zunin. Contact: The First Four Minutes. New York: Ballantine, 1972.

N. A. "Average Salaries...And Why They're Not So Average." Occupational Outlook Quarterly, 25 (Fall 1981): 24- 25.

N. A. "Human Ills of 'WIN' Women in Job Search Shouldn't be Ignored, 'MDRC' Study Warns." Employment and Training Reporter (September 1, 1982): 8-9.

N. A. "The Myth of the Vanishing Middle Class." Business Week (July 9, 1984): 83, 86.

N. A. "BLS Reports on Displaced Workers." News, U. S. Department of Labor, Bureau of Labor Statistics (11/30/84).

N. A. "Work Interruptions and the Female-Male Earnings Gap." Monthly Labor Review, 108 (February 1985): 50-51.

N. A. "Comparable Worth Settlements." Monthly Labor Review, 109 (March 1986): 43.

N. A. "New Data on Workers Belonging to Unions, 1986." Monthly Labor Review, 110 (May 1987): 36.

INDEX

ABOUT THE AUTHORS

Robert Wegmann is a professor of sociology at the University of Houston - Clear Lake. UH-CL is an upper level school; that is, it has no freshman or sophomore students. The average student age is in the early thirties. Therefore, finding, changing and choosing occupations and jobs, and how best to go about these processes, are critical personal issues for many in the student body.

Bob's first exposure to employment and training issues came in 1970, while serving on the staff of the Subcommittee on Employment, Manpower and Poverty of the U.S. Senate. This interest was rekindled several years later, and he now teaches graduate and undergraduate courses dealing with career development. Much of his research has been concentrated on job search training groups and their outcomes; he has published several articles on this topic. He is also the author of a book, *How to Find a Job in Houston*, which grew out of the university courses he teaches.

Miriam Johnson brings both extensive practical experience and a solid research background to the study of unemployment. Working for the employment service in California, she dealt on a daily basis with people looking for work. Realizing that many of those who asked her help were failing to obtain employment because of their poor job search skills, she began running group sessions in San Francisco for inner city residents. She was able to show them how the employment process works and how to approach the important steps in this process more efficiently. Miriam has since written extensively about ways to make the Employment Service more effective, and has played a major role in studies of labor market operations funded by the Department of Labor. More recently, she served as the public member of California's Advisory Committee to the Bureau of Employment Agencies (a regulatory body), and was research director for a major study, done under contract to the Department of Labor, on the "state of the art" in job search training for youth and adults.

Robert Chapman's experience has been in career counseling and outplacement in the private sector, particularly with Fortune 500 companies. He is a management consultant who has worked individually with corporate executives, and also with groups drawn from virtually every corporate level, from president to secretary. He has consulted with firms that were planning major staff reductions and trained internal consultants to run career centers and conduct outplacement efforts within their own companies.

Bob's initial interest in helping others look for work came while doing an internship involving social welfare and mental health programs for poverty area residents. This interest was pursued during his doctoral studies. His appreciation of the need to understand employment issues became most intense when he found himself both unemployed and thinking through a major change of career direction. He successfully moved from director of residential treatment programs for emotionally disturbed children to business consultant. Bob first worked with Hay Associates, and then with Drake Beam Morin, Inc. In 1983, he founded King, Chapman and Broussard, Inc., a consulting firm specializing in outplacement and career consulting, management of cultural changes in organizations and general management consulting. The firm has offices in Atlanta, Dallas, Denver, Detroit, Houston, Los Angeles and San Diego. Bob has also been active in the Association of Outplacement Consulting Firms. He has served as a director for three years.

Two of us (Wegmann and Chapman) have recently written a book to assist the unemployed individual to both choose and find an appropriate job (*The Right Place at the Right Time*, published by Ten Speed Press). In bringing out this second edition of *Work in the New Economy*, we express our equally strong interest in assisting those who work with the unemployed. If our continuing efforts contribute to shorter job search periods and more successful outcomes, then we will have done what we set out to do.

The Authors
June, 1988

ACKNOWLEDGEMENTS

Over the years, the authors have learned a great deal about the job search process from other researchers, employment service personnel, vocational counselors, personnel officers, leaders of group job search programs and, above all, from the unemployed themselves. To all of those who helped us understand this most difficult human and social problem, we express our appreciation.

Personnel at the Library of Congress, the Department of Labor, the Department of Commerce and the University of Houston - Clear Lake library were very helpful as we gathered information on the changing economy and the employment process. They gave much needed assistance in locating both published and unpublished data. Garth Mangum provided comments and suggestions as the first edition of this book evolved. Joseph Fischer, Philip Norris, Jeffrey Power and Kimberly Robinson read an earlier draft, and made useful comments. Any misunderstandings, errors or omissions are, of course, our responsibility.

The various drafts of the first edition were efficiently handled by the UH-CL Word Processing Center. We appreciate the assistance of Anna Mae Bozsin, who operated the center. The university awarded Robert Wegmann a sabbatical semester and other released time to work on the first edition. This help is gratefully acknowledged.

Kathy Kirchner and Bipin Patel of the UH-CL Computer Center translated the first edition from a mainframe-oriented word processor to microcomputer disks. Pam Sisk duplicated the second edition, and helped with other clerical chores. Their help is gratefully acknowledged.

ORDERING INSTRUCTIONS

Order Form

Work in the New Economy • Revised Edition • 300 pp. $14.95
Mail To: **JIST Works, Inc.** • 720 N. Park Ave • Indianapolis, IN 46202
Phone Orders And Information: **800/648/5478** or use **317/637/6643** for calls from Indiana, Canada and outside the continental United States.

Number Of Copies _____

Ship To:

Name _____

Title_____

Org'n _____

Street*_____

City_____

State _____ Zip _____

Phone (____)_____

*We cannot deliver to P.O. Boxes via U.P.S.
❑ Check or money order enclosed
❑ Charge to my credit card (call in your order)

Quantity x $14.95 = Subtotal $ _____

IN Res. add 5% Sales Tax   _____

Shipping ($1.50 each)   _____

Total   _____

Orders must be prepaid unless previous credit arrangements have been made.

Call for quantity discount information.

Distributors, libraries, institutions, bookstores and individuals order from **JIST Works, Inc.** using the order form above. Call for quantity discounts at **800/648/5478** or **317/637/6643.**

JIST will provide *free review copies* to journalists and book reviewers. Instructors considering this book for class assignment may obtain a free review copy under certain conditions. Please make requests on your institutional letterhead including your title, the course name and the number of students.

Members of the American Association of Counseling and Development, the College Placement Council and the Association Marketplace direct your orders to: American Association of Counseling and Development, 5999 Stevenson Avenue, Alexandria, VA 22304, 703/823/9800.